THE
CASE
FOR
CHANGE

SEYMOUR B. SARASON

THE
CASE
FOR
CHANGE

Rethinking
the Preparation
of Educators

Jossey-Bass Publishers · San Francisco

Substantial discounts on bulk quantities of Jossey-Bass books are available to corporations, professional associations, and other organizations. For details and discount information, contact the special sales department at Jossey-Bass Inc., Publishers. (415) 433-1740; Fax (415) 433-0499.

For international orders, please contact your local Paramount Publishing International office.

Manufactured in the United States of America on Lyons Falls Pathfinder Tradebook. This paper is acid-free and 100 percent totally chlorine-free.

The ink in this book is either soy- or vegetable-based and during the printing process emits fewer than half the volatile organic compounds (VOCs) emitted by petroleum-based ink.

Library of Congress Cataloging-in-Publication Data

Sarason, Seymour Bernard, date.
    The case for change : rethinking the preparation of educators / Seymour B. Sarason.
      p. cm. — (Jossey-Bass education series) (Jossey-Bass higher and adult education series)
    Includes bibliographical references and index.
    ISBN 1-55542-504-6
    1. Teachers—Training of—United States. I. Title. II. Series. III. Series: Jossey-Bass higher and adult education series.
    LB1715.S24 1993
    370.71'0973 — dc20   92–29937
                                              CIP

FIRST EDITION
HB Printing   10 9 8 7 6 5 4 3 2   *Code 9308*

A joint publication in

The Jossey-Bass Education Series

and

The Jossey-Bass
Higher and Adult Education Series

Contents

ix

Preface

Schools of education have always had their critics. Some of these critics have taken delight in exposing the foibles, fallacies, fads, and fashions of schools of education—all for the purpose of demonstrating that these schools attract students who, having been symbolically "injured" at birth with a low IQ, then unknowingly suffer the insult of being subjected to an indoctrination by a faculty incapable of logical thinking, of feeling at home with a complex idea, or of running against the tides of convention. Although I understand the frustration of these critics, I cannot agree with what I have concluded is the basic point, the action point, of their diverse criticisms: throw one set of rascals out, put in the "right" kind of people, and all good things will follow. It is neither that simple nor historically defensible. The most damning critics have come from other parts of the university (for example, arts and sciences) that now or in the past would have absolutely nothing to do with the field of education. So when these critics vent their spleen at these schools of education, especially their preparatory programs, it does not necessarily mean that their criticisms are invalid, but it does mean that the critics and their fields have been and still are part of the problem and not the solution. At the very least, they are amazingly, unforgivably, and scandalously ahistorical.

I have been a psychologist for over fifty years—when you say more than half a century it seems longer. Except for four of those years, I have been in and around universities, prestigious or otherwise. My experience may be atypical, my perceptiveness may be limited, my sympathy for the underdog too intrusive and distorting. With those caveats, I have to say that when I compare the personnel of schools of education with those in other parts of the university, I see little difference between them in the way wisdom, denseness, imaginativeness, arrogance, and intellectual flexibility, curiosity, or rigidity are distributed. If there is a difference, it is not one that makes a difference. That conclusion flies in the face of conventional academic wisdom. But if I restrict that conclusion to how these other fields have understood the substance and context of education problems and processes, the critics betray a degree of ignorance and bias no less than that of those they criticize. I do not say this from any stance of superiority. It took me years, in and around schools, to appreciate how complex the problems are and how they still bear the imprint of a long national and institutional history. One thing I have learned: the problems we deal with were not "willed," nor was the response to those problems solely or even primarily a kind of conspiracy of educators intent on foisting on an unsuspecting public strange, wrong, or subversive ideas. Educators have played their parts, but there have been many other actors on the societal stage. If you like to play the game of blame assignment, few fields will keep you as occupied as education.

I am no less critical of preparatory programs for educators than the most splenetic critics. But mine is not an ad hominem critique, and it is not one that in any way suggests that improvement in these programs can be achieved by add-ons, new courses, or any other form of remedial cosmetics. Unlike almost all critics, save John Goodlad, what I advocate is a complete *conceptual* redesigning of preparatory programs. We have had a surfeit of recommendations from task forces and commissions about the crisis in education, and in each of these reports there is a sentence or so (rarely more than that) that says we need "better-trained" teachers. Nothing is said about administrators, even though one of the obvious features of the school culture is the adversarial relationship between teachers and administrators.

And what is obvious? Let me mention but four such points here. The first is that preparatory programs very inadequately prepare educators (teachers *and* administrators) for what life is like in classrooms, schools, and school systems—a point long apparent to educators. The second is that as long as efforts at educational change focus on the repair of existing problems and for all practical purposes ignore primary prevention, the need for repair will *increase*. The third is that preparatory programs, far from being based on a primary prevention orientation, unwittingly contribute to the manufacture of problems. And the fourth is that we have been both unable and unwilling to confront and accept the fact that primary prevention courses of action require a long-term perspective, that is, they have none of the politically sexy attractiveness of quick fixes. There is really a fifth obvious point, obvious to educators but not publicly expressed: however morally and politically justifiable, the repair effort is doomed to disappoint us. That, I hasten to add, is no justification for giving up on repair—you don't turn your back on pressing problems about which you must do something—but it is justification to look to whatever you can do to prevent the incidence of problems. That is why this book looks at preparatory programs for educators. You start where you can, where your experience has led you, even though you know you are dealing with part of a horribly complicated drama. I can assure the reader that I know that what I deal with is only part of the problem. At the very least, I hope this book puts some conceptual flesh on the bones of the cliché that we need better-trained educators.

What I have to say in this book rests on two related assumptions. The first is that we should prevent in students the intellectual viruses of low motivation, a lack of intellectual curiosity, a devaluing of the life of the mind, boredom with subject matter, and the attitude that there are two distinctly different worlds: that which is inside of schools and that which is the "real" one outside of schools. That is putting it negatively. Put positively, it is our obligation to nurture and support in students their ever present curiosity and desire to understand themselves and the world they live in. You can count on that curiosity and desire. Our task is to recognize, harness, and exploit those characteristics. The second and related assumption is that unless the conditions exist wherein the educators of these students can experience a sense of learning, growth, and personal and intellectual change for themselves, they cannot create and sustain those conditions for their students. Those conditions do not now exist for educators. What we now have are conditions inimical to both assumptions or goals. Musicians say that the Beethoven violin concerto is not for but against the violin. Schools today are against, not for, productive learning on the part of students *and* educators. Students begin their schooling, and educators enter their profession, eager to learn, to absorb, to "grow up," to make a difference, to feel worthy and respected, not passively to await a future but to reach for it. Rarely does it work out for them as they hoped. And if we do not face up to those disappointments, I am forced to this prediction: the maxim that says the more things change, the more they remain the same will be invalidated. Things will get worse.

Acknowledgments

I take personal pleasure in acknowledging the aid, encouragement, and friendship of Ed Meyer in the writing of this book. He has had several careers, one of which was as a high school teacher of science. He has been dubbed the Minister for Responsible Disturbance, an apt title for someone unable to suffer fools gladly, never in awe of those who in proclaiming educational policy betray their ignorance of what life is like in our schools and who indulge the tendency to blame the victims: students *and* educational personnel. And, of course, I shall always be grateful to Lisa Pagliaro for her graciousness, efficiency, and strange ability to read my handwriting. I thank God for big favors.

New Haven, Connecticut   Seymour B. Sarason
January 1993

The Author

Seymour B. Sarason is professor of psychology emeritus in the Department of Psychology and at the Institution for Social and Policy Studies at Yale University. He founded, in 1962, and directed, until 1970, the Yale Psycho-Educational Clinic, one of the first research and training sites in community psychology. He received his Ph.D. degree from Clark University in 1942 and holds honorary doctorates from Syracuse University, Queens College, and Rhode Island College. He has received an award for distinguished contributions to the public interest and several awards from the divisions of clinical and community psychology of the American Psychological Association, as well as two awards from the American Association on Mental Deficiency.

Sarason is the author of numerous books and articles. His more recent books include *The Predictable Failure of Educational Reform: Can We Change Course Before It's Too Late?* (1990), *The Challenge of Art to Psychology* (1990), *The Making of an American Psychologist: An Autobiography* (1988), and *Caring and Compassion in Clinical Practice: Issues in the Selection, Training, and Behavior of Helping Professionals* (1985). He has made contributions in such fields as mental retardation, culture and personality, projective techniques, teacher training, the school culture, and anxiety in children.

For Elizabeth Lorentz,
friend and colleague

THE
CASE
FOR
CHANGE

Chapter One

A Litany
of Inadequacies

Years ago some obviously wise person said that the most important decision you have to make when you decide to write a book is what you are *not* going to write about. If I had any doubts about that advice, they were dispelled when I started to think about this book. Decisive in that agonizing awareness was a casual suggestion my friend Bruce Thomas made that I "might" want to look at *The Story of the Eight-Year Study with Conclusions and Recommendations* (Aikin, 1942), which was written under the aegis of the Commission on the Relation of School and College, a creation of the Progressive Education Association in 1930. The commission's focus was on secondary education. And what were the inadequacies of high schools as seen earlier in the twentieth century?

1. Secondary education in the United States did not have clear-cut, definite, central purposes.
2. Schools failed to give students a sincere appreciation of their heritage as American citizens.
3. Our schools did not adequately prepare students for the responsibilities of community life.
4. The high school seldom challenged the student of first-rate ability to work up to the level of his or her intellectual powers.
5. Schools neither knew their students well nor guided them wisely.
6. Schools failed to create conditions necessary for effective learning.

1

7. The creative energies of students were seldom released and developed.

8. The conventional high school curriculum was far removed from the real concerns of youth.

9. The traditional subjects of the curriculum had lost much of their vitality and significance. "The purposes they should serve were seldom realized even in the lives of students of distinguished native ability" (Aikin, 1942, p. 7).

10. Most high school graduates were not competent in the use of the English language.

11. There was little evidence of unity in the work of the typical high school.

12. The absence of unity in the work of the secondary school was almost matched by the lack of continuity.

13. Complacency characterized high schools generally.

14. Only here and there did one find principals who conceived of their work in terms of democratic leadership for the community, teachers, and students.

15. Principals and teachers labored earnestly, often sacrificially, but usually without any comprehensive evaluation of the results of their work.

16. The high school diploma meant only that the student had done whatever was necessary to accumulate the required number of units.

17. The relationship between school and college was unsatisfactory to both institutions.

Apparently, the arena of education does not look very different to the critics of today. If the commission had done no more than give us a litany of inadequacies, its report deserved the amnesia that was its fate, but it went far beyond such a litany. It outlined, developed, and implemented the most ambitious, well-described, honest, carefully researched study of *institutional change* ever done in education. I know that is quite a statement. I entreat the reader to scrutinize the study's methods, findings, and conclusions. I doubt that anyone who reads the report will fail to ask: why has that study gone unrecognized, unutilized, and undiscussed?

So what do I do? Summarize that report? I was tempted to do that but it would not be directly relevant to my major purpose: to rethink the preparation of educators.[1] So I shall not fully elaborate on it. It is not surprising that I latched on to the following two statements from the report:

> Teachers were not well equipped for their responsibilities. They lacked full knowledge of the nature of youth—of physical, intellectual, and emotional drives and growth. They understood little of the conditions essential to effective learning. Relation of the school to the society it should serve was only dimly perceived. Democracy was taken for granted, but teachers seldom had any clear conception of democracy as a way of living which should characterize the whole life of the school. Very few were capable of leading youth into an understanding of democracy and its problems, for they themselves did not understand [Aikin, 1942, p. 9].

> It was in no spirit of sweeping condemnation that the members of the Commission viewed the work of the secondary school in the United States. Their criticism was not so much of others as of themselves. They realized that many shortcomings were due to the amazing growth of our schools, *to the necessity of employing inadequately prepared teachers,* and to lack of time

---

[1]I have been unable to determine why the *Story of the Eight-Year Study* did not have an impact and has gone unrecognized. Almost all of the individuals who oversaw that study have long since died. The most likely explanation is that the study was published not long after we entered World War II, a time when the attention of everyone was far from the arena of public education. Having lived through those war years I should remind the reader that for the first two years of the war it was not at all clear that we could defeat the German, Italian, and Japanese military machines. Indeed, the manpower needs of our military appeared to be of such a large scale that it seemed as if many colleges might have to close their doors. It was not a time conducive to debate about school reform.

to adjust the work of the school to new responsibilities. But understanding of the conditions which produced weaknesses in our schools did not lessen the
Commission's conviction that earnest attempts to remove them should be made at once. The co-operation
of more than 300 colleges and universities was sought
and secured in 1932 [pp. 11–12, italics mine].

Those statements contain, explicitly and implicitly, my
justification for writing this book. As these extracts clearly show,
the commission understood well that the process of *repairing* our
secondary schools would have been far easier if the preparation
of educators (teachers *and* administrators) had been more adequate to the realities of schools and their problems. That is to
say, more realistic preparatory programs for educators could
serve the goal of *preventing* problems.

I have five major goals in this book. The first is to persuade the reader that the repair of existing problems, however
necessary and morally justified, can no longer be at the expense
of efforts at primary prevention, that is, a reduction in the incidence of new cases with a particular problem in a particular
cohort. The repair effort deals with problems that already exist
and the prevalence of which has been more or less determined.
The preventive effort seeks to lower the incidence of new cases
having those problems, thus reducing the need for repair. If the
repair effort needs no justification, the fact remains that such
an effort is not only horribly complicated but very problematic
in outcome. The track record of the repair of our schools is not
encouraging. In fact, it is on the dismal side, which is why *The
Story of the Eight-Year Study* is so refreshing and important. This
is not to say that the preventive effort is anything resembling
a simple, nonproblematic affair. When the Salk vaccine to prevent polio became available, no one had to convince the general
public to have their children inoculated. In regard to the prevention of many educational problems, we cannot count on such
willing compliance and support. The daily problems educators
must deal with leave them too overwhelmed to give serious
thought to prevention. And there has been little educational

leadership to inform the general public about the whys and wherefores of prevention. At the same time that no one denies the need for prevention—to do so would be like favoring sin over virtue—the reality is that almost all of our thinking, actions, and funding have gone into repair.

The second of my goals is to convince the reader that one way, and it is only one way, to take prevention seriously is to confront the inadequacies of preparatory programs for educators. If, as John Goodlad has said, we need completely to redesign preparatory programs, it is because such redesigning would better prepare educators to prevent as well as to repair *some* of our most thorny problems. Such redesigning is no panacea; it is not the universal solvent for all of our problems. It is one way to take action, a way most educators in their heart of hearts have acknowledged privately to be very important. We do not lack for problems that should be prevented. Nothing in the pages that follow should be interpreted as suggesting that if we redesign these programs the gray, threatening clouds will disappear, the sun will shine, and all will be well. I do not expect readers to agree with some of my specific suggestions. I can assure them that I in no way harbor the thought that I have cornered the market on wisdom or truth. If I am realistically modest on that score, I am nevertheless certain that as long as preparatory programs remain as they are, cosmetically adding this or that course or this or that requirement, or continuing to confuse ends and means, change with innovation, our schools will always require an increase in efforts at repair.

The third goal is to help the reader understand that in redesigning preparatory programs we seek to prevent problems in students *and* teachers. As long as teachers are viewing themselves as powerless as well as intellectually and personally alone and lonely, lacking the feelings associated with productive learning and growth, plagued with feelings of guilt because they do not know how to be helpful to many of their students, angered by the knowledge that they count for little or nothing in decision-making and policy matters, aware that they are settling into a routine that is the enemy of change, content to survive, and fearful of new ideas—if the incidence and strength of these and other feelings and attitudes remain as they are, there is no basis whatsoever to expect that student outcomes will generally improve. What happens to teachers — emotionally, intellectually, and socially — very much affects how children experience classrooms and learning. And if what happens to teachers when they become independent professionals is untoward in its consequences, it is to a large extent a result of preparatory programs unconnected to the real world of classrooms, schools, and school systems. The adversarial relationship between teachers and administrators is not unrelated to the nonexistence of overlap between preparatory programs of these two groups. Why should they understand and appreciate each other? Why should they be able to work together to their mutual advantages? If, as I have, the reader scrutinizes the plethora of reports — from presidential commissions, state commissions, foundation task forces — he or she will not quarrel with two conclusions: little or nothing is said about how administrators need to change, and whatever is said about preparatory programs is superficial in the extreme, and superficial is a charitable adjective to describe these reports. But that is what happens when we look at the problems almost exclusively in the framework of repair. Where and how were these professionals prepared? You do not have to be especially wise to conclude that some of the problems that plague our schools have to reflect some of the limitations of preparatory programs.

The fourth major goal of the book is to help the reader understand that efforts at primary prevention will not bear fruit except over a long period of time.[2] That has been, and may continue to be, the kiss of death to the preventive orientation. Today we use the phrase *quick fix* as a pejorative, that is, a short-

[2]I ask the reader to keep in mind that when I use the word prevention, I mean more than the prevention of pathology. A colleague of mine, Elizabeth Lorentz, to whom this book is dedicated, put it well: "We have to unimprison ourselves from the medical way of thinking about prevention: the prevention of a particular pathology. Let us not forget that no less important, and ultimately more important, is prevention as the *promotion* of health. And let us remember that when we talk about deficits we refer not only to an inadequacy in performance of some kind but, more frequently, to a *lack* of information, opportunity, or motivation" (personal communication).

sighted, deceptively adequate, ultimately wasteful expenditure of time, energy, and money. But that is precisely what we have done and seem to be continuing to do in matters educational. Quick fixes are bad enough, but when they are reincarnations of earlier fixes — indeed, the degree of similarity is frequently startling — one gets more than bored at the reinvention of educational wheels. In responding to the case I make for recasting preparatory programs from a preventive orientation, I ask the reader to keep in mind the history of quick fixes and the intractability of our schools to our efforts at repair.

The final goal of this book is to help the reader see that the inadequacies of our schools *and* of our preparatory programs were not willed; no one set out to produce these inadequacies, there are no villains, and ad hominem invectives are as unwarranted as they are unproductive. Yes, there are vested interests, there are different points of view, history is always a variable, and the necessity or pressure for change brings out the best and worst in us. Few things have been as insidious in the current and past debates as the (not so) implicit contempt that so many critics express toward educators: blaming their genes, IQs, inadequate grasp of subject matter, an allergy to creativity, and more. That they are blaming the victim can never occur to these critics whose capacity to oversimplify is apparently bottomless.

Chapter Two

Unused Personal Experience

Let us begin with the obvious: no one denies the need for educational reform, and it is not clear if or how it can be accomplished. The rhetoric is accompanied by passion, exhortation, and apocalyptic visions of a deteriorating America. If you took seriously the hard sell for educational reform, you would be justified in concluding that the general public is unaware of or too unconcerned about the quality of our schools. Otherwise, why the hard sell? No such hard sell is necessary, and those who employ it know it. No one has to be convinced about the need for accountability, for maintaining standards for performance, for not requiring policemen in schools to protect students and teachers, for engendering higher levels of motivation in students, for parent-family involvement, for preparing students who will be better able to compete in the marketplace, and on and on. Is the hard sell necessary, perhaps, because the general public no longer has confidence in the reforms or the reformers?

In the 1930s John Gunther wrote *Inside Europe,* consisting of assessments of each European country in that troubled decade. Each chapter had an italicized "saying" below the main title. For the chapter on Austria, which followed the one on Germany, Gunther wrote: "In Germany the situation is serious but not hopeless. In Austria the situation is hopeless but not serious." There are people today who regard our schools as Gunther did Austria. There are others who regard them as Gunther did Germany. In my experience, most people — especially those who in one or another way paid their dues in the educational reform movement — cannot make up their minds. They

8

feel they must be hopeful at the same time that reality does not seem to justify hope.

What, then, is the reason for the hard sell? In my opinion, the purpose is to appear to be *doing* something, to appear to be taking a *new* direction, to justify renewed hope. This is not to say that officialdom — from the president, to the secretary of education, to state governors, to commissioners of education, to superintendents of schools, to boards of education, and, of course, some foundations and teachers' and administrators' unions — is merely acting, colluding in a charade, going through the motions. I would be less than candid if I said that there were no elements of a charade. I have been around too long and observed too many "policymakers" to believe that the educational reform movement does not contain its share of con artists. But in the main, the motives of most policy people are pure, their commitment is a serious one, and their anxiety real. Unfortunately, their knowledge, their *experienced* knowledge of educational reform is too frequently nonexistent or superficial. And to add ignorance to inexperience, for most of these people history is either bunk or started yesterday. If my experience is in any way representative, the great majority of policymakers have read next to nothing about the history of reform. They can sound very impressive when they describe how children are robbed if they do not know how to read or, if they once did, never open a book again. Is it asking too much to expect that policymakers will take seriously for themselves what they advocate for others?

I do not expect the president of the United States to be knowledgeable about education. Let me hasten to add that if I do not expect him (and someday her) to be knowledgeable, it is not because he is without personal experience. If only because he has been a student in the elementary and high school grades, the president is capable of knowing what, when, and where he experienced pleasure in learning, and the characteristics of educational contexts in which he was bored to tears or mischief or failure or sleep. Yes, anyone who has been through the grades has experience relevant to educational reform. Whatever the reason, that experience is unused.

When we go to our physician we expect that he or she will be knowledgeable about the clinical and research literature, an expectation which, unfortunately, is too frequently unjustified. But *our* expectation is certainly justified. So, when the physician prescribes a course of action, we want to feel that his attempt to "reform" our body is based on whatever knowledge exists about our constellation of symptoms: what works, what doesn't work, what is clear, what is up in the air. If we independently were to learn that the physician hardly reads in the literature, we would not return. In regard to educational innovations, the existing literature may not be helpful. This is no reason whatsoever not to proceed, but it does require that the public be made to understand that what is being recommended has to be considered "iffy" in outcome.

I am not suggesting that the literature on the history of educational reform is a gold mine of proven fact and well-sifted, evaluated experience. It isn't. But neither is it devoid of ideas, lessons, or suggestions worthy of reflection and emulation. Indeed, insofar as the reform process is concerned, leaving goals aside, the literature has become refreshingly mature, comprehensive, and plentiful. That this literature paints a dispiriting picture of the process, the goals of which are rarely attained, is disappointing, but at the least we are given concrete illustrations of what not to do. If the reformers do not read, however, the number of illustrations our journals and books contain will increase.

I have never read anything by an elected official (such as the president, a member of a board of education, a chairperson of a legislative committee) that reflected his or her *personal* experience in schools. In fact, in the entire literature, reference to personal experience is very rare. I'm quite aware of the arguments against using personal experience to prove anything or as a basis for a policy recommendation. But what if there are certain types of personal experiences that are so general, so illuminating, so important that they should not be dismissed on grounds of subjectivity? The one and only example I can give is from a short piece in *Education Week* for March 1, 1989. The article is by Thomas Kean, at that time governor of

New Jersey.[1] It is a remarkable piece in two respects. It marks the first time (in my experience) that a high government official laments that arts education is not considered an absolutely *basic* component of education: not a luxury, a frill, an add-on but a *basic*. So the governor says: "While a back-to-basics movement has figured prominently in the reform agenda of recent years, one 'basic' has not been taken along for the ride on the bandwagon: Arts education" (p. 36). That Governor Kean was not mouthing empty clichés can be seen in his appointment of a task force to outline an arts curriculum for kindergarten through twelfth grade and to seek ways to provide the money and teachers the expanded arts education would require.

The second remarkable aspect of the article is more germane to the role of personal experience in the formulation of educational policy. Here is a short paragraph from it:

"No doubt the skepticism of many Americans towards arts education is born of personal experience. Too many of us can remember classes in which art meant learning a simple tune on the recorder or making a macrame potholder for our mothers. And we can all recall English classes in which studying literature meant reading the occasional novel or poem and certainly never included creative writing of our own. Though such experiences are more a symptom of the problem we face than a critique of arts education, they hold sway over parents and educators alike" (Kean, 1989, p. 36).

The classrooms that Governor Kean was describing, far from being intellectually stimulating and engendering a sense of personal satisfaction and growth, were uninteresting, boring, and devoid of personal meaning. He was using personal experience to pinpoint a problem that everyone — and "everyone" is only a slight exaggeration — has experienced in a greater rather than lesser degree. And his indictment goes beyond education in the arts. What are the implications of that indictment for educational reform? The governor does not ask or pursue

---

[1]In my book *The Challenge of Art to Psychology* (1990a) I reproduced Governor Kean's article and discuss it at length. Here I can only summarize aspects of his piece and of my analyses of the governor's recommendations.

the question. He uses personal experience to state a crucial problem and for that he deserves credit for clarity and courage, but
in failing to pursue the implications of the problem he is prevented from seeing that his recommendations are doomed to
failure. Nevertheless, in that very brief article the potency of
using personal experience is made clear. Indeed, it is the personal experience of people, professional or lay, with educational
reform and reformers that makes it so difficult for them to decide whether our schools are Gunther's Austria or Germany.
Using personal experience to inform educational policy may be
a double-edged sword, but that characteristic is no warrant to
ignore such experience. That is precisely what has been ignored
by almost all reformers, *their* personal experiences.

I am told that when someone talks at a meeting of Alcoholics Anonymous they begin by saying, "I am an alcoholic."
No ifs, ands, or buts. And those who hear those words know
from personal experience not only what those words mean but
also what difficulties had to be overcome to say those words out
loud and, no less important, the mine field of temptations that
have to be resisted if actions are to be consistent with those words.
The articulation of the words is one thing; actions consistent
with them is quite another. Analogously, it is as if Governor
Kean had said, "What goes on in our classrooms is, from my
personal experience, anti-educational, however unintended. This
must not be allowed to go on." But it does and will go on as
long as we cannot bring ourselves to say, "We have been wrong.
We have not faced the realities of our personal experience. We
have tried this and that to no avail. We are ready to own up
to our past failures. It is no longer enough to say things will
work out, and that we have come through worse problems." We
have much to learn from the self-deceptions of alcoholics. We
are still employing our ifs, ands, and buts.

My previous book *The Predictable Failure of Educational Reform* (1990b) was not an exercise in nihilism or hopelessness but
an effort to identify some core issues which, because they have
been ignored or glossed over, guarantee that efforts at reform
will largely be failures. It is a book in which I sedulously avoid
scapegoating, which would have been justified only if individuals

or groups willed the current inadequacies of our schools. There are no such villains. Our task would be incomparably easier if such villains existed. Being imprisoned in tradition, being resistant to and fearful of anything other than superficial change and window dressing, puzzled by the failure of past efforts, allergic to fads and fashions, disenchanted with quick fixes — such attitudes and reactions are not those of villains.

That book was a very personal statement. What was so encouraging to me was the number of people, none of whom I have ever met, who wrote to say that their personal experience was not only similar to mine but led them also to similar conclusions. I am aware that authors tend to hear from the converted. In reality, I was emboldened to write that book because over the decades I have listened to countless people say what I later wrote in it. More specifically, they were saying that something was fundamentally wrong and that reform efforts were not addressing it. In truth, the book contained the experiences of multiple authors.

It is fair to say that it was an attempt at etiological diagnosis, an effort to isolate what I consider some of the most important factors without which we cannot explain the discrepancy between a disturbing condition and the efficacy of our reform efforts. If everyone is in agreement that we are faced with a set of problems that we have to do something about, and if in the post–World War II era serious people have committed themselves to valiant efforts at reform, why have the results been either so modest, minuscule, or nonexistent? That was the question the book tried to illuminate. It was not about what to do; it was about how we have been thinking, what axioms we have unreflectively accepted as right, natural, and proper, and alternative ways we should begin to think.

There is one point in the book that deserves emphasis here because it reflects a truly revolutionary change, a change that has already taken place but that is hard for people to articulate for diverse reasons. I refer to the fact, and I consider it a fact, that an increasing number of people in and around the educational arena no longer believe either that underfinancing is a root cause of the problem or that increased expenditures will solve the problem to any discernible extent. That belief, I should hasten to add, does not reflect an unwillingness to increase expenditures or an attitude of malign neglect or a decision that existing resources need only to be reallocated in more judicious ways, but rather that there is no reason to believe that the direction of proposed reform efforts will be productive. Up until very recently the articulation of such a belief would have been regarded as reactionary in the extreme, an example of callousness, a refusal to redress past and present inequities. I am sure there are people for whom such attributions would be appropriate. They are *not* the ones I am talking about. That belief is one that has been expressed to me privately by countless educators who feel guilty that they harbor such thoughts and are puzzled (too weak a word) about what they should think and do. What they think in the quiet of the night they fear to express in the light of day because if they did so, *they* would be blamed for the failures.

Some would argue that for so many people to have been driven to such a belief is bad news. I would argue that the good news is that these people are being driven to a reexamination of treasured beliefs. And when I say driven I mean just that: we have not wanted to go to where we seem to be arriving. Being driven to a truly revolutionary conclusion is unsettling.

In that earlier book (Sarason, 1990b) I refer several times to the constitutional convention of 1787 when representatives of each of the colonies met over a period of months to forge a new basis for governance. Some were reluctant participants, they differed widely in political outlook, they were far from unanimous in philosophy and values, and they were zealous partisans for the social and economic interests of their regions. There were times when it appeared that agreement on fundamental issues would be impossible. But there was one undeniable bond that kept them going and facilitated a transcendence of their differences: the existing Articles of Confederation, hastily drawn up after the revolution, were not working, and the ways that they were failing were endangering the fledgling country. The members of that convention could no longer afford to evade the inadequacies and potential dangers of the Articles of Confederation. What is wondrous is how the convention participants faced and dealt with the realities of what was and the necessity to give concrete expression to a new vision.

There is another feature of the convention that bears on our current educational scene. The participants agreed that their deliberations would be held confidential as a way to ensure that they would all feel free to raise and explore any attitude or idea or suggestion without fear of condemnation. They knew the problems were complicated, that there was more than one way of thinking about them, and that the stakes were too high for them to be satisfied with quick fixes. They also realized that thinking through the consequences of proposals was as thorny as it was necessary, that there was a difference between compromise and submission, and that tradition was not to be treated lightly at the same time that one needed to be prepared to depart from it. And they prevailed on the press of the times not to publish anything about the deliberations. And, wonder of wonders, the press agreed and respected the agreement! That comes as close to an operational definition of a secular miracle as I know, equaled only by the document that finally emerged.

In matters educational we are in desperate need of a constitutional convention — not just another meeting bemoaning the sad state of affairs, not more proclamations of virtuous intent, of people talking past each other, or of adversarialism untempered by sustained, face-to-face discussion. And not more debates carried out in public, guaranteeing that the news bite on the evening news or the brief article in the newspapers will convey simplicity and ignore complexity.

Such a convention is not in the cards for educational reform. (Can you imagine forty or fifty "leaders" holing up for three months or for as long as it takes to arrive at agreement?) I have had frequent fantasies about such a convention. After all, if I will not be there, I can at least imagine what it would be like and what I would say.

These fantasies have led to this book. In the following pages I propose courses of action I would dearly love to discuss with others who may disagree with me or, if they agree, see pitfalls I have not. As important as the actions I propose are the problems they seek to address. It is one thing to disagree about actions; it is quite another to disagree that there is no problem justifying those actions. So, for example, I shall have much to propose about the selection and preparation of educators. If you think that their selection and preparation are a relatively minor problem, or, worse yet, no problem at all, you will obviously find my proposals an example of misplaced emphasis, a making of a mountain out of a molehill. Similarly, when I propose a time perspective for educational reform that is vastly different from that which undergirds present efforts, I expect two types of disagreements: one agrees in principle with my statement of the problem but regards my proposal as socially unacceptable and, therefore, self-defeating. The other disagreement challenges the way I formulate the problem, seeing my definition of it as essentially a misdiagnosis of the capacity of complex organizations to change.

In the following pages I make relatively concrete proposals about some important problems. In my previous writings I have tried to analyze them in order to clarify them, and I have given special attention to the reasons efforts at reform have fallen short of the mark. Therefore, in what follows I shall not advance a comprehensive conception of these problems, and I shall not repeat all the factors on which implementation has foundered. Inevitably, I shall have to go over some old ground.

I entreat the reader to distinguish between a problem and the actions I suggest. And I further ask the reader to take seriously the horrendously complex nature of these problems. Mencken had it right when he said that for every problem there is a simple answer which is wrong. Indeed, what may discourage a reader of the following pages is how complicated the problems are. Too many reformers and policy makers are guilty of the grossest kinds of oversimplification, not the least of which are the nonsensical beliefs — for which not a shred of evidence exists — that you can legislate motivation, that a "shape up or ship out" approach heightens student interest, curiosity, and performance, and that making test scores public will bring about a change for the better, in ways never specified. In regard to publishing test scores the rationale seems to be "the truth shall set you free." Test scores are facts, not truths.

Before presenting what I consider to be my most important proposal, it is necessary that I devote several chapters to demonstrating how complicated the problems are. I do this as much to caution the reader against underestimating their complexity as to indicate how egregiously lopsided reform efforts have been in regard to complexity. As I hope to make clear, given that complexity—even leaving aside the feckless consequences of dealing with it—we are faced with two alternatives for action: to continue to try to *repair* existing problems or to take *preventive* actions. Of course we will and should continue to ameliorate existing problems but that is no justification for failing, as we now are, to take prevention seriously. The problems are too many, too complicated, and too resistant to past efforts for us to expect that the nearly exclusive dependence on repair will have discernible positive consequences.

Chapter Three

Underestimating Complexity

When someone advocates improvement of the quality of education, we cannot judge their advocacy unless we know who they are, that is, in what relation they stand to schools and the decision-making process. If the advocate for such a laudable goal is a classroom teacher, we assume that he or she is in a position to change something in a single classroom. We take for granted that whatever resources the teacher has are relevant to the goal of improving the educational experience and performance of students in that classroom. Let us imagine a teacher who has become convinced that instead of teaching by the "whole class" method, he or she will divide the pupils into small working groups in which students will take on more responsibility for their own learning: they will no longer be passive recipients of teacher input and direction, they will learn to use each other to handle assignments, they will have a more personal stake in what they do. Whether the teacher is right or wrong in being convinced is not at issue. The point is that we assume the teacher can institute such a change; we applaud a teacher who is dissatisfied with the way things have been and sets out to "reform" his or her classroom. One classroom, one teacher, one effort at improvement.[1]

---

[1]The clearest, most succinct and balanced presentation of the theoretical basis of cooperative learning is that by Shlomo Sharan (forthcoming). As he points out, cooperative learning is a generic name that refers to several methods for the organization and conduct of classroom instruction, each method constructed on the basis of different theoretical orientations. His focus is on one type of "Group Investigation." What is so refreshing about this paper is that Sharan emphasizes,

But when teachers advocate educational reform, however, they almost never are referring to what they can or should do in their own classrooms. They refer to people and factors outside the classroom, which they see as being in need of change that would presumably have a positive impact on what happens in classrooms. Indeed, it almost has the status of a law to say that those who advocate an educational reform seek not to reform themselves but to change someone or something else. So, let us imagine that the teacher who gave up the "whole class" method of teaching concludes at the end of the school year that the change has had dramatically positive results, by whatever criteria one could employ. And now that teacher, stimulated by success, seeks to convince other teachers and the principal to change their attitudes and practices. Whereas before we could take for granted that in the single classroom the teacher had the resources, the responsibility, and the authority to institute a change, we cannot take for granted that in seeking to effect a change in all classrooms in that school the teacher has similar powers and responsibility. In fact, we would be justified in assuming that the teacher has taken on a task for which he or she is not prepared by formal training or even knowledge. Is that teacher perceived by others as a leader, an opinion maker? Does the teacher have the interpersonal skills to undertake such a task? Is the teacher willing to devote out-of-school time to discussing the issues and problems the change would require? Are there forums in that school at which the changes can be raised, discussed, and judged? Does the school or school system have resources and supportive services that can be utilized?

---

as he has in other writings, that for a teacher to *unlearn* the traditional "whole class" method of teaching and to *learn* and *appropriately* apply small group methodology is a personally and intellectually demanding and even upsetting process. That process is well known to the psychotherapist who having worked only with individual clients decides to try his or her hand at group psychotherapy. It is a different ball game, not one in which good intentions are sufficient. I have personally observed classrooms organized on a small group methodology but which in practice were suppressed with all of the features of the whole class method. A good example is given in Chapter 13 where I discuss David Cohen's observations of a teacher who prided herself on her use of cooperative learning.

It is infrequent, bordering on rare, for an individual teacher to try to have an impact on an entire school. For one thing, there is nothing in the preparation of teachers that is relevant to such a task. And, as I have said countless times in the past, the culture of schools is inimical to collegiality in regard to intellectual-education-reform matters. But even leaving these facts aside, teachers can relate "war stories" about what can happen to those who try to change something outside of their classrooms, or about what happens to teachers who are the objects of someone else's proposal for reform.

There have been times, however, when a teacher has not been intimidated by others' failures and has spearheaded actions that changed a school in important ways. And in recent years, formal, system-initiated changes have taken place that give teachers responsibility to make changes. (Just as some teachers have organized their classrooms to give more responsibility to students, there are schools where teachers are being given new responsibilities.) Two problems have arisen. These were predictable, except no one dealt with the predictable. The first is that the new responsibilities required attitudes, knowledge, and understanding for which teachers had not been prepared. Learning to act in ways consistent with new roles collided with the need for and difficulty of *unlearning* old ways. At best, learning new ways is difficult; at worst, the old ways win out rather quickly. The second problem is that teachers vastly underestimated what one confronts in *sustaining* a change. In brief, what many teachers have learned is that reforming an existing organization and its problems is best left to those with unfulfilled reservoirs of masochism. There are exceptions, of course, and in later pages I shall return to why they have succeeded and are so rare.

Let me now give an example of a proposal that contrasts to existing practice, a proposal that illuminates the difference between repair and prevention. It is a proposal I first floated in 1975 (Sarason, 1976) and have managed to refloat every time I have talked with groups of educators, and those times have been many. Two points are noteworthy. First, never has any person disagreed with the proposal. Second, no one has seen

fit to take it seriously in practice. In part, failure to implement
the proposal may be explained by the fact that I stand in no
formal relationship with a school and school system. There are
other reasons, which will become clear after I present the proposal. Here is how I put it in 1976:

> I must confess that when I hear people say "we want
> to meet the needs of all children so that each child has
> the opportunity to realize his potentials" I do not know
> whether to laugh or cry—to laugh because behind that
> statement is the invalid assumption that to accomplish
> these goals all we need do is to hire more and more
> of the kinds of personnel who now inhabit our schools.
> This assumption, even if it were true, is scandalously
> unrealistic. And I want to cry because that well-in-
> tentioned statement fails to recognize that the prob-
> lem primarily reflects our accustomed ways of think-
> ing of what a teacher is, how a classroom should look,
> and how a school should be organized.
>
> Let me give an example with which most adults
> are familiar. When do most parents come to their
> child's school? One of these times is when they have
> been asked to come to discuss a problem in connec-
> tion with their child. That is to say, they come *after*
> the school is fairly sure there is a problem, and usually
> that is well after the school found itself asking *if* there
> was a problem. The other time is several weeks after
> the school year has begun, when there is "open house"
> or "parent's night" usually in conjunction with the first
> PTA meeting. Parents are encouraged to come and
> visit their child's classroom, meet the teacher, hear
> about the curriculum, and to talk with the teacher
> about their child, if they so desire. These evenings
> are, by common consent, among the most uncomfort-
> able, unsatisfying social rituals invented by humans—
> albeit one of the less hostile examples of man's inhu-
> manity to man. At the end of the evening everyone
> breathes a sigh of relief that this charade is over, that

a function designed to be informative and to redound to the interests of children has been lived through without casualties (except for the purposes for which the meeting was intended).

Is there another way of thinking about how to get parents and teachers meeting around the individual needs of children? Can this be done so that the interests and knowledge of both stand a chance of being articulated in a way which could be used to meet the needs of individual children — at least to recognize these needs to a greater extent than they now are? Suppose that before the first day of class appointments are made with the parents of each child. (To make it possible for both parents to come, teachers would be available in the evenings and even over a weekend — you deliberately and willingly adapt to the circumstances of parents and not vice versa.) And suppose that the teacher said to the parents: "I was eager to get together with you before class begins because I wanted to learn as much as possible about your child so that I can be of as much help to him (her) as possible. Obviously, you know your child extremely well and even after I have gotten to know him I will not know him in the same way you do. You know his likes and dislikes, his strong points and weak points, what turns him on and what turns him off, what works with him and what doesn't. You know a great deal I ought to know if I am to treat and teach your child in ways suited to him — some ways are more suitable for some children than they are for others. So you can see that if I am to help your child you have to help me with what you know."

Note that you cannot talk to parents in this way unless you truly believe that what they can tell you will be helpful to you in your relationship with their child. If you view parents as hopelessly prejudiced and blind about their child, as people who do not or cannot recognize positive and negative features in their child, as people who would rather withhold than reveal information about their child — if you tend to view parents in these ways you usually structure your relationship with them so that you end up proving you were right in the first place. If, however, you are not intent on proving your superiority to parents, your all-knowingness, and you have no trouble accepting as a fact that parents can be helpful to you, that they can reveal "bad" things about their child, that indeed many parents want to do just that without the fear that it will be held against their child, you will learn a great deal which will help you react differentially to their child. In short, I am not suggesting role-playing but rather some values and a way of thinking about how you learn about individual children and how you begin a relationship with parents that is not likely to become an adversarial one, or one in which people talk to and not with each other. Whatever its other benefits would be, the relationship I am suggesting is far more humane than the dishonesties of Parent's Night or the usual after-school parent-teacher conference characterized by as much openness and candidness as a high-stakes poker game. Can there be any doubt that my suggestion holds out greater hope than present practice that a teacher will learn something which could be useful in meeting individual needs? To follow my proposal requires no additional money or personnel, just another way of thinking. But where will teachers be aided to think in these ways? As we (Sarason, Davidson, and Blatt, 1962) pointed out years ago: even though talking to parents is considered a crucial function of the teacher — a function they are *required* to perform — they receive absolutely no instruction for the function in their training. Similarly, even though principals and other administrators spend a fair amount of their time organizing and running meetings, they too receive no exposure in their training to the issues (technical, theoretical,

and moral) contained in such a function. Unless one
believes that performing such functions is a matter
of genes or divine guidance the issues have to be
directly confronted in training [Sarason, 1976, p. 578].

The obstacles to implementing such an approach are
several. First, it requires a sincere belief that parents have knowledge important to your purposes. That, it must be emphasized,
does not mean that what they tell you is hands-on-the-bible truth.
Let us remember that that is no less true for what *we* know and
say. No less than parents, our knowledge and explanations are
inevitably incomplete and in certain respects wrong. But the
purpose of putting the cards on the table is to alter, enlarge,
and combine differing perceptions and understandings. More
than that, the purpose is to gain commitment from the participants to take on new, shared responsibilities. Educating children is not and should not be the sole responsibility of educators.

A second obstacle, of course, is time, the ubiquitous variable. In my 1976 remarks I said that the approach requires
another way of thinking, not more money and new personnel.
It is unlikely that all teachers would be willing to give that time
freely. If that is true, it says less about greediness than it does
about the adversarial relationship between teachers and administrators. There is one conclusion I have come to from my experience and that of others: when teachers, indeed all educators,
come to see that a course of action is in their self-interest — that
it will be personally, intellectually, and educationally productive —
time as an obstacle is surmounted. One of the reasons most reforms fail is that they deal with the "form" of a problem and
not its substance or context. You can proclaim the virtues of
parental involvement, you can even legislate such involvement,
but if you are ignorant of or insensitive to how the parties define
their self-interests, you are engaging in self-defeating actions.
You are making problems, not preventing them. The words *self-
interests* tend to be viewed as reflective of selfishness or callousness. I trust it is clear that when I use those words I am referring to how people define themselves in regard to roles, goals,
and obligations. It is glib to say to a group of educators, par-

ents, and others that "we all share the commitment to a quality education for our children." Everyone nods in agreement but no one is prepared to acknowledge that different groups do not define their roles and obligations to that commitment in the same ways. To ignore those differences or to assume that goodwill alone will solve them is the grossest of misunderstandings of the nature, power, and inevitability of perceived self-interests.

This chapter is a plea that we face up to the complexity of the problems reforms are intended to ameliorate. I have begun with the examples of *a* teacher and *a* classroom, *a* teacher and *a* school. And I have used proposals of modest scope, each intended to repair an unsatisfactory state of affairs. Let us now turn to far more ambitious proposals.

There have been three revolutions in American education. The first was legislation making schooling universal and compulsory. That revolution was powered by diverse considerations, values, and national self-interest. However unassailable the goal, it brought in its wake a host of problems, a form of organization and administration, a view of professional responsibility, a mode of selecting and preparing personnel, a conception of a classroom and a school that we continue today to grapple with, to try to reform. One could argue that we are unjustified in criticizing the proponents of compulsory education for failing to anticipate problems; in those late nineteenth- and early twentieth-century days the level of sophistication about children and schooling was understandably meager and, as a result, the proponents underestimated the complexity and consequences of their proposals. That argument assumes, however, that since those days we have become so much more sophisticated that we do not underestimate complexity, we take more seriously what children are, and, therefore, we do a better job in obtaining desired outcomes. That assumption, I need to believe, is one with which no sane person would agree. We have traveled far but those desired outcomes seem always to be receding before us just beyond our horizons. We are kin, not strangers, to those early proponents. We have learned a great deal about problems, we have been sobered and chastened by our efforts to deal with them, but what we have learned seems to have little or no payoff. In some inchoate way we know that the problems are horribly complex and in the quiet of the night we wonder whether they are remediable.

But there is one other answer to those who feel it is unjustified to pass judgment on those early proponents. Even in the early days there were individuals, well known nationally and internationally, who were incisive critics of schools. I refer specifically to John Dewey, although there were others. Dewey's great contributions were in the illumination of the minds of children and in the concrete ways educators could capitalize on that illumination to encourage a child's personal and intellectual growth. Dewey was not an armchair philosopher. He created his own school at the University of Chicago precisely to test his ideas in the crucible of practice. And Dewey understood one thing that was never taken seriously: education was not an isolable field separate from other fields of theory and practice. *Education was a social science* and to the extent that it was embedded in the social sciences we stood a chance of comprehending the complexity of the problems education faced. Unfortunately, the social sciences had other agendas, none of which was education. In this regard I urge the reader to read Dewey's presidential address to the American Psychological Association in 1899 (Dewey, 1975 [1913]).

In the ordinary household Dewey was not a familiar name, but in the household of education it was illustrious. Many educators supported his ideas, writings, and school. Dewey spent much time stimulating, encouraging, and helping others implement his ideas in their individual schools and school systems, but in just a few years it became clear that the sought-for reforms had not taken.

Why? That is a very complicated question and I will respond to only those parts that have answers most relevant to my present purposes. First, Dewey did not understand that because much of what he had learned came from a lab school experience, generalizations were quite risky. Put in another way, Dewey never confronted the problem of how to reform a school; *he* had *created* the lab school, he did not have to *reform* an existing one. In fact, in the process of creating the lab school Dewey sought to *prevent* the problems he saw plaguing many schools. As I pointed out years ago (Sarason, 1989 [1972]), the process of creating a new setting is not for the fainthearted or the light-headed or those with tunnel vision. Nevertheless, it is a process in which those creating the new environment very consciously seek to prevent some perceived defect or inadequacy of existing similar ones. No one creating a new setting seeks literally to replicate existing ones similar in function and purpose; the new environment is always viewed by its creators as superior in some ways to these other settings. In creating the lab school, Dewey knew what he wanted to prevent. He did not have to make a lab school over; insofar as the lab school is concerned, Dewey was not a reformer. He was a creator out to demonstrate, among other things, that he could prevent classrooms from being places where "commanders" poured in facts into children who were required to be passive, conforming recipients, presumably unable in any way to participate in the structuring of their learning.

The second reason for the failure of Dewey's ideas to take hold is that despite his extraordinary sensitivity to how children think and grow, how in the modal classroom the creative spark in them is unrecognized, diverted, or extinguished, how schools rest on the assumption that children are not curious about their world and are not question-asking organisms — despite his exquisite sensitivity to children, Dewey seemed peculiarly uninterested in why teachers teach as they do and, fatefully, why they would resist changing their practices. But there is more to it than that: Dewey understood that classrooms, schools, and school systems are very complicated affairs, which may be the understatement of the decade, but he seemed to underestimate the practical implications of this reality for the change process. Whenever you have people who are in formal relationships with each other and who differ widely (and sometimes wildly) in age, role, gender, power, background, race, ethnicity, and ambitions — in a classroom, a school, a school system — you have a complexity which, if not intended deliberately to defeat reform, is mightily resistant to it.

It is not because Dewey is one of my heroes that I believe

he understood that complexity, at least up to a point. Whether he did or not, in practice he ignored it. He seemed to operate on the assumption that good intentions allow you to surmount the problems that arise when you seek to change what individuals and organizations do, *even when these individuals and organizations proclaim their desire to change.* If we have learned anything with near certainty, both from the organizational and psychotherapeutic literature, it is that those who seek to change find themselves at some point resisting change. If Dewey's ideas did not take hold, it was not because those who were implementing them were unusually dense, or superficial, or not sufficiently motivated. For the most part, they were bright people eager to reform and improve inadequate schools. But, like Dewey, they did not comprehend what they were up against when they took reform seriously.

The second revolution was started by the Supreme Court's 1954 desegregation decision. No one expected the Court to come up with a blueprint to implement its legal decision. The nearest it came to the arena of action was the admonition that the decision be carried out with "deliberate speed." There are at least two ways you can explain the use of that phrase. The first is that the Court understood that desegregation could not be accomplished in a matter of months or even a few years and, therefore, it avoided setting deadlines. There is nothing in the decision to suggest that the justices had the foggiest idea of the dynamics their decision would set off so that decades later desegregation would seem as unattainable as ever — indeed, that three decades later some influential black educators and elected officials would call for segregated schools.

But the Supreme Court consists of lawyers, not of educators or of those in allied fields. In matters educational the members of the Supreme Court are part of what may be called the educated public. These distinctions aside, lumping all of these groups together, what were the reactions to the decision? There were three. One was opposition from those who viewed desegregation as calamitous and sinful. One was relief — from North and South, blacks and whites — that an egregious wrong could no longer be sanctioned by law. One was the expectation and hope that the mandated changes would occur in the foreseeable future and with minimum discord. That there would be discord and problems was taken for granted but there was also the hope that in the not-too-distant future right would prevail over wrong. One other reaction has to be noted: the expectation that implementation would encounter a rougher road in the South than in the North.

Before commenting on these reactions, I have to tell the reader that I could write a fair-sized article, even a book, cataloguing my mistakes in comprehending the response of individuals and organizations to the pressure for change. That article or book would not contain my reactions and predictions in regard to the 1954 decision. Never have I felt more alone than when I listened to presumably knowledgeable people express the belief that the goal of desegregation was near at hand — if not next year or in five years, then not long after that. It was obvious to me that these people, in and around schools, were underestimating enormously the complexity of the object of change and were coming up with proposals that would transform complexity into an impossibility. Unfortunately, I was right.

One can argue that revolutions are inevitably messy, devouring affairs, if only because an old tradition — with its associated attitudes, expectations, morality, and worldview — is being supplanted by a new one. There are winners and losers, the haves and the have nots, the powerful and the powerless, the good guys and the bad guys. But unlike most revolutions marked by spontaneous, militant uprisings, the one sparked by the desegregation decision was not spontaneous. It was a consequence of a legal decision by judges who dimly, if at all, sensed what the consequences might be. And if that was understandably true for the Court, it was less understandable (to me) in the case of those policymakers, legislators, and educational practitioners, theorists, and researchers seeking to implement the decision.

I trust that the reader will not interpret these remarks as in any way suggesting that I think the Court erred in its decision. Further, I trust the reader will not conclude that I believe

if we had truly recognized the complexity we faced, the outcomes would have been dramatically more positive. Maybe yes,
maybe no. What I am suggesting is that today we acknowledge
that the complexity of the reform process was vastly underestimated. Why own up to it today? Because the history of educational reform since 1954 contains little evidence that we have
drawn the appropriate lessons. On the contrary, the reform
movements have come and gone without providing us a convincing explanation of their failures. I have discussed this di-
lemma in four previous books: *The Culture of the School and the
Problem of Change* (1982), *Schooling in America. Scapegoat and Salvation* (1983), *The Predictable Failure of Educational Reform* (1990b),
and *The Challenge of Art to Psychology* (1990a). I will not repeat
here what is in those four books.

In a fascinating and predictable way the third revolution
was sparked by the second. I refer to Public Law 94-142, passed
by Congress in 1975 and titled the Education for All Handicapped Children's Act. As in the first two revolutions, that legislation was intended to affect every school in every state.

I have to explain why I describe this third revolution as
predictable. Revolutions, like most if not all human actions, have
predictable and unpredictable consequences. I know of no public
educator who predicted that the 1954 decision would be interpreted by parents of handicapped children as providing the rationale for requiring schools to cease segregating handicapped
children in special classes, and, in addition, to cease refusing
to accept children who by traditional standards were deemed
uneducable. Put in another way, in the language of the legislation, handicapped children deserved the opportunity to be in
the least restrictive environment. Special classes were separate
and unequal.

Professionally, I grew up, so to speak, in the field of mental
retardation and special education. I, like others in the field, did
not need to be told that we had two school systems: regular and
special. And guess who were the second-class citizens? With the
1954 decision a number of parents, parent organizations, and
their lawyers quickly saw the applicability of that decision to
the education of all handicapped children. Their efforts culmi-
nated in the 1975 legislation.

Two goals of that legislation are most relevant to my present purposes. The first is implicit and moral. As in the 1954 decision, Public Law 94-142 centers around this question: How do we want our children to learn to be sensitive to and tolerant of differences in others? How should or can such sensitivity and tolerance be discussed, learned, and reinforced in classrooms? When the Supreme Court struck down the doctrine of "separate but equal" it did so in large part by the argument that segregation has negative consequences for the segregatees *and* segregators. Similarly, segregation in our schools on the basis of handicap was seen as unjust to and restrictive of handicapped children as it was a creator and sustainer of prejudice and stereotypes in "regular" children.

Historically, there were several major arguments in favor of special classes but none was as persuasive as the one asserting the anti-educational consequences of heterogeneity in the classroom. That argument had three parts: heterogeneity vastly complicates the teacher's task, it reduces the time available to the more able, and it further erodes a low self-esteem in the less able. What got lost over the years in the heterogeneity versus homogeneity controversies was the reality that no selection procedure — be it an intelligence or personality or achievement test, or combination of them — eliminates heterogeneity. Classrooms inevitably vary in degree of heterogeneity, and bringing handicapped children into regular classrooms would increase but not be a *cause* of heterogeneity. If that had been recognized, a most fundamental question could have been addressed: how well is heterogeneity, narrow or wide, handled in the regular classroom? That question would have brought to the fore an obvious feature of teachers, principals, and administrators: the pressure they exert to remove from classrooms children who in one or another way interfere with "normal" routine.

It has never been a secret that many children who were (and many who still are) removed from the classroom were not handicapped in any clinical sense but were victims of classroom atmosphere, practices, and goals. It would be both surprising and amazing if that were not the case because the preparation of educators and the rationale for structuring classrooms in schools give overwhelming emphasis to the learning of content and academic skills, not the confronting and accommodation by students of differences among them. No one, of course, would deny the importance of such confronting and accommodation, and no one would say that they are ignored or glossed over. But the historical record belies such good intentions. Segregating diverse students for diverse reasons has long been the rule, not the exception. Historical record aside, we have no secure basis for believing that sensitivity to and tolerance of differences are desirably handled in the modal classroom.

I am not scapegoating educators. I am criticizing their preparation, which ill prepares them for how to use heterogeneity in the classroom to help students understand their moral obligations to the omnipresent fact of differences among them. That criticism, however, has to be seen in the light of one other fact: to cope seriously with the moral implications of heterogeneity requires *classroom time;* and in light of the emphasis, the near-exclusive emphasis, on acquiring content and academic skills, such time is not available. Any activity that cuts into achieving these important but narrow educational goals is viewed as an interference and a distraction. In the culture of the school everything takes a backseat to those narrow educational goals. This perspective is justifiable only if you do not view schooling as a moral enterprise but rather as one in which understanding and tolerating differences, whatever their nature, are luxuries unnecessary for living in a democratic society. And it is justifiable if you believe that people are born fair and wise. That these are unjustifiable positions is precisely what the 1954 desegregation decision and the 1975 legislation for the handicapped brought to the fore and challenged.

What have been the consequences of the 1975 legislation? One has been that those handicapped children who heretofore were not in schools are now there but in segregated settings, usually in *special* schools. In regard to other handicapped children, they spend part of each day in "resource" rooms or "self-contained learning centers." In elementary schools especially, those labeled handicapped (but educable) are frequently in special classrooms although they may eat, play, go to assemblies, and take music classes (where available) with "regular" children.

I do not wish to convey the impression that school personnel consciously seek to subvert the intentions of the legislation. That is usually not the case, although it is true that many educators resent the resources provided to these children and programs. And yet, paradoxically, it is those additional resources that have allowed educators to label children as handicapped so as to get them services ordinarily not available to children in regular classrooms. Since the passage of that legislation in 1975, the number of children labeled handicapped has steadily and dramatically increased each year. This growth has less to do with the appropriateness of such labeling than with the inability of teachers to deal with heterogeneity in the classroom. As a result, more children today spend part of the school day outside their regular classroom than ever before. My experiences of sitting in on "placement" meetings force me to conclude that this increase derives in part from the lack of understanding and skill of many teachers in coping with heterogeneity. No less than the mislabeled children, teachers are also victims — of their preparation and the pressure to have their pupils learn content and academic skills.

I do not underestimate the difficulties of teachers in coping with marked heterogeneity. If you are the parent of two or more children, you can begin to comprehend what teachers are up against with a classroom of many more unique characters. As one teacher said to me, "Since parents do not do a particularly outstanding job dealing with the differences among their children, why do they expect us to do better with twenty or more students?" It was that same teacher who told me that even with her own three children she never had enough *time* to deal as effectively as she should with each child or a child's relationships with siblings. How many times have teachers expressed guilt because they could not deal adequately — either because of lack of understanding or sheer time — with the diversity among their pupils? Too many times. It is the source of that guilt that plays into the tendency to segregate children.

I have been discussing a key goal of the 1975 legislation in which a primary concept is the least restrictive alternative, that is, to give handicapped children the opportunity to be educated with "regular" children, not apart from them. I have tried to indicate what predictable problems such a goal would engender. How would teachers of regular classrooms react to and cope with the grab bag of diagnostic categories encompassed by the term *handicapped?* On what basis does one decide what would be the least restrictive alternative? Does that phrase refer to existing alternatives — which means a special program or a regular one — or does it require developing a variety of alternatives? What administrative problems would arise between those responsible for handicapped children and those responsible for regular children? Considering that special and regular classroom teachers have different professional preparations and certifications, how will the regular teacher integrate the handicapped child into the classroom in ways that are educationally and interpersonally productive for all concerned? How will administrators cope with the resistance of teachers to an increase in the heterogeneity of students? One can go on and on if one is knowledgeable about the history and segregated place of special education and how they are reflected in the culture of schools: attitudes, organization, allocation of resources, and hierarchy of values. Segregation is always reflective of culture and desegregation is always a challenge to that culture, especially if the challenge is a mandated one for which no welcome mat has been rolled out.

A second goal of the complicated 1975 legislation — a very explicit goal — was called by one individual who played an important role in formulating the legislation the "civil rights guts" of the act. Briefly, *no* decision about a handicapped child could be made unless parents were part of the decision-making process and, if they did not approve of a decision, they had avenues of appeal. As that person said to me, "What we intended was once and for all to make it impossible for school personnel to ignore parental rights, needs, feelings, and ideas in regard to their handicapped children." Several years after the 1975 legislation, Michael Klaber and I (Sarason and Klaber, 1985) had occasion to review the research literature on how frequently and well that goal was achieved. The results were predictably sad. My own personal experience in several urban school systems is that results are worse than sad. This outcome is explainable only in part by professional attitudes toward the role of parents in educational decision making. No less important, the writers of the legislation vastly underestimated three very predictable characteristics of a process involving diagnosis, discussion, and placement options: it takes time, knowledge, and a reality that provides more than one or two options for action. Given an increase in the number of children labeled handicapped, why engage in a complicated process when you know beforehand that existing alternatives and services are narrow in the extreme? And why make recommendations that the school, from an economic and educational standpoint, is unable and unwilling to accept?

I participated in a meeting called by the American Psychological Association in response to concerns of school psychologists. They were troubled by their role on placement teams having the responsibility, mandated by the 1975 legislation, to develop individual programs for handicapped children. What troubled them was a conflict between their professional obligations to a child and administrative pressures (sometimes fiats) to make only those recommendations the school could implement without additional expenditures or new programs or even a reallocation of existing resources. I do not mention this as criticism of educators who, I know, do not possess bottomless pits of money but only again to make the point that efforts at educational reform ignore what is knowable and predictable.

I did not present the three revolutions to labor the obvious point that the objects of educational reform are complicated. My purpose was twofold. First, to ask, again, why is that complexity so underestimated? Is it that the pressure to take action causes you to ignore or forget what you know, because if you don't ignore or forget, you will be in the untenable position of proceeding, knowing you are going to fail? Is it that the pressure to initiate reforms according to a fiscal or school calendar — you *must* begin by a certain date and you *must* show results by a later date — adds to the pressure? Is it that these pressures inhibit a thoughtful consideration of the universe of alternatives for action available to you and, no less fateful, prevent you from changing your plans when you see that what you are doing is misfiring? Is it that a passionate commitment to a set of ideas and actions makes you insensitive to glaring signs that you are wrong? Is it that the interpersonal problems any meaningful reform effort engenders — problems stemming from personality differences, power relationships, misinterpretations, and past history — cause you to explain things in terms of individuals and the systemic context fades out of your consciousness?

Or was I wrong, or at least much too charitable, when I said reformers really know that the problems are complicated? How many times have people poured out their dysphoric feelings to me in regard to their failures at reform, vividly describing one explosion after another on their excursion over the minefields of implementation? *And this is from people whom I knew had read the critical and analytical literature on reforms, but who describe their experiences as if they were totally ignorant of such writing.* Again, I do not say this from any stance of superiority. Quite the contrary, like the anti-hero in the musical *Pal Joey,* I could write a book about ignoring in action what I truly knew in an abstract, conceptual way. There is knowing and there is knowing. Over the decades I have known many deservedly noted people in child development. If they agree on anything, it is that knowing the principles of child development was one thing, applying them appropriately to their "real, live" children was quite another. I shall return to these issues later in this book.

Suffice it to say here that the "trick" in a reform effort, from the moment of its conception, is how to develop some kind of forum to prevent you from unduly underestimating complexity. The reformer needs to be able to say, "I have met *an* enemy, and it is I and, therefore, I need some external source of control." That is preventive thinking in regard to a predictable set of experiences. In the normal course of living, keeping ourselves honest is not easy. Keeping ourselves honest when we engage in a meaningful reform effort should be regarded as probably impossible. If you accept that, you are playing it safe.

My second purpose in using these examples was as a way of approaching what is central to this book: the prevention, not the repair, of problems. Conventionally, we distinguish between two types of prevention. In primary prevention we seek to prevent or at least dramatically to reduce the incidence of appearance of a problem. In secondary prevention we seek to ameliorate or prevent the further adverse consequences of a problem that already has arisen. It is secondary prevention that has been a distinguishing characteristic of the educational reform movements, that is, these reforms are geared to do something about problems that have been identified and require action. Low motivation, dropouts, low achievement scores, school behavior problems, inadequate or outmoded curricula, teacher incompetency or inadequacy, failure to articulate and maintain standards of performance, stultifying bureaucratic organizational styles, poor teacher morale, parental indifference or noninvolvement — one can generate a long list of problems in reaction to which a reform effort has been mounted. The results have not been encouraging. This explains, in part, why the most frequent fantasy among educators centers around creating new schools, starting from scratch and building into the new school ideas, procedures, organizations, forums, and values that will prevent the emergence of the problems that plague existing schools.

Beginning in the sixties we witnessed the mushrooming of alternative schools, deliberate efforts to take *primary* prevention seriously. In almost all these instances the schools were created by educators who no longer wanted to spend their days dealing with problems caused in measure by the ways conventional schools were conceived, organized, and run. Over the years I have visited several alternative schools and have had the opportunity to talk with many more individuals with responsibilities in or for these schools. Unfortunately but quite understandably, they are too busy administering their schools to write up their experience in ways that would permit us to judge the degree of their success.[2] And, of course, we will never hear from those whose alternative school failed or went out of existence, a not-infrequent occurrence.

Let us assume that the schools I visited and the schools

---

[2]An exception here is Trickett's (1991) *Living an Idea,* which is about one of the oldest alternative schools in the country. It is a book well worth the reader's attention.

of those people with whom I have spoken have been relatively successful in preventing, either in part or whole, certain problems from ever arising. I have to say that when I have talked to these people they have conveyed to me a sense of gratification and achievement strikingly different from what I hear from educators in conventional schools. Granted that subjective reports contain self-serving, self-deceiving elements, and granted that we lack confirming data, these individuals could not, as one person said, "ever go back to my old school."

So let us make an assumption about relative success and turn to one reaction I have gotten from most of these individuals. It is not one reaction but an interrelated set of reactions. It goes this way: "We know our schools are different, so different that when we talk to educators in conventional schools we really aren't communicating. We know what *they* are saying, but they really don't understand what *we* have done and why. Sometimes they do seem to understand, but they don't act on it. When you criticize schools as you frequently do, why is it that you don't say anything about *our* schools. We do exist, but no one seems to know it."

My answer is in several parts. The first is that I have unbounded respect (and sympathy) for anyone who, taking primary prevention seriously, creates and sustains actions consistent with such a goal. Second, all these instances involved local people reacting to local conditions to create *an* alternative educational site. They did not seek to test and implement their ideas in ways that would influence any other site; that was not their intent. Indeed, they had to devote time and energy to protect their efforts from outside interference, opposition, or resentment. Third, with the exception of Trickett's study (1991) we have nothing resembling a secure basis for understanding why and to what degree any of these alternative schools was successful. The issue is only in part the extent to which a preventive effort was successful; no less important, *and from the standpoint of replication more important,* is how this was accomplished. We need to know the leadership, constituencies, resources, organizational style, development and transformations, time perspective, mistakes, serendipity, personnel selection and turnover—factors that make up a complicated narrative that should seek less to persuade than to force us to conclude that we are being given a no-holds-barred, warts-and-all account that tells us what happens when visions power actions. (Trickett's book about an alternative high school, which may be the oldest alternative school in the country, is not a small volume, containing as it does evaluation data and a refreshingly comprehensive, candid account of the school's development.)

The fourth part of the answer is that however successful these alternative schools may be, and even if they were to double in frequency each year over the decade, they would represent a very small fraction of all schools in the country. But they have not doubled in the past decade (they may actually have been reduced in frequency) and they will not double in the next one. The point that deserves emphasis is that alternative schools have not and probably will not have a *general* influence. They are and will remain important but narrow examples of the prevention of major problems in a school.

If in the sixties primary prevention had informed the thinking of national policymakers, legislatures, and funding agencies (including foundations), they would have seen alternative schools as potentially so important and instructive that they would have seized the opportunity to study them comprehensively. After all, one does not have to be especially bright to conclude that preventing problems is a lot more desirable and efficient than repairing them. At best, there were small programs to fund and develop alternative schools but no money whatsoever to study and evaluate them. The policy seemed to be, "We want to encourage alternative schools precisely because they hold out the promise of demonstrating the prevention of problems. But we are not very interested in the degree to which that promise is fulfilled. So, go ahead and in a year or so please tell us how it worked out. Your word is good enough for us."

The alternative school movement was reinvigorated in the sixties as part of a general rebellion against many features of our major societal institutions. Within the past year or so President Bush and his educational advisers have given, at least on the level of rhetoric, new life to creating alternative schools.

Unlike the rhetoric of the sixties, this is not part of a rebellion against societal traditions generally; rather, it seems to reflect the implicit assumption that going the route of reforming existing schools has not been and will not be productive.

Unfortunately, policymakers in Washington are saying nothing that indicates they have anything to learn from the history of alternative schools. That is true in the sense that this history provides us only the most sketchy pictures of what these schools were like, and virtually no data by which to judge outcomes. But that is precisely the point: *there is nothing in the presidential rhetoric to suggest that these new initiatives will be described in ways permitting us to draw conclusions about why A succeeded and B failed, why A seemed to succeed and then deteriorated, and so on. And there is nothing to suggest that the federal policymakers understand that if you go the route of primary prevention, you are obligated to state clearly what you seek to prevent and by what criteria you will judge success.* The icing on this cake of vexation is that there is no suggestion that they know how complicated the creation of an alternative school is, *if only because the new school is part of an existing school system.* It is not dyspepsia or nihilism that makes me cynical, but I predict that this ignorance of the complexity of creating a new school having distinctive goals, a self-sustaining supportive ambience, and the capacity to study dispassionately the achievement of goals, will lead to unrealistic timetables, a downplaying of problems, early disillusionment, and, of course, a scapegoating of educators who colluded in the well-intentioned imitation of experimentation.

Unlike a person who wants to create an alternative school, or a small core group seeking to reform an ongoing school, or a superintendent who wants to reform a school system, the president and his advisers explicitly seek courses of action that will impact on schools generally, nationally. They know, of course, that no one approach will have an encompassing effect and that even a combination of approaches will fall short of total impact. What they do not seem to know is how complex both primary prevention *and* reform are. And by "know" I mean that they have a firm grasp of the major *predictable* problems such efforts will encounter and, as a consequence, a realistic time perspective from which to judge funding and outcomes.

A story is appropriate here. It concerns the creation of Job Training Centers or Camps during the war on poverty in the sixties. (One such camp was high up in the Catoctin Mountains not far from Washington.) It occurred to Patrick Moynihan that these centers were conceptually similar to those of the Civilian Conservation Corps (CCC) created during the Great Depression of the thirties. What could be learned from that earlier experience? Moynihan, good academic that he was (and is), went back to pore over what had been written that would be relevant and helpful to the new program. To his amazement and chagrin he found there was nothing to read. There was no institutional memory, no basis for utilizing that earlier experience as a guide to the new effort, an experience that presumably had been productive. As Moynihan expected, the ahistorical attitude was one factor that contributed to the failure of the new program. The stance that the world was born yesterday is a feature of President Bush's initiative today in regard to the creation of new model schools. I reserve for the next chapter another story of a presidential initiative of which neither President Bush nor a large foundation were, as they should have been, aware.

If we have not learned as much as we would have liked, we have learned a good deal about why efforts at educational reform and primary prevention have been so disappointing. It would be good if policymakers were aware of what we have discovered; it would be even better if they took it seriously. If they did, they might learn that the problem, initially at least, is not financial or motivational; rather, it requires gaining a firmer understanding of the complexity involved in creating new settings or reforming existing ones.

We did not get to the moon because we wanted to and we were willing to appropriate the money. We achieved that feat because over many decades we had acquired the *cumulative* knowledge that said it could be done. When in his inaugural address President Kennedy said that by the end of the decade we would place a man on the moon, he had good reason to believe that it could be done. Given the existing knowledge, he was articulating a realistic time perspective. He did not say that the effort would be devoid of mistakes, miscalculations, or appalling catastrophes. More lives have been lost in the space program than in educational reform. And when these events happened, we mourned at the same time we were forced to realize they were predictable — unpredictable as to when, where, and why, but actuarially quite predictable. They were in the cards.

Similarly, it is in the cards that new educational initiatives will have their failures and, I have to predict, will be an overall failure because of two factors: our underestimating the complexity of what we are up against and our inability or unwillingness to utilize the cumulative experience we have acquired. History is not bunk, past failures do contain productive lessons, and intractability says more about our imprisonment in tradition and convention than it does about impossibility.

To be in favor of primary prevention (or educational reform) is not inherently virtuous. Too often such phrases, however well intentioned, are empty, bordering on sloganeering. Similarly, it is not an expression of wisdom to say problems are complex. So what else is new? What we must do, after acknowledging the complexity and our past fecklessness in dealing with it, is try to map the universe of alternatives available to us. In past efforts at such mapping, primary prevention has been given short shrift. To an overwhelming degree the emphasis has been on repair. In the pages that follow I make an effort to redress the imbalance in some small measure.

In the next chapter I shall begin to indicate what you must confront if you begin thinking in terms of primary prevention. We will be confronted by a deceptively simple question: what do you want to prevent? That seemingly straightforward question will bring to the fore, as it has in the past, diverse and controversial answers mirroring different views of what people are and should be, what as a society we are and should be, and, fatefully, whether we are willing to take the long view. Primary prevention of any important problem requires the long view, which is why we much prefer quick fixes. And preference for quick fixes is enhanced by the realization that an effort requiring the long view is only one among many possible efforts. How many long-term attempts to prevent cancer have been fruitless? In regard to many other diseases, why do we so willingly accept and support long-term efforts, many of which, we know, will turn out to be instructive but unproductive in regard to prevention? We do so because we want and need to believe that in some ultimate sense we have no moral alternative. That does not mean that we stop grappling with problems as they confront us now. To continue struggling with existing problems is no less a moral imperative than one that seeks to prevent them from ever occurring.

By the end of this book the reader may conclude that whatever I will have concretely suggested about primary prevention and the long view is incomplete, or wrong, or unrealistic, or an indulgence of unjustified hope, or some combination of all of these. That reader may be right, but I urge him or her to distinguish between the need for the long view and my particular, perhaps idiosyncratic, use of it. Let us not throw the baby out with the bath water.

Chapter Four

Prevention and the Long-Term View

There may be no universal law governing this, but one is wise to assume that any major problem is, directly or indirectly, related to other major problems; therefore, there is no single course of action that will eliminate the problem you seek to prevent. It is also safe to assume that the problem has more than one cause and that it is nearly impossible to deal *effectively* with all of them simultaneously. So, for example, in the case of cancer, we believe that among the suspected causes are smoking, diet, pollution, genetics, and more. No one preventive effort can deal with all of these. Consequently, we are always faced with this question: given our present state of knowledge about the etiologies of a problem, where should we concentrate our efforts? We cannot proceed as if all etiological factors will be equally fruitful in the degree to which their prevention will reduce the incidence of the condition. That does not mean, of course, that we take one route only. But since we do not live in a world of limitless resources and our knowledge is always conditional and incomplete, we have to make decisions about priorities. It may turn out that our priorities were wrong or ill advised, in which case we must decide again about new priorities.

This is not an issue peculiar to primary prevention efforts. If anything is a distinguishing feature of the educational reform movement it is the number of different approaches that have been tried, the inevitable reordering of priorities, the coming and going of "solutions" and "answers." It is tempting, but it would be wrong, to say that educational reforms have been like fads and fashions. Those who have proclaimed a new approach have been serious people dissatisfied and critical of what has been tried by others. Where these people can be faulted is in their tunnel vision: confusing an answer with the whole solution, unaware that they are conceiving the problem as independent of other problems, and, too frequently, ignorant that their nostrum was prescribed and tried by earlier reformers. They have no priorities; they have *an* answer. Modesty and humility have not been distinguishing characteristics of educational policymakers and reformers. Those characteristics are attained after failure.

    I write these words at the same time that the following appeared in *Education Week* (September 25, 1991). Here are the opening paragraphs of the long article:

> Three years after the Annie E. Casey Foundation committed $50 million to an ambitious five-year effort to raise student achievement and stem dropout rates, teenage pregnancy, and youth unemployment in five cities, project participants' initial enthusiasm and optimism has been tempered by a healthy dose of reality.
>
>   "This was the first time we had a five-year commitment and a sense of quite a bit of money to work with to address youth issues comprehensively," recalled James Van Vleck, a retired Mead Corporation senior vice president and the chairman of the interagency collaborative overseeing the grant in Dayton, Ohio.
>
>   "It made us think it was going to be a piece of cake," he said.
>
>   But Casey Foundation executives and project leaders now admit that the "piece of cake" was much bigger and more difficult to digest than they had first imagined.
>
>   They recount story after story about how complicated it has been to coordinate the efforts of a wide range of youth-serving institutions, including schools and human-service agencies.
>
>   They talk about the difficulties of implementing change from the top down and of the price to be

paid for not including educators fully in the process. And they tick off the problems that come with expecting results too quickly and now acknowledge that it will take much longer than originally anticipated to bring about lasting change.

"As we've sobered up and faced the issues," Mr. Van Vleck said, "we have found that getting collaboration between those players is a much more complicated and difficult game than we expected."

I confess that it is hard, really impossible, for me to react charitably to this report. It is easy to give brownie points for good intentions, but how do you grade an effort that managed to make every mistake predictable from similar past efforts? How should you react to an endeavor so ignorant of the cumulative wisdom gained from these past efforts? The Casey Foundation program exemplifies an attempt at primary prevention of certain problems that required *initially* the reform of the relationships within and among diverse agencies. As I said earlier, proclaiming the virtues and goals of primary prevention does not earn you a badge of honor when you are ignorant of what you need to accomplish for your objectives to be realized. Primary prevention does not avoid complexities; it brings them to the fore. To forget that, assuming you once knew it, is to be governed by a time perspective guaranteed to defeat you.

Apparently no one at the Casey Foundation saw the similarity *in principle* between their goals of primary prevention and those that powered the curriculum changes of the sixties. Let me illustrate by the new math which, if not heralded as a panacea, came uncomfortably close. The primary prevention goals of the new math were explicit and several: to prevent in students an aversion to math, to instill in them an enjoyment of math, to bring about a higher level of math skills and performance, and to increase the number of students desirous of pursuing a scientific career needed by a scientific-technological society. As a nation, we were told, we could not afford to let a bad situation become worse. We had to prevent in future generations what had happened to past ones.

The new math (as well as the new physics, new biology, new social studies), consistent with the rationale of primary prevention, was *not* geared to be helpful to individuals with existing problems in math; it was *not* a clinical or repair or rehabilitative effort. It was geared to influence the total population of students in ways that over time would discernibly decrease the incidence of untoward attitudes and deficits related to math. It is important to emphasize that primary prevention is not oriented to this or that *individual* but rather to a class of people within which, it is hoped, the incidence of a problem or condition will decrease. It is the difference between trying to get someone who smokes to give up the habit and trying to persuade people not to take up smoking. One could as well use obesity, drugs, and alcohol as examples.

The new math was a disaster. It is not being unfair to say it had iatrogenic consequences: it made a bad situation worse. The Casey Foundation had millions of dollars and good intentions. The new math advocates had a new curriculum and good intentions. The Casey Foundation was ignorant of the school and agency cultures. The new mathers were ignorant of the culture of schools, life in the modal classroom, the preparation of teachers, what was involved in helping teachers *unlearn* conventional ways of thinking and teaching, and the helplessness of parents for whom the new math was a foreign language.

If it is understandable that the Casey Foundation did not see kinship with the new math debacle, it is scandalous that they were unaware of President Nixon's Experimental Schools Program (ESP). That program not only had the support of the president but also that of the president's Science Advisory Committee and the top officials in the Department of Health, Education, and Welfare. The ESP was based explicitly on a recognition of the inadequacies of past efforts, a recognition that was as refreshing as it was singular. Very briefly, the ESP rested on several considerations:

- Past federal efforts to improve and change schools were largely failures.
- Federal programs had a buckshot quality: there was a pro-

gram for this part of the school system and for that one; there was a program for this educational problem and for that one. It was as if the federal government kept reacting to whatever problem was brought to its attention. Sequence and interconnectedness were not important.

- The federal government should provide the resources for *comprehensive* change in a school system, that is, sufficient resources to permit a school district more meaningfully and efficiently "to put it all together" in a single direction.

- There was merit in the complaints of local districts that federal imposition of programs, or too many intrusions by federal personnel into planning at the local level, robbed local people of initiative, creativity, and control. In the ESP local people would have more control over ESP projects. If local districts were sincerely given the opportunity to change their schools in ways they considered most appropriate, one could then count on their commitment to initiate and sustain the change process.

- Federal efforts to evaluate past reform efforts had been inadequate and they bore no relationship either to changes in federal policy or to local program management. The ESP would use innovative and rigorous social science methodology to understand and assess the change process better. Indeed, somewhat less than one-third of the sixty to seventy million dollars that the ESP would cost would go to an evaluation scheme no less comprehensive than the changes that local districts would bring about in their schools.

The ESP was a disaster and anyone who has any doubts on that score should read Cowden and Cohen's (n.d.) federally sponsored assessment. Obviously, the Casey Foundation did not do so.

Most assuredly, I gain no satisfaction from having predicted the failure of the ESP, but one had to be inordinately obtuse not to have made such a prediction. Somewhere near the point when the policymakers were to decide which school districts would be part of the ESP, I was asked to come to Washington to advise on these decisions. It was a chaotic visit on several scores. Federal personnel felt tremendous pressure to launch ths well-publicized program as soon as possible, preferably yesterday. I could not decide whether the pressure was more internal or external, although as the meeting wore on the internal drive seemed to be the major source. That feeling of pressure seemed very much related to the federal personnel's vast underestimation of how much time it would take to select school districts. Because the local districts would have the most to say about how they would bring about comprehensive change, that kind of freedom made the task of selection very difficult. How does one choose on the basis of a written grant request (and telephone calls) except by resorting to one's own conception about how comprehensive change *should* be accomplished? That issue came quickly to the fore when one perused the written documents at different stages of their submission; they were vague statements of virtuous intent, giving one no sense of security about how "comprehensive change" was being defined. However committed federal personnel had been to the idea of local initiative and control, that commitment quickly began to dissolve as they concluded that local districts were defining comprehensive change in strange and various ways. The written documents were more like inkblots, forcing the reader to intuit what local districts meant by what they said and wrote. The truth is that the local districts were as much at sea about the meaning of "comprehensive change" as the federal personnel were.

My second contact with the ESP was a year later when I was asked to assess the plans and resources of a private consulting firm seeking the contract for the first in a series of evaluation studies. By this time most of the local districts to be part of the ESP had been chosen and their final grant applications were made available to us. Each application was no less than four inches thick and weighed five or more pounds. Their bulk was matched only by their lack of substance. That may sound like an excessively harsh judgment, but no one at this second meeting came to a contrary conclusion; it was obvious to everyone that these applications presented no focus to evaluate — no conceptual or procedural framework. It was painful to observe the staff of the consulting firm, a methodologically sophisticated group, trying to reconcile their desire to get the contract with the inkblot character of what they were supposed to do. The federal staff wanted a rigorous evaluation, but they had maneuvered themselves into a classically tragic situation in which the beginnings already contained the seeds of everyone's ultimate defeat. This judgment is well documented by Cowden and Cohen (n.d.) and will not be further discussed here.

I did not relate this and other experiences merely to indicate that initiating, managing, and sustaining "comprehensive" change involving schools and community agencies are complex affairs. Nor was it my intention to add to the collection of horror stories. My use of these instances was the basis they provided to make several points. The first is that any effort at primary prevention in schools, geared as it almost always is, to the prevention of student problems, cannot ignore the necessity for the adults (professional or lay) who will implement the effort to change in ways consistent with that effort. Put another way, the effort always will require that these people literally *reform* their attitudes and practices. To put it more baldly: these people have to be seen initially as part of the problem, not as tailor-made for the solution. I am in no way suggesting that they should be viewed as clinical specimens possessing characteristics absent in "us." Like us, they come to the effort with attitudes and practices that contributed to the need for the new effort. To ignore this point, to proceed as if verbal agreement and commitment are sufficient for change, is defeating of one's goals.

This is why I said earlier that proclaiming adherence to the goals of primary prevention is not inherently virtuous. To achieve these goals requires processes and a long-term time perspective too frequently overlooked or egregiously oversimplified, which is another way of saying that your conception of the particular conditions you seek to prevent was woefully incomplete. The goals of primary prevention rest on some understanding of the factors contributing to the conditions you seek to prevent. In the case of our schools those conditions are *in part* always a reflection of the attitudes and practices of those who participate in the new effort.

The second, obviously related to the first, is that the goals of primary prevention are achievable only if the dynamics of secondary prevention have been successfully overcome. If those participating in the effort are *part* of the problem, how can you dilute the adverse consequences of their overlearned attitudes and practices? To get to the point where primary prevention becomes a possibility, you must have successfully confronted and overcome the consequences of these past attitudes and practices.

The third point is less obvious than the first two. Is it not a fateful mistake to formulate the goals of primary prevention *only* in terms of what you want to prevent in pupils? If it is indeed true that educational personnel are part of the problem, should we not be paying more attention to how we might select and prepare these personnel so that they will be less of a problem than they are now? Can our colleges of education better prepare personnel so as to make the achievement of primary prevention goals less messy, less of a failure than such efforts have been in the past?

What is it you want to prevent? That question has been almost always answered in terms of students. But if anything is clear from the history of educational reform — and anyone who has attempted any degree of educational change will attest to this — it is that what you want to prevent in students depends on the "reforming" of existing personnel and that is a task we do not do well. If we looked anew at the selection and preparation of educational personnel from a primary prevention perspective — informed as that should be by the cumulative wisdom attained from the failures of school reform — might not that be productive? Is not such a perspective long overdue?

Schools of education have never been without their critics. The most frequent and damning criticisms have been that those seeking careers in education are intellectually of mediocre quality, they are inadequately steeped in subject matter and/or they are steeped in stultifying pedagogical methodologies, and in the classroom they are unimaginative, conforming, and unstimulating. If you had to summarize the thrust of these criticisms it would be that educational personnel are not the intellectuals their critics are. There is a kernel of truth in these criticisms, but only a kernel. I shall have more to say about this in later chapters. At this point in our discussion I wish only to indicate that examining the selection and preparation of educational personnel from a primary prevention perspective is long overdue. If we could start from scratch and design programs to prepare educational personnel — taking into account what we have experienced and learned about the difficulties of changing attitudes and practices of those personnel once they are in schools and socialized into the culture of schools — would we not do a better job of preventing problems in students *and* educators, and would we not make the task of implementing and sustaining reform in schools less of a mine field of explosive failures? In my fifty years of experience in and around schools and educators I have heard only a handful of people say that their preparation was adequate for the realities of classrooms and schools. Apart from criticism of educators by others, educators are, generally speaking, very realistic critics of their professional training.

The past failures of educational reforms have brought in their wake the conclusion that the problem is not in a primary sense a financial one but a lack of knowledge about what will work. Here, too, there is a kernel of truth but one that has been dangerously and wrongly misused. When in the past I have expressed a similar conclusion, it was always from the standpoint that reform efforts reflected diagnoses and conceptions guaranteed to be ineffective, and to proceed as if increasing expenditures would be fruitful was an invitation to disillusionment. This conclusion in no way implied that if we altered our view of things, money would not be a problem. Rather than lacking knowledge, we had gained a degree of cumulative wisdom that ought to be taken seriously. To argue, as did Secretary of Education Alexander recently, that increased expenditures were not justified by existing knowledge speaks volumes about what he and his advisers do not know about what has been learned. Let us take Head Start as an illustrative case.

Head Start was powered by a diagnosis as correct as it was unverbalized. It was a program, the first, to take primary prevention seriously. If disadvantaged children were given an appropriate preschool experience, as children from more affluent backgrounds received, there would be a reduction in that group's incidence of school failure and low academic achievement. The diagnosis had several parts. The first was that these children were intellectually capable of normal educational achievement. Why, then, did so many of them not achieve once they started school? The second part of the diagnosis was that there was something in their backgrounds (familial, cultural) that was either "missing" or ill suited for school learning, that is, the "problem" was in these factors, not in the children. What went unverbalized was the clear implication that schools were and had long been ill suited for these children: *schools* were a problem. The third part, also unverbalized, was based on a theory of "contagion": when these children entered school they caught the virus of disinterest, low motivation, and alienation. Head Start was to be a form of *inoculation* against catching the virus.

What has been the result? No one claims that Head Start has been a dramatic success, but on the basis of available evidence no one can claim that it has been a failure. That evidence indicates that there has been a decrease in the incidence of school failure or academic retardation. However, if one takes seriously the unverbalized contagion part of the original diagnosis — a part which is no less applicable to many so-called advantaged children — one has to ask why the inoculation should have been expected to have truly dramatic results? *You could justifiably argue that if the culture of schools was part of the problem and not the solution, then the results of Head Start are indeed dramatic, that there was and is a "ceiling effect" imposed by the culture of schools, limiting what Head Start could accomplish — an effect against which any inoculation could be only partially effective.* For too many students, advantaged or disadvantaged, schools are uninteresting, unstimulating places.

Now let us return to Secretary Alexander who, on the MacNeil-Lehrer news hour on October 2, 1991, stated that before the government increased expenditures for new educational reform effort, we needed to have more secure knowledge about what works. To this Jonathan Kozol, also on the panel that night, asked, since there was evidence that Head Start enjoyed some success — a conclusion the secretary had agreed with on

that and previous occasions — why is it that there were no programs for the *majority* of children eligible for Head Start? The
Secretary was momentarily nonplussed and then spoke about
the funding limitations imposed by the current recession, a reply that did not, of course, explain why in the more affluent
eighties the same situation obtained.

We do not lack knowledge about the fruitfulness of primary prevention efforts in regard to education. I do not want
to overevaluate what we know but neither do I want to ignore
the ignorance belied by statements from officialdom. I think we
know more about how to prevent problems than how to "solve"
them once they have appeared. It is understandable that, faced
with pressing, complicated, socially unsettling problems in education, people seek ways of repairing them. And it is understandable if they want near-term solutions. When you are, so
to speak, on the firing line, the long-term view seems neither
practical nor attractive. Nevertheless, the imbalance between
the support and encouragement of repair and primary preventive efforts is inexcusable, costly, and ultimately self-defeating.

Over the past fifteen years there has been a fair amount
of research on helping children acquire social problem-solving
skills. The available evidence is clear that these efforts do prevent untoward behavior in students. I am aware of only one
study that has attempted to provide a more solid basis for evaluating a social problem-solving curriculum by targeting an entire K-12 school population. (Most studies have been more
modest in their research goals, working with small samples of
differing ages.) As luck would have it, that study was carried
out by my next-door colleague, Roger Weissberg, now at the
University of Illinois in Chicago. It is not my purpose here to
discuss his published and unpublished findings, which substan-
tiate the results of others about the preventive efficacy of these
curricula. My purpose is to stress that it took Weissberg ten
years to convince the school system that it was in its self-interest
to encourage him to take on the entire system.

Anyone who reads his publications will get only the faint-
est idea of all he had to do in his truly heroic effort to reach
the point where he could apply to an entire school system popu-

lation what he had demonstrated in previous, discrete studies. When he writes up those experiences, it will not be a small volume. It would be unfair to say that he got to that point despite, not because of, the school system; but it would not be unfair to say that at each step of the way he had to overcome every obstacle ever described about what one encounters in introducing an innovation into the culture of schools. Weissberg began with the long-term view; the school system did not. Plagued as it was and is with every major educational and social problem characteristic of an urban school system, that system understandably (but not excusably) was more interested in repairing problems than in preventing them. Its budget accurately reflected its support of primary prevention: no support. Ten years earlier the system had "allowed" this new Yale faculty member, Roger Weissberg, to initiate some small studies. If at that time he had articulated his long-term goals, plainly stating the futility of putting all resources into repair, at best he would have been laughed at and at worst asked to peddle his wares elsewhere. Taking the long-term view is not a distinguishing feature of the thinking of educators. I do not say this unkindly but as an observation that illustrates what the primary prevention orientation is up against. And, lest one fall into the trap of scapegoating educators, remember that the long-term, primary prevention view is not a characteristic of funding sources: local, state, and national governments, foundations, and the private sector.

It would not be far off the mark to say that for ten years Weissberg was a "salesman," spending countless hours convincing educational policymakers (the board of education, the superintendent, and his administrators) *and* teachers to cooperate in his endeavors. Teachers already feel overburdened and overwhelmed by underachieving students; they experience constant pressure to raise achievement scores and regard themselves as undervalued, misunderstood, and unfairly criticized. These are not feelings and attitudes conducive to warm acceptance of a new curriculum they did not ask for, another instance of having imposed on them something about which they had no say, another "something" for an already crowded day, a something

that appeared to have nothing to do with reading, math, or social studies, a something *they* would have to learn. All this Weissberg knew; he also knew that sensitively, diplomatically, and
closely monitoring the implementation was a can of worms. Getting up a curriculum was one thing; getting it appropriately put
into classroom practice is another. A curriculum is *not* contained
in a written document; it is that plus a set of ideas, conceptions,
values, and procedures intended to create an atmosphere, not
an empty, impersonal ritual devoid of personal significance both
for students and teachers. Implementing a curriculum is not
like following a recipe in a cookbook.

Let us assume that the research on problem-solving skills
has validity as one approach to primary prevention. Several
questions arise. Considering that the psychological principles
undergirding these curricula are not new and not very complex,
why do teachers need to be reminded of them? Why are these
principles either absent or unsystematically applied in the classroom? Is it unreasonable to expect that in their training teachers
would have acquired an understanding of these psychological
principles, would have experienced what is involved in acting
in accord with them, and would not look upon such actions as
an intrusion on "real" learning, such as in math, social studies,
and science? Is it unreasonable to expect that the preparation
of teachers would require less heroic efforts on the part of someone like Weissberg, less need to be monitored in the implementation process, and more reason for the Weissbergs of this world
to be less necessary? When you look at the preparation of teachers from a primary prevention perspective, you come up with
a suggested program radically different from what now exists.

What about the preparation of administrators? Why is
their preparation so unrelated to the realities they will face? Why
should one expect them to think preventively when that way
of thinking is absent from their preparation? I must use an example I have used frequently in the past. Administrators spend
a lot of time organizing and conducting meetings. It is no secret
that faculty meetings are not in the category of humane and
interesting experiences. They are relatively brief affairs in which
a principal reads the latest directive from "downtown," reminds

faculty of this or that, announces this or that change, and that's that. Some teachers take notes, others sit with folded hands, all stare at the slow-moving clock. *I am describing the manufacture and reinforcement of problems: the engendering in teachers of the belief that it is in no way their meeting, that they have no voice in any important educational decision, that there is no collegiality, no discussion of ideas, interesting and/or stimulating, and that there is no point in rocking the boat.* That's what I mean by the manufacture and reinforcement of an important school problem.

I once had the opportunity to survey the training programs for educational administrators. As I expected, not one program exposed its candidates to how one might think about meetings: how to prepare for a meeting, who has or should have input in formulating an agenda, what it means to respect the ideas and feelings of participants, how to avoid the countless ways by which to produce silence and conformity and to avoid controversy. In short, who "owns" the meeting? Administrators regard teachers the way teachers regard children: individuals who possess no assets, for whom direction must be provided, who have to be protected against their lack of knowledge and sophistication, and who, because of these deficits must be provided direction and external control. For the situation to be otherwise would occasion surprise. I am neither caricaturing administrators nor scapegoating them. To do so would be to blame the victim. I know there are exceptions, but the exceptions I have known existed before training, not because of it.

It is not my purpose to review the research literature on approaches that appear to have an acceptable degree of validity in regard to the primary prevention of school problems. (In *The Predictable Failure of Educational Reform* [1990b] I use the research literature on cooperative learning as an example.) All of these approaches are based on studies carried out in existing schools, which means, as in the case of Weissberg, that masochistically inclined researchers prematurely aged getting to the point where they could appropriately test their preventive efforts. Their numbers are predictably minuscule compared to those researchers who never published their findings because of failure due to ignorance, or an unwillingness or temperamental inability

carefully to oversee the implementation, or a shrinking from
the recognition of the complexity of introducing something new
into a resistant, uncomprehending host organism.

Again, I am not assigning blame. I am describing a
tragedy in which the thinking and behavior of the actors are
quite understandable but who by virtue of their parts are fated
to defeat each other. The history of educational reform has its
tragic features.

Insofar as primary prevention is concerned we know a
good deal more than one would think from the pronouncements
of policymakers. That does not mean that we know as much
as we would like or that what we do know has the most solid
of foundations. Where we have been shortsighted is in the un-
due emphasis on applying that knowledge to existing schools.
The purpose of this chapter has been to suggest that we look
at the selection and preparation of educators from the perspective of what we have learned about primary prevention. We are
not faced with an either/or decision. We are faced with how to
begin unimprisoning ourselves from a way of thinking that does
not allow us to raise and think through the question: can we
come up with new ways of selecting and preparing educators
which over time would decrease the incidence of educational
problems, reducing thereby the time, energy, and waste atten-
dant on the repair problems?

Anyone familiar with my writings will not be surprised
that my final example concerns question asking in the classroom. The research literature is painfully clear: the rate of question asking by students is not far above zero, the rate of question
asking by teachers in social studies periods is astronomical,
speaking comparatively. I have never met an educator who considered those findings acceptable or justifiable. Children are *par
excellence* question-asking organisms, endlessly curious about
themselves, others, and their worlds. Freud said that dreams
were the royal road to the unconscious. Analogously, one could
say that question asking is the royal road to knowledge and
learning.

So what do we do? Round up scads of child developmen-
talists, psychologists, and other types of consultants who will

be assigned to schools to help teachers think and act differently in regard to question asking? That is as shortsighted as it is unfeasible. Should we not ask what it is about the preparation of educational personnel that contributes to a classroom regularity that *nobody* can justify, that contributes mightily to making classrooms uninteresting places? This is not a plea intended to undermine any effort by any educator, school, or school system to begin to change an undesirable, anti-educational, antiintellectual classroom regularity. It is a plea that we reexamine preparatory programs in which candidates absorb conceptions, and implement under supervision, of what children are, their uses of their curiosity, and what that means for how classrooms are structured and managed. When will we begin to take primary prevention seriously?

The Federal Drug Administration does not permit the marketing of any medication, whether for the purposes of primary or secondary preventions, unless carefully controlled clinical trials meet certain criteria, one of which is that there are no serious, unmanageable, or life-threatening side effects. No medication gives perfect results. It is noteworthy that as I write these words the FDA has relaxed its criteria in regard to a new drug that may ameliorate the course of AIDS, and it has done so because of the crisis proportions of the condition and the public clamor that we cannot afford to wait until we have the total answer. In regard to education we are faced with a crisis for which past efforts have been ineffective and current efforts and plans, largely replays of those past efforts, will be no more effective. To illustrate why I make this prediction I discuss in the next chapter a recent Carnegie Commission report on K–12 math and science education. That chapter is prologue to a proposal which, if in education there was an analogue of the FDA, would arouse more controversy than the Carnegie Commission report. The time is past when we can continue on our present course.

Chapter Five

"Second Best: Secondary Prevention"

In the early seventies I was asked by an under secretary in the then Department of Health, Education, and Welfare (HEW) to serve on an advisory committee which would have two purposes: to survey the sections of the department that produced educational reports and materials and to make recommendations for wider, more effective dissemination of those reports. At that first meeting the under secretary revealed that her attempt at a survey had both surprised and overwhelmed her; although she knew that there were many parts of the department that prepared educational materials (for example, teaching materials, research reports, conference proceedings), she did not expect the number would be as high as seventy. Indeed, she said that she could not give us an accurate number. No less bothersome to her was the unconnectedness of the parts. Not all parts of that vast, sprawling department prepared educational materials directly relevant to schools but there was no doubt that the bulk of those materials were intended to be of use in schools. It is a credit to her reality testing that she recognized there was no way *she* could reorganize, or restructure, or meaningfully interconnect all the relevant parts, each of which seemed to have a different and autonomous mission. In brief, she described precisely the same kind of problem that the Casey Foundation attempted to but did not solve: to bring all of the pieces together. And that was precisely what Nixon's Experimental Schools Program tried and could not do.

I was relieved that the under secretary did not ask us seriously to discuss how she might better interconnect the diverse parts. Understand that I am not opposed to interconnectedness, which would be like being opposed to virtue, motherhood, and the flag; but interconnecting autonomous parts is a horrendously complicated, conflict-arousing task of repair that requires, among other things, a kind of *sustained* personal, intellectual, vision-stimulating leadership that is in very short supply. Leadership does not confuse administrative interconnectedness—producing new, impressive flow charts with multidirectional arrows going to and from hierarchically arranged boxes—with the eliciting of a willingness to redefine goals and practices. I have never undertaken such a task but those efforts I have observed or read about have forced me to conclude that this confusion between administrative reorganization and intellectual-attitudinal change is the rule and not the exception. It is not an impossible task but it requires a concatenation of people, leadership, resources, and time that is very rare. It is a task of repair for which the odds are overwhelmingly against you. It is not, initially at least, a matter of funding. It is a matter of gaining acceptance of a new vision, of a new definition of the *substance* (not the adminis-tration) of the problem. That is especially the case in matters educational where intractability to previous reform efforts has been a distinguishing feature.

The under secretary wanted us to focus on dissemination. There was, she correctly said, no evidence that disseminated materials changed anything. More cautiously, there was no evi-dence that if the materials changed anything or anyone any-where, these changes were justified by the costs of preparing and disseminating those materials. There was agreement on several points. First, many of the reports were required by the bureau or division that funded research and too frequently those reports were either self-serving or drew conclusions that went beyond the findings. Second, these reports very much tended to be written in ways that made replication impossible. Third, disseminating materials to people on various mailing lists guar-anteed that wastepaper baskets would not remain empty. Fourth, educational personnel were not avid readers; they were too taken up with problems of daily living to spend leisure time reading reports on the research literature generally.

Now let us turn to the 1991 Carnegie Commission report *In the National Interest. The Federal Government in the Reform of K–12 Math and Science Education.* This report, we can assume, will be nationally disseminated. My guess is that those who peruse or truly read it will feel comforted that a distinguished group of people is not only alarmed by the problem but offers concrete steps to deal with it. It is a report not without virtues. It is also a report that contains nothing new and makes little effort to explain past failures. It is another example of believing that an arena — this time involving the reform of math and science education — was born yesterday!

Let us start with one of the report's virtues.

> In the year 2000, when the national goals agreed upon by the President and governors call for American students to be "first in the world" in mathematics and science, one American child in four will be poor; one child in three will be a minority group member; and one child in twelve will lack the English language proficiency required for learning. School reform alone will not suffice to address these sources of disadvantage. Yet the Task Force on K–12 Mathematics and Science Education is convinced that education is the best hope for all children, and that math and science skills are especially critical for good jobs, for further education, and for effective participation in an increasingly technological world. We also believe that rapid progress is possible, despite the aspects of disadvantage that beset many schools, students, and families [Carnegie Commission, 1991, p. 7].

I consider it a virtue that the report alerts the reader that our schools are faced with problems not of their making and which make their educational task extraordinarily difficult. That is a glimpse of the obvious too many people choose to ignore, permitting them to expect that schools are a kind of universal solvent for social-economic-political-cultural-moral problems. That is why I entitled one of my books *Schooling in America. Scapegoat and Salvation* (1983). Our country has long regarded education as a form of secular salvation; when salvation is not forthcoming, we scapegoat our schools.

But what about the last sentence in the quotation that says "rapid progress is possible" (p. 7)? On what diagnosis, on what lessons from previous research and experience is that judgment made? Would the writers have made a similar judgment about problems (such as cancer or schizophrenia) for which causes, known and unknown, are many and complex, for which billions of dollars have been expended for a new age of discovery that has yet to arrive, and about which experts today take a more humble stance? Of course we have learned a good deal about these problems but not enough to conclude that "rapid progress is possible" (p. 7).

At the turn of the century medicine made a virtue of its ignorance: it correctly told the public that it could not say if and when major diseases would be conquered; there were too many unknowns, existing knowledge was too inadequate, and there would be many instances in which promising research would turn out to be sterile. What medicine did promise was to do its best and not to mislead the public that solutions were at hand. Even so, the history of medicine is replete with those who proclaimed "answers" that were wrong.

I consider it inexcusable that the Carnegie Commission neither justified that last sentence or elsewhere in the report told the reader that what it was recommending, however thoughtful and well intentioned, was inevitably iffy in outcomes. It is understandable if the commission felt a need to appear hopeful. To give up hope is inexcusable, but that is no warrant for couching hope in unrealistic terms. The more that is done, the more people will come to believe that the situation is both serious and hopeless.

Why the commission?

The charge given the Task Force by the Carnegie Commission was to examine how the federal government *is organized* to make decisions and implement change in the reform of math and science education, and to identify *changes in organizational structure* and *decision-making processes* that will help the federal government to be an effective partner in education reform. Why focus on math and science education when the schools are beset with systemic problems not specific to any subject and by teaching problems *in every subject* area? There are at least two reasons why the federal government should pay special attention to math and science education: the increasing demand for numeracy and problem-solving ability in tomorrow's world, and the federal government's special responsibility for assuring the nation's technical capability to address national goals for the economy, environment, health, and security.

The Task Force shares with most Americans a sense of urgency for *bold* initiatives that will provide *real* help to the nation's schools and renew public confidence that dramatic progress can be made. There is no shortage of motivated Americans with good ideas about how to serve our children better. In short supply, however, is the institutional capacity *to aggregate enough resources,* to build a national consensus for action, and—most important—*to persist with a specific program of reform long enough for it to take effect, at least a decade and maybe two.*

The federal government should, therefore, support the most promising initiatives in the country and build a constituency for launching them on a scale that will make a substantial difference in every school in America. The Task Force recommendations are intended to help the federal government identify the best responses to the challenges and support them more swiftly, wholeheartedly, and intelligently [Carnegie Commission, 1991, pp. 7–8].

The italics are mine and are for the purpose of emphasizing that a major purpose of the commission was to interconnect or reorganize a variety of autonomous agencies, the kind of interconnections in principle so zealously sought for by the Casey Foundation, Nixon's Experimental Schools Program, and identified but left alone by the HEW under secretary I discussed earlier. What the Casey Foundation and Nixon's efforts sought to interconnect was small potatoes compared to the scope of the Carnegie Commission.

The Task Force devised a strategy for math and science education reform with four elements.

Commit to change both how schools are organized and run and what goes on inside the classroom. This requires the action of two lead agencies, the Department of Education and the National Science Foundation, working together through new mechanisms for collaboration with each other and with other agencies.

Deploy the resources of the technology-based agencies of the federal government to improve math and science education and to expand the supply of professionally trained scientists and mathematicians serving the nation as teachers and technical professionals.

Leverage state and private initiatives and support effective change through greater emphasis on flexible, competitively evaluated funding mechanisms and the best available understanding of the education system and of teaching and learning strategies.

Build an informed, broadly participatory, and productive collaboration among leaders of states and communities, federal agencies and Congress, private institutions, and the technical community, using a variety of new institutional mechanisms to ensure that federal activities are both effective and supportive [Carnegie Commission, 1991, p. 8; italics mine].

Anyone familiar with the federal bureaucracy—or with any large bureaucracy, public or private—has to give the commission credit for courage and ambitiousness. But several questions arise. The first is why similar efforts in the past have been so ineffective? After all, when President Carter and the Congress set up the department of education it was explicitly "to bring together" heretofore unrelated efforts to improve education. Give education the representation it deserves, use existing and additional resources more efficiently, pay more than lip service to a national educational policy, support and act on existing and new knowledge — do this and more and our schools will improve. Why did it fall so short of the mark? That question is not addressed by the commission and, yet, the answer is clearly relevant to what the commission proposes. Is it that the commission believes it was a mistake to have assumed that a department of education alone could deal effectively with educational problems, administratively unconnected with other federal agencies seeking to influence educational policy and practice? Is that why the commission now recommends a greater degree of interconnectedness? But how significant is it that connectedness was not a distinguishing feature *within* the department of education? And what significance should be given to the observation that in his campaign for the presidency Ronald Reagan promised to eliminate the department of education? How was that message interpreted by all the parts of the government with an educational mission?

History is always a variable, not as abstract knowledge of the past but in terms of its effects on and continuation *in the present*. In matters educational, history is not a museum of conceptual and attitudinal relics. It is a ubiquitous presence. To ignore or to forget that is to increase geometrically the chances that the more things change the more they will remain the same. History contains a lot of bunk, but history is not bunk.

Finally, let us listen to the commission's recommendations about priorities:

> Foremost among the federal responsibilities is the leadership role of the President himself. **The Task Force urges the President to use the full prestige and influence of his office to mobilize all Americans for a sustained, national, bipartisan reform effort.**

The Task Force developed specific recommendations for action by federal agencies in the following areas:

- **Provide fully qualified math and science teachers for every school** by recruiting teachers from under-represented groups; creating a single professional path to either teaching or practice in mathematics and science; and enhancing the knowledge, skills, and motivation of current teachers.
- **Decide what students need to know and know how to do by establishing requirements for the jobs of the future.** Engage the business community, scientists, and citizens in this effort. Develop methods of assessment appropriate to this goal.
- **Strengthen educational systems research and establish broad-based support for basic cognitive and applied learning research and field testing of innovations.** A coordinated reform effort requires systems research and "systems engineering" based on the best analytical understanding of the K–12 education system.
- **Ensure diffusion of successful innovations:** process access for all schools and all students to tested educational improvements and support their successful adoption. Do not be satisfied with successful demonstrations alone.
- **Empower all federal science agencies to take leadership roles in the reform of K–12 math and science education.** Every science agency of the government should have an explicit education charter defining the responsibilities to address precollege issues that lie within the agency's special technical expertise and human resource requirements.
- **Encourage private sector development of educational materials, curricula, textbooks, and software for new educational technology.** Educa-

tional innovations in the private sector not only make significant educational investments but are able to diffuse innovations throughout the country.

- **Support science centers and museums, educational television, and other sources of "informal" education.** Nontraditional education is a powerful way to motivate students and interest parents in the serious study of mathematics and science and to explode negative stereotypes of science and scientists.
- **Provide an information and referral service to document innovations and help innovators locate federal support for K–12 math and science activities.** Individuals outside the federal agencies have difficulty in locating the correct agency through which to gain access to program materials, services, and information [Carnegie Commission, 1991, p. 9].

Why do I find the Carnegie Commission report disappointing? After all, in terms of stated goals it is laudable, especially in several respects: the emphasis it gives to the need for understanding why more productive learning does not occur in the classrooms; its underlining of the importance of a better understanding of how classrooms are embedded in and adversely affected by schools and school systems; its support for the need to support truly radically new conceptions of what schools can and should be; and the crucial importance of recognizing that "reformed schools" will "have the same parents, the same students, and much the same educational process, *until* [italics mine] those schools adopt content standards for what students should know, and until that content is embodied in new curricula taught by better-trained teachers and measured by better assessment methods" (Carnegie Commission, 1991, p. 23).

The report is disappointing because it rests on a very incomplete and flawed diagnosis. It confuses cause and effect. The explicit diagnosis is that student disinterest and poor achievement in science and math is, in large part, a consequence of poor teaching. Put another way, if educators generally—not only those in math or science—were better prepared, classrooms and schools would not be as ineffective as they are. Yes, the report recognizes that there are other etiological factors but where it is most clear and concrete is in its focus on the inadequacies in the attitudes, thinking, knowledge, and practices of school personnel. It is to the credit of the commission that it does not descend to a polemic against educators. I have to assume that the commission members truly believe that educators have not *willed* the present situation, that they are not engaged in a conspiracy to defeat reform, that they were not born with their inadequacies. Nevertheless, you cannot read the report without concluding that the inadequacies of educators are a very important part of an explanation of the present, undesirable situation; that is, the inadequacies of students are in part an effect of inadequate educators: their understandings, their curricula, their pedagogical conceptions and practices. Cause and effect. *But is it not then quite likely that the inadequacies of educators, like those of their students, are in part a consequence of their teachers, their preparation?* If that is so, as we (Sarason, Davidson, and Blatt, 1989 [1962]) pointed out long ago, why is the Carnegie report virtually silent about the preparation of educators? Saying, as the report does, that we need better-trained teachers I can only regard as equivalent to silence. The report emphasizes, as it should have, why we should focus on children and teachers in classrooms, but it has nothing to say about what educators experience in *their* classrooms in *their* preparatory programs.

How should we understand that silence? I said before that the diagnosis was incomplete. I did not say it was wrong. Nor did I say or imply that I am opposed, or even reluctant, to support any serious effort to "reform," to help existing schools and their personnel. But I fault the commission for not taking its diagnosis seriously or far enough.

There are possible explanations for the silence. One is that the commission members are simply unknowledgeable about the preparatory programs for educators (not only those for teachers). Most of those on the commission are scientists who are comprehensively knowledgeable about how people in their fields are selected and educated. I would predict that if directly asked they would say that their students are *educated* for and in their fields, they are not *trained* in the sense that dogs are trained to be obedient. Yes, they would say, there are elements of training in the preparation of their students but the overarching goal is to acquire knowledge, conceptions, attitudes, and ways of thinking that will permit them to be self-directed, self-critical, and desirous and capable of new learning. Science, they would say, is at its root a moral enterprise in which the more you know the more you need to know — enterprise that requires a respect for changing truths and the rules of evidence, based on the knowing and confronting of the human mind as both our greatest ally and foe.

Education for science is far more than training. So, when the commission says that we need "better trained" teachers (1991, p. 23) — they do not say "better trained" administrators — is it being a carping critic to ask what they mean by "better trained"? Is it unfair to say that the commission is hoist with its own petard because having identified a problem, it cannot ignore it? After all, it has not identified a piddling problem but an extremely important one which, if not addressed, pulls the rug from under its major recommendations. For example, take the following statement from the report: "Most efforts at school reform, including those to which President and governors are committed, are aimed at improving overly regimented schools staffed by dispirited teachers and attended by unmotivated students. These efforts are meant to produce fully functional institutions with properly trained, motivated teachers who use modern materials and teaching methods in creative environments and develop strong incentives for student progress" (Carnegie Commission, 1991, p. 15).

Let us again credit the commission for candidly stating that we are dealing with problems that in part reflect anti-educational atmospheres intrinsic to the culture of most schools. But the commission does not suggest that the effort to change those atmospheres, and let us assume they are successful, will dramatically compensate for "improperly trained" teachers who do not use "modern materials and teaching methods" (p. 15). What the commission is suggesting is that comprehensive improvement will require "better" personnel. And in emphasizing "modern materials and teaching methods" the commission is talking about training, not education, and by that emphasis reinforces imagery they would decry in the preparation of scientists. To equate better training of teachers with better materials and methods is the height of irony because the one criticism made over the decades of the preparation of educators — and by people identical in background and affiliation to those on the commission — is that the preparation of educators gives too much emphasis to materials and methods. Or did the commission mean more than those sentences suggest? If they did, why the silence? I do not expect commission reports to offer detailed recommendations. At their best they give us blueprints. The blueprint given us by the Carnegie Commission is unaccountably silent about a problem it has identified.

Another possible explanation for the silence is that the commission was centered on reform and not prevention. Confronted as its members were with the seriousness and enormity of the problems of our schools, it is understandable if their basic focus was on how to repair them. This position makes thinking about primary prevention seem like a luxury. But, as someone said, to understand all is not to forgive all. In the case of primary prevention it seems that we have to be driven to take it seriously, to alter the imbalance between repair and primary prevention. Let me illustrate this with the work of Emory Cowen.[1]

Thirty-five years ago Cowen initiated a project in the secondary prevention of untoward behavioral patterns in elementary school children.

The realization that help for young children at risk was not available either when, or in the amount, needed was the motor force that started Primary Men-

[1]The quotations from Emory Cowen are from an unpublished paper he gave as an invited speaker. I am grateful for his permission to quote from that address ("Primary Prevention, Children, and Schools," October 1991, Winnipeg, Canada). By my latest count 278 publications have come from the project. A complete bibliography can be obtained from Emory Cowen, Department of Psychology, University of Rochester, Rochester, New York 14620.

tal Health Project (PMHP). We decided to focus scant
professional resources at the primary level in a program for early detection and prevention of school
maladjustment. Although we realized that reallocat-
ing resources in a finite system required compensa-
tory cutbacks, we hoped that the new approach would
minimize later more serious problems and, with that,
the need for services at the upper levels. That decision was PMHP's midwife. It has been central to the
project's ways ever since.

   Thus, PMHP can be seen as one way of addressing perceived insufficiencies in past mental health
approaches. Its key technologies were to detect risk
signs in children early-on and to provide prompt,
preventively oriented help.

To my knowledge, Cowen's project in secondary prevention is
the most sustained, most scrupulously evaluated, and most carefully disseminated of its kind. The results have been more than
encouraging and are in line with the more modest research efforts
of others. Anyone who states that we are without knowledge
in matters of prevention should read the papers and books of
Cowen and his colleagues. (Roger Weissberg was a student and
colleague of Cowen.) To study a particular set of problems for
thirty-five years one deserves an A for persistence. Crowning
that persistence with valid, practical results is rare indeed.

   Fifteen years ago Cowen came to a conclusion about his
work in secondary prevention:

   Without demeaning our own effort we end up with
   the Avis-like conclusion that PMHP, conceptually,
   is only second best. Although the approach is realistic, responsive to present realities, and much prefer-
   able to established, rutted, school mental health practices, it does not come to grips with the heart of the
   problem. And the heart of the problem was primary
   prevention.
      Though we did not fully realize it then, we were

setting a future agenda pivoting around the challenge of moving from ontogenetically early secondary prevention toward true primary prevention, i.e., developing effective ways to promote wellness in young children from the start. This new agenda did not mean abandoning PMHP; rather it meant building on it in more basic, primary ways. Indeed, the climate of trust and credibility that PMHP has created in schools over many years was a key factor in facilitating this new thrust [Cowen and others, 1975, p. 370].

There were three focuses to the new effort (which did not mean abandoning the research on secondary prevention): providing competence training or social problem solving; modifying classroom environments and practices to enhance adaptive outcomes; preventing or minimizing the negative sequelae that often follow divorce. The most recent addition to these research goals was explained this way by Cowen:

Our newest primary prevention trip is called the Rochester Child Resilience Project. Although the RCRP is still largely at a generative level, I am absorbed by the issues that power it and hopeful that its findings will ultimately address a vexing social problem. Quite beyond exposure to individual stressors, many children in modern society grow up in worlds of chronic and profound buffetings, aptly labelled by Garmezy as "stressors of marked gravity." For many kids, these grim realities have grave consequences. Yet others, propelled by a special resilience stemming from sources not fully understood, surmount such profound adversity — indeed, show unusual adaptive skills and competence in the face of it. These children have variously been called invulnerable, invincible or resilient. Garmezy spoke of them as healthy children in unhealthy environments. Werner described them as children who, notwithstanding heavy exposure to life stress, "worked well, played well, loved well and expected well." These are the *survivors* who come somehow, in nature's crucible, to find adaptive ways of coping with stressors of marked gravity and thus achieve a sense of control of their destinies. How does this happen? What factors enable them to beat the heavy odds? And how can such information be harnessed to forestall the devastating effects of chronic life stress and, more basically, to promote wellness in kids at grave risk?

Let us not gloss over several features of Cowen's work. It took a long-term view on his part to convince schools, school systems, and school districts to initiate primary prevention programs. He had established his credentials to them and had demonstrated the validity of his ideas and programs in secondary prevention. When he proposed researching primary prevention projects they saw it as in their self-interest to collaborate with him. He was not perceived as a university professor eager to make a time-limited excursion into schools, as an outsider who would come and go according to his self-interest. No less important, he demonstrated in action that he understood schools and their personnel, he was not the all-knowing, truth-proclaiming educational missionary bringing the message of salvation to ignorant primitives. He had a message, but, excellent clinician that he is, he did not underestimate what would have to happen for that message to be heard and accepted. He stayed the course.

The Carnegie Commission is absolutely correct when it says that the fruits of the reforms it suggests may not become manifest for decades. The commission should have added — could have added if it took the history of reform efforts seriously — that implementation of those reforms was not a task of engineering, not a matter of "applying" knowledge. On the contrary, reformers are confronted with a truly basic problem: what do we have to know about a "system" — its organizational structure, its relation to history and tradition, its selection of personnel and rites of passage, its cultural dynamics and how they affect and illuminate roles and relationships, its definition of "insiders" and "outsiders," the basis for its behavioral and programmatic regularities? How should all of this serve as a basis for a reform effort? It is not a matter of "delivering" ideas, curricula, or programs. It is not a matter of broadcasting. It is a matter quite familiar to the anthropologist trying to understand a foreign culture. Before going into the field the anthropologist tries to absorb all that has been written about a culture, knowing full well that the knowledge is incomplete and in undetermined ways wrong or misleading, and that when he or she arrives on the scene the shock of reality cannot be avoided.

Complicated? Yes, but unavoidable. Reforming schools is dangerous if you are seeking to change a system about which your preconceptions are very incomplete or simply wrong. Cowen learned all this from his early failures and mistakes (which he fully acknowledges); that is why he became such a superb anthropologist of our schools. The Carnegie Commission could have made a singular contribution if it had indicated that spearheading a reform effort was not for everybody. Better not to engage in reform than to engage without the knowledge, wisdom, personal style, and persistence such an effort requires. If love is not enough, neither are good intentions. The power to lead does not necessarily translate into the power to be influential. Indeed, the history of school reform suggests that the exercise of power for purposes of change too frequently has engendered passive resentment and resistance dooming the effort.

To Cowen's credit, he came to see that however successful his secondary prevention efforts, those efforts were "second best." His efforts could not alter the number of *new* cases that appear in a particular time period in a particular cohort or age group. Just as there was an imbalance in school reform between primary and secondary prevention, that imbalance was mirrored in Cowen's program. It is in the failure to suggest redressing that imbalance that the Carnegie Commission, like almost every other such group, missed an opportunity to be instructive.

Again, the question has to be asked: can we select and prepare educators better prepared to prevent problems in school children? A more interesting way to put it is this: if you were presented with the opportunity to start a new school of education, how different would it be, and why, from what such schools are today? In thinking about this fantasy several cautions should be observed. The first is to avoid scapegoating, in this case schools of education. It is one thing to criticize; it is another to resort to ad hominem attacks. Schools of education are not dens of iniquity, populated by people without minds, unmotivated to make schools better. There is much to criticize, but let us keep in mind that schools of education in our universities have *never* been viewed with enthusiasm or acceptance but always as second-class citizens; this position is reflected in their funding, political power, and status.

The reasons are historical and many. That state universities have schools of education says much more about the imperatives of legislative or public policy than it does about recognition of education as an intellectually legitimate arena of research and practice. Many elite universities and colleges do not have even a department, let alone a school, of education. Yale, for example, had a graduate department of education, eliminated it in the fifties, and now has a minuscule undergraduate program for those considering a career in secondary education. Given my interests I would bemoan this history. Bemoan until I realized one day that Yale was so inhospitable to education as an area of academic interest and concern that it was doing the field a favor by staying aloof. (Cary Cherniss's dissertation on education at Yale is fascinating reading [1972].) There is Teachers College, which Columbia University tolerates but does not support. Yes, we have much to criticize but if we seek to intervene — or to indulge in the fantasy I propose — let us acknowledge that schools of education (like a school in a school system) are part of a system whose dominant values and attitudes influence such schools. We will gain nothing by scapegoating, except to underline the power of self-fulfilling prophecies.

Also, we should not gloss over the reality that the one "system" having the greatest and most influential transactions (directly and indirectly) with a school system is higher education. To deal with the two as if they are not interacting systems — as if you can change one without changing the other—should be considered impossible, or at least off limits.[2]

Still another caution is that we try, initially at least, not to be constrained by what preparatory programs are today, that we not fetter ourselves by what we consider "practical." It is one thing to be practical in the realm of action; it is quite another to be practical in the realm of thinking, proposing, and taking the long-term view. What is required today is a vision of what should be, a vision that begins to gain a public currency that is the stuff of debate, controversy, and stimulus to change. Being practical in the short run is no virtue if it is not a step toward the realization of a vision. We have had a surfeit of seemingly practical ideas and interventions that have been failures precisely because they were not powered by an overarching vision.

We are used to hearing that we should be pragmatic, that we should heed William James's criterion of the "cash value" of our actions, that is, we should judge those actions by their consequences, by the degree to which they "work." But what does it signify about matters educational when they have not worked? The virtue of pragmatism is in the degree to which it sensitizes us to reexamine the sources of our failures, to understand better the sources of our impractical actions. If the cash value of our efforts is nil, should we not ask whether the guiding vision powering those efforts was deficient? Faced as we are with pressing, complicated problems we are forced to act, and we should. But that does not absolve us of the responsibility for trying to take distance from what we are doing in an effort to flush out and critique the basis for the vision undergirding our efforts. When you *have* to act—when the pressures are inexorably moral, social, and political—you have reason enough to assume that the cash value of your amelioration will not be high. Crises, we must not forget, are not conducive to self-

---

[2]It is to the everlasting credit of those who spearheaded *The Story of the Eight-Year Study* (which I discussed in the first chapter) that they took seriously the interacting influences of public schools and higher education. So, for example, they obtained from three hundred colleges and universities a waiver of the usual entrance criteria for the thirty high schools in the study, with fascinating and positive results.

examination, let alone the long-term view. If it is not conducive, it is not impossible. To regard it as impossible or wantonly impractical, or as an indulgence of pie-in-the-sky musings, we stand an excellent chance of losing the battle and the war.

Up to this point I have been making a case for giving more attention to a primary prevention approach to our educational problems, and I have suggested that we adapt that approach to the selection and preparation of educational personnel. In the pages that follow I will elaborate on that suggestion. As we shall see, giving substance to that suggestion is no easy matter. The reader can be assured that although I have no doubt whatsoever that a primary prevention approach to the preparation of educators will in the long run decrease the incidence of problems, I am quite aware that the fruitfulness of that approach will depend in part on changes elsewhere. That approach will stimulate changes in other places, and those changes will in turn affect the course of that approach. My task is not only to avoid oversimplification but also not to be overwhelmed by complexity. As for complexity, I am sure the reader will come to feel kinship, if not agreement, with me.

In the next chapter I will discuss an instance, most instructive, of an effort to adapt the primary prevention approach to the preparation of professional personnel. It concerned physicians at the turn of this century, a time at which the quality of medical practice was coming to be recognized as woefully inadequate and to a significant extent iatrogenic.

Chapter Six

When Medical Education Was Anti-Educational

The 1910 Flexner Report on Medical Education in the United States and Canada was sponsored by the Carnegie Foundation for the Improvement of Teaching. Abraham Flexner, a graduate of Johns Hopkins, had been a high school teacher, established his own private school, and in 1908 wrote a book critical of American higher education. That book led to the invitation from the Carnegie Foundation to study and report on educational programs of American medical schools. Flexner was a prolific writer who later in his career was the first director of the Institute of Advanced Study at Princeton.

He visited 150 medical schools then in existence, almost a total sample. The following excerpt from his report lays the groundwork for his findings on medical education:

> Between 1810 and 1840, twenty-six new medical schools sprang up; between 1840 and 1876, forty-seven more, and the number actually surviving in 1876 has been since then much more than doubled. First and last, the United States and Canada have in little more than a century produced four hundred and fifty-seven medical schools, many, of course, short-lived, and perhaps fifty still-born. One hundred and fifty-five survive today. Of these, Illinois, prolific mother of thirty-nine medical colleges, still harbors in the city of Chicago fourteen; forty-two sprang from the fertile soil of Missouri, twelve of them still "going" concerns; the Empire State produced forty-three,

79

with eleven survivors; Indiana, twenty-seven, with two
survivors; Pennsylvania, twenty, with eight survivors;
Tennessee, eighteen, with nine survivors. The city of
Cincinnati brought forth about twenty, the city of
Louisville eleven.

These enterprises—for the most part they can
be called schools or institutions only by courtesy—
were frequently set up regardless of opportunity or
need; in small towns as readily as in large, and at times
almost in the heart of the wilderness. No field, however limited, was ever effectually preempted. Wherever
and whenever the roster of untitled practitioners rose
above half a dozen, a medical school was likely at any
moment to be precipitated. Nothing was really essential but professors. The laboratory movement is comparatively recent; and Thomas Bond's wise words
about clinical teaching were long since out of print.
Little or no investment was therefore involved. A hall
could be cheaply rented and rude benches were inexpensive. Janitor services was unknown and is even
now relatively rare. Occasional dissections in time sup-
plied a skeleton—in whole or in part—and a box of
odd bones. Other equipment there was practically
none.

The teaching was, except for a little anatomy,
wholly didactic. The schools were essentially private
ventures, money-making in spirit and object. A school
that began in October would graduate a class the next
spring; it mattered not that the course of study was
two or three years; immigration recruited a senior class
at the start. Income was simply divided among the
lecturers, who reaped a rich harvest, besides, through
the consultations which the loyalty of their former students threw into their hands. "Chairs" were therefore
valuable pieces of property, their prices varying with
what was termed their "reflex" value: only recently a
professor in a now defunct Louisville school, who had
agreed to pay $3000 for the combined chair of physi-

ology and gynecology, objected strenuously to a division of the professorship assigning him in physiology, on the ground of "failure of consideration"; for the "reflex" which constituted the inducement to purchase went obviously with the other subject. No applicant for instruction who could pay his fees or sign his note was turned down.

State boards were not as yet in existence. The school diploma was itself a license to practice. The examinations, brief, oral, and secret, plucked almost none at all; even at Harvard, a student for whom a majority of nine professors "voted" was passed. The man who had settled his tuition bill was thus practically assured of his degree, whether he had regularly attended lectures or not. Accordingly, the business throve. Rivalry between different so-called medical centers was ludicrously bitter.

Still more acrid were — and occasionally are — the local animosities bound to arise in dividing or endeavoring to monopolize the spoils. Sudden and violent feuds thus frequently disrupted the facilities. But a split was rarely fatal: it was more likely to result in one more school. Occasionally, a single too masterful individual became the strategic object of a hostile faculty combination. Daniel Drake, indomitable pioneer in medical education up and down the Ohio Valley, thus tasted the ingratitude of his colleagues. As presiding officer of the faculty of the Medical College of Ohio, at Cincinnati, cornered by a cabal of men, only a year since indebted to him for their professorial titles and profits, he was compelled to put a motion for his own expulsion and to announce to his enemies a large majority in his favor. It is pleasant to record that the indefatigable man was not daunted. He continued from time to time to found schools and to fill professorships — at Lexington, at Philadelphia, at Oxford in Ohio, at Louisville, and finally again in that beloved Cincinnati, where he had been so hardly served. In the course of a busy and fruitful career, he had occupied eleven different chairs in six different schools, several of which he had himself founded; and he had besides traversed the whole country, as it then was, from Canada and the Great Lakes to the Gulf, and as far westward as Iowa, collecting material for his great work, historically a classic, *The Diseases of the Interior Valley of North America* [Flexner, 1960 (1910), pp. 6–8].

Here are some highlights from Flexner's findings:

1. Sixteen of 155 medical schools required one year of college work, "six more, now demanding one year of college work will . . . require a second; and several more . . . will shortly take the step from the high school to the two year college requirement" (p. 28). Fifty medical schools required a high school education. The remainder "ask little or nothing more than the rudiments or the *recollection* of a common school education" (p. 8, italics mine).

2. A fair number of medical schools were unconnected to a hospital or university. They were commercial enterprises, some of which spent more on advertising than on buying laboratory materials. More than a few universities that had medical schools took no responsibility for them in regard to admission, quality standards, or financial support.

3. Medical training was hardly informed by advances in such fields as physics, chemistry, and biology.

The state of medical education at the turn of the century was best summarized by Henry Pritchett, president of the Carnegie Foundation, in his introduction to Flexner's report:

The striking and significant facts which are here brought out are of enormous consequence not only to the medical practitioner, but to every citizen of the

United States and Canada; for it is a singular fact that the organization of medical education in this country has hitherto been such as not only to commercialize the process of education itself, but also to obscure in the minds of the public any discrimination between the well trained physician and the physician who has had no adequate training whatsoever. As a rule, Americans, when they avail themselves of the services of a physician, make only the slightest inquiry as to what his previous training and preparation have been. One of the problems of the future is to educate the public itself to appreciate the fact that very seldom, under existing conditions, does a patient receive the best aid which it is possible to give him in the present state of medicine, and that this is due mainly to the fact that a vast army of men is admitted to the practice of medicine who are untrained in sciences fundamental to the profession and quite without a sufficient experience with disease. A right education of public opinion is one of the problems of future medical education.

The significant facts revealed by this study are these:

(1) For twenty-five years past there has been an enormous over-production of uneducated and ill trained medical practitioners. This has been in absolute disregard of the public welfare and without any serious thought of the interests of the public. Taking the United States as a whole, physicians are four or five times as numerous in proportion to population as in older countries like Germany.

(2) Over-production of ill trained men is due in the main to the existence of a very large number of commercial schools, sustained in many cases by advertising methods through which a mass of unprepared youth is drawn out of industrial occupations into the study of medicine.

(3) Until recently the conduct of a medical school was a profitable business, for the methods of instruction were mainly didactic. As the need for laboratories has become more keenly felt, the expenses of an efficient medical school have been greatly increased. The inadequacy of many of these schools may be judged from the fact that nearly half of all our medical schools have incomes below $10,000 and these incomes determine the quality of instruction that they can and do offer.

Colleges and universities have in large measure failed in the past twenty-five years to appreciate the great advances in medical education and the increased cost of teaching it along modern lines. Many universities desirous of apparent educational completeness have annexed medical schools without making themselves responsible either for the standards of the professional schools or for their support.

(4) The existence of many of these unnecessary and inadequate medical schools has been defended by the argument that a poor medical school is justified in the interest of the poor boy. It is clear that the poor boy has no right to go into any profession for which he is not willing to obtain adequate preparation; but the facts set forth in this report make it evident that this argument is insincere, and that the excuse which has hitherto been put forward in the name of the poor boy is in reality an argument in behalf of the poor medical school.

(5) A hospital under complete educational control is as necessary to a medical school as is a laboratory of chemistry or pathology. High grade teaching within a hospital introduces a most wholesome and beneficial influence into its routine. Trustees of hospitals, public and private, should therefore go to the limit of their authority in opening hospital wards to teaching, provided only that the universities secure suffi-

cient funds on their side to employ as teachers men who are devoted to clinical science.

In view of these facts, progress for the future would seem to require a very much smaller number of medical schools, better equipped and better conducted than our schools now as a rule are; and the needs of the public would equally require that we have fewer physicians graduated each year, but that these should be better educated and better trained. With this idea accepted, it necessarily follows that the medical school will, if rightly conducted, articulate not only with the university, but with the general system of education. Just what form that articulation must take will vary in the immediate future in different parts of the country. Throughout the eastern and central states the movement under which the medical school articulates with the second year of the college has already gained such impetus that it can be regarded as practically accepted. In the southern states for the present it would seem that articulation with the four-year high school would be a reasonable starting-point for the future. In time the development of secondary education in the south and the growth of the colleges will make it possible for southern medical schools to accept the two-year college basis of preparation. With reasonable prophecy the time is not far distant when, with fair respect for the interests of the public and the need for physicians, the articulation of the medical school with the university may be the same throughout the entire country. For in the future the college or the university which accepts a medical school must make itself responsible for university standards in the medical school and for adequate support for medical education. The day has gone by when any university can retain the respect of educated men, or when it can fulfill its duty to education, by retaining a low grade professional school for the sake of its own institutional completeness [Flexner, 1960 (1910), pp. x–xi].

Flexner's contribution was in outlining and justifying a four-year medical school program, one that sought to provide and integrate hands-on laboratory and clinical experience with closely supervised hands-on interactions with ill people. What we call modern medicine has several sources, not the least of which was Flexner's candid, critical, controversial report. He pulled no punches. He called a spade a spade. Someone has said that he was the right man at the right time with the right backing (moral and financial) to coalesce in one report a changing worldview about science and societal obligations.

What is the relevance of Flexner's report to our current concerns and efforts to improve our schools? One way to answer that question is that it never entered Flexner's thinking to come up with recommendations for improving the practice of *existing* physicians. It was not because Flexner on principle would have been opposed to such efforts, just as no one today is opposed to efforts to influence and improve the thinking and practices of educational personnel *now* in our schools.[1] Indeed, in the post–World War II era we have expended billions of dollars in such efforts, with outcomes pleasing to nobody.

Another way to answer the question is to say that implicitly Flexner was guided by the primary prevention model: if we changed, improved, enlarged, and deepened the preparation of physicians we would, over time, more successfully prevent many illnesses, and in the case of other illnesses secondarily prevent or ameliorate untoward sequelae. If that rationale was implicit — and it is my guess that it was so obvious to Flexner that he did not feel the need even to couch it in terms of prevention — there was one basis for it about which he was most explicit: science had given us new knowledge and skills that could and should inform both primary and secondary prevention. Why were we not using that knowledge and those skills? How

---

[1]Lest I be misinterpreted, on average, the quality of the education, intelligence, motivation, and even professional preparation of educational personnel in our schools are vastly superior to the quality of these attributes in those who were physicians at the turn of the century. However, that comparison in no way justifies ignoring the dysfunction between the realities of our schools and the needs and inadequacies of educators. And some of the deficits of the contemporary physician are similar to those of educators.

could they inform medical education? Those are the questions Flexner posed and answered.

One other point was explicit in his report: the hoped-for consequences of his primary prevention model would only become apparent over decades. Flexner was a realist. He knew the resistance his recommendations would encounter. Some of the sources of resistance were understandable and could not be glossed over. Some of the resistance he regarded, correctly, as self-serving, illogical, and socially unjustified. But whatever the sources of resistance, Flexner kept his and the reader's eyes on what had to be done. In terms of his goals he had twenty-twenty vision. He had a vision, a belief, a faith. He was like the biblical prophets: unwilling to excuse social injustice, stupidity, and irresponsibility, compelled to remind people of their moral obligations to themselves and to each other. His report is a moral, not a scientific, treatise. Let us listen to Flexner (1960 [1910]):

> So far we have spoken explicitly of the fundamental sciences only. They furnish, indeed, the essential instrumental basis of medical education. But the instrumental minimum can hardly serve as the permanent professional minimum. It is even instrumentally inadequate. The practitioner deals with facts of two categories. Chemistry, physics, biology enable him to apprehend one set; he needs a different apperceptive and appreciative apparatus to deal with other, more subtle elements. Specific preparation is in this direction much more difficult; one must rely for the requisite insight and sympathy on a varied and enlarging cultural experience. Such enlargement of the physician's horizon is otherwise important, for scientific progress has greatly modified his ethical responsibility. His relation was formerly to his patient — at most to his patient's family; and it was almost altogether remedial. The patient had something the matter with him; the doctor was called in to cure it. Payment of a fee ended the transaction. But the physician's function is fast becoming social and preventive, rather

than individual and curative. Upon him society re-
lies to ascertain, and through measures essentially
educational to enforce, the conditions that prevent disease and make positively for physical and moral well-
being. It goes without saying that this type of doctor
is first of all an educated man [p. 26].

The values expressed in this excerpt are unassailable.
However, the passage ignores an issue that will occupy us in our
reexamination and discussion of the preparation of educational
personnel. It is less an omission than an uncritical acceptance
of an assumption that, in part at least, is invalid. Before iden-
tifying the issue I must inform the reader that in recent decades
the medical community has been criticized on the grounds that
too many physicians lack the attributes of caring and compassion, that in their interactions with patients they are insensitive
to the patients' needs and feelings, to a degree that engenders
silence, passivity, and hostility. A not-infrequent consequence
is that the physician is robbed of information relevant both to
primary and secondary prevention. These criticisms come not
only from the general public but also from prestigious groups
of medical educators.[2]

Flexner says virtually nothing about caring and compassion in physicians. Indeed, except for his forceful emphasis on
preparation in science as a prerequisite for entrance to medical
school, he does not discuss criteria for selection. That omission,
it is safe to assume, in no way reflects Flexner's insensitivity to
the importance of these personal characteristics in physicians.
If the omission points to anything, it is Flexner's assumption —
one of those "of course" assumptions — that people who sought
a career in medicine were prompted by a *calling,* a term he explicitly uses almost in passing.

Today, that term has an antique flavor, sounding like a

[2]The reader may wish to consult my *Caring and Compassion in Clinical Practice* (1985)
in which I discuss the issue of caring and compassion in five professions: physicians in general, psychiatrists, clinical psychologists, lawyers in family practice,
and public school personnel.

remnant of long ago when it was the rule, not the exception, to believe that one's plans and life had transcendental origins and meanings. It was not that one exercised no choice in the matter but rather that the choice had to reflect the feeling that, in a larger moral-ethical-spiritual scheme of things, one had a special place: a role that uniquely integrated one's special interests and abilities with the rendering of a service. And to be "called" meant that you took on the obligation to be governed by the rules and traditions of that larger, transcendent scheme of things. A calling presented you with an opportunity to serve; it also meant that you would be governed by a "higher" set of moral-ethical obligations, which, precisely because of their transcendental significance, meant that the needs of those one served took precedence over one's own. It was expected that "calling" would frequently require self-sacrifice.

Living as most of us do in a very secular world, in which a phrase such as "transcendental scheme of things" smacks of mysticism and superstition, it is hard for us to comprehend the concept of a "calling." But for Flexner, as for many others of his time, that was no problem. The idea that one embarked on a medical career for monetary or purely personal reasons was an idea that Flexner derogated.

Flexner's conception of what should be appropriate motivation for entering a medical career was in no small part a reaction to the practice of many medical schools to entice students to their programs because they would lead to monetary rewards. In some cases, Flexner points out, the advertising budgets of these schools were larger than the budgets for laboratories! No, for Flexner, it was morally inadequate to seek a medical career for financial gain. The physician had to have "higher," more morally demanding, less personal reasons. For Flexner, the physician's obligation to the sick and to the larger society took precedence over personal aggrandizement in any manner, shape, or form.

There are those who would argue that Flexner had an idealized image of what kind of person a physician should be, an image no more found in 1910 than among "real" physicians today. That may be the case, but it should not obscure the fact that what exercised Flexner was the number of people who were entering medicine for the wrong reasons: for narrow, personal, selfish reasons.

There is a major blind spot in Flexner's report, a consequence of his exclusive, indeed obsessive, concern with scientific training — its direct impact on selection of students, its control over the curriculum — and his complete inability to consider the unintended negative consequences of his recommendations. In the realm of human affairs, there are always unintended consequences. It is one thing to force oneself to recognize that brute fact and to try, albeit always imperfectly, to get some sense of the realm of unintended consequences. It is another to proceed as if we live in a world where one's intended consequences will be the only consequences. Illusions are governed by our wishes, and nowhere is this better illustrated than by the frequency with which we restrict our thinking to intended consequences. This is said not as criticism of Flexner, let alone as blame, but as recognition of Flexner's humanity.

In terms of the medical curriculum, Flexner was faced with the practical problem of what could reasonably be included in four years of medical school. It seems clear that from the outset he had concluded that a scientifically based medical education could not be achieved within those four years unless the foundations were begun in the undergraduate years and, in addition, there were postgraduate opportunities for keeping up-to-date on scientific and technological advances. Sophisticated curriculum developer that he was, Flexner knew that time was a most precious commodity, to be apportioned in ways that did not do violence either to the letter or the spirit of the goals of integrating science and medical practice. The basic medical sciences, as Flexner conceived them, were to be assimilated not as arid, isolated bodies of knowledge but in relation to a stepwise series of exposures to clinical phenomena and practice. Every step of the game was to serve the purpose of deepening the integration between knowledge and application.

Flexner was not out to train technicians of limited knowledge and skills who dispensed their wares in uncritical, even mindless kinds of ways. That, of course, was the kind of physician he saw being produced by the bulk of medical schools. Flexner's aim was to forge a new kind of professional, steeped in and dedicated to science and its application to medical practice. That would take time and a special kind of educational ambience in which this new type of physician would be nurtured.

Flexner did not assume that this integration would take place by itself or by a social osmosis or by the consequences of the right intentions. It could occur only if that integration was the central focus of student and faculty, not only informing what goes on but also justifying vigilance and efforts at improvement.

There were many questions Flexner never asked: How do we ensure that the medical student becomes a caring and compassionate physician? By what educational procedures do we instill and judge a student's understanding not only of a person's symptoms and bodily condition but of that person's experienced plight? If we seek to engender in the student a scientific conscience by which the student and we will judge action, what should be the substance of that other conscience that tells us what we "owe" others in our interpersonal, social commerce with them? Are there values or considerations that justify restricting the scope of the effort to recognize and dilute the personal and familial anxiety, pain, and misery accompanying physical illness? Are the symptoms of these accompaniments — their prevention as well as dilution — less important than symptoms of bodily malfunction? Can we arrange a productive wedding between science and medicine without a destructive divorce between medicine and the caring, compassionate stance and action?

If Flexner did not ask these questions, it is because he was making at least two "of course" assumptions. The first was that those who would be attracted to the new medicine would be selflessly dedicated, interpersonally sensitive people prepared to deal with all aspects of the pain and misery of illness. The physician was not only to be a scientist in the narrowest sense; he was to be someone with "insight and sympathy," an "educated man" (Flexner, 1960 [1910], p. 26).

By "an educated man," Flexner meant someone steeped in the humanities: those traditions and bodies of knowledge concerned with the nature and vicissitudes of people's moral and

ethical relationships to each other, what humans "owed" to fel-
low humans, the "shoulds and oughts" that have liberated humanity from superstition, selfishness, and tyranny. It is to Flexner's everlasting credit that he saw the sciences basic to medicine
as an inadequate instrumental minimum for the education of
the complete physician.

The second "of course" assumption Flexner made was that
the medical student would be constantly and vigilantly guided
by teachers who themselves were "educated men." These teachers
would be more than scientists, ever alert to the dangers of a
narrow technical training. Flexner points out that the medical
student, unlike the engineering student, "handles at one and the
same time elements belonging to vastly different categories: physical, biological, psychological elements are involved in each
other" (Flexner, 1960 [1910], p. 23). It would be the prime
responsibility of the teacher to ensure that these categories would
be integrated. The medical school professor would be the ex-
emplar of the complete physician, not of the narrow scientist.

In short, if Flexner did not pursue certain questions, it
is not because he deemed them unimportant. On the contrary,
he considered them the most important questions. His failure
to pursue them is because he assumed they would be answered
in three ways: a broad undergraduate education, a self-selection
factor that would "call" to medicine individuals with the appropriate vision and motivation, and a medical school ambience that
exposed the student to teachers who approximated the ideal of
the scientific, caring, compassionate, socially responsible physician. How else can one explain his proposing a medical school
curriculum that from beginning to end concentrated on what
Flexner himself considered to be "inadequate instrumentally"
(Flexner, 1960 [1910]) as a basis for medical education? The
quotation earlier that ended with Flexner's "educated man" appears on page 26 of the report. The rest of the report contains
nothing relevant to the contents of that stirring paragraph.

What evidence did Flexner have for the validity of his "of
course" assumptions? The evidence — spread throughout his
report — lent little or no credence to these assumptions: the great
majority of medical schools lacked the appropriate ambience;

those who entered these medical schools generally had the wrong motivations; and most medical students had completed an undergraduate education vastly deficient to the one on which Flexner pinned his hopes. There were a few medical schools that Flexner considered as models of what he was proposing; he refers to Johns Hopkins in terms of reverence. But a close reading of the report suggests that this handful of medical schools met Flexner's approval because they based their curriculum on the basic sciences, not because he had any evidence that they attracted, selected, and educated the type of student who approximated Flexner's ideal physician.

I am not being critical of Flexner. His report deserves praise, not criticism when one considers the year the study was done, the sorry state of medical education, the partial and often complete lack of a relationship between medical schools and universities and between medical schools and hospitals, the slowness with which advances in science and technology were filtering into medical training, the commercialization of medical education, and how frequent it was for the medical students to have only two years or less (and sometimes none) of college. But it is not criticism to say that Flexner, like us, was possessed by a worldview resting on axioms that are unarticulated precisely because they seem so natural, right, and proper. The process by which we are socialized into society is one by which we assimilate axioms requiring no articulation. They are self-evidently "right." They are silent but bedrock to our view of what the world is and should be. These axioms do not become blind spots (that is, they are not recognized as such) until events in the larger society force us to challenge what was heretofore unchallengeable.

Flexner lived at a time when science as salvation, as the force for human progress, as the universal solvent for human misery, had become an unarticulated part of the worldview of the "educated man." This axiom did not permit Flexner to inquire into possible unintended negative consequences of a medical school curriculum that from beginning to end riveted on science and technology, that, indeed, even required suffusing the undergraduate curriculum with the same ambience. He assumed that his dramatic proposals would not alter the characteristics of those who would self-select themselves for a career in medicine, that somehow or other caring, compassionate, selfless behavior (in contrast to caring, compassionate, selfless rhetoric) would not be in conflict with assimilating the substance of the new curriculum, that such behavior would be both engendered and reinforced by the student's mentors: these assumptions Flexner was unable to state and, therefore, examine or challenge.

By definition, unintended consequences are not predictable. But it is one thing to propose policies completely insensitive to the inevitability of unintended consequences and quite another to be aware of that fact and deliberately to try to fathom what some of these unintended consequences might be, even though one knows that such fathoming will at best be very incomplete. If the road to hell is paved with good intentions, a major ingredient in the pavement are the unintended consequences to which one's passions and do-good tendencies precluded awareness. By and large, the professional views the do-gooder as someone who vastly oversimplifies the realities with which their proposals must deal, unaware of the myriad negative ripple effects the proposals could have. In that sense, one has to say that Flexner was the typical do-gooder. Yes, and paradoxically, he was a very sophisticated do-gooder; but to the extent that he could see medical education only as an onward and upward course on which there were no potholes about which one had to worry, Flexner was a do-gooder. He lived at a time when the "educated man" had yet to learn about potholes.

If Flexner can be faulted for anything, it is his failure to take seriously something that he notes and indicts: the commercialization of medicine. His indictment is of the many medical schools of the day that were explicitly in business to make money and of those individuals attracted to the profession for the same reason. Flexner did not confront the implications of our being a capitalist society — a characterization I do not use pejoratively — in which in countless ways the desire for individual material gain, indeed aggrandizement, is stimulated and reinforced, in which success is too often equated with what Veblen termed *conspicu-*

ous consumption, in which striving for upward social mobility is a socially accepted goal. Possessed as he was by the concept of the "educated man," which in his day referred to a relatively small elite in terms of socioeconomic status, Flexner assumed that such individuals were somehow devoid of the seamy aspects of the motivation for pecuniary gain.

Similarly, if his indictment did not refer to the relatively few medical schools of which he approved, it was again because he assumed that, populated as they were by educated men and by medical students with the appropriate college education, economic considerations were not important in terms either of individual motivation or of institutional organization.

Flexner had a very narrow conception of how the nature of the society inevitably became reflected in the institutions it spawned. He had a very clear and inspiring conception of the kind of physician the society needed, and he knew how the abstraction we call science — its truth-seeking and moral traditions — should be assimilated into the outlook and practices of physicians. However, to his everlasting credit, Flexner understood, as his words plainly convey, that, although these scientific underpinnings were necessary, they were far from sufficient. There were other "more subtle elements" even more important. In regard to these elements, however, as "specific preparation is in this direction much more difficult, one must rely for the requisite insight and sympathy on a varied and enlarging cultural experience." Why is that preparation much more difficult? What does Flexner want us to understand by "varied and enlarging cultural experiences"? Why is he here so vague and general about elements that he considers the most important of all, while he is so concrete and detailed about scientific training? If the preparation of these elements is so important and much "more difficult," how does one justify reliance on something vague and ink-blottish as "varied and enlarging cultural experiences"? Flexner "solved" the problem essentially by ignoring it, by resorting uncharacteristically (for him) to expressions of hope and of unalloyed optimism about the benefits of formal education. What Flexner glossed over, together with his science-filled curriculum and his narrow conception of the kind of society he lived in (and we continue to live in), set the stage for those subsequent cyclical reports bemoaning the dilution of caring and compassionate behavior among medical students and physicians generally.

In the field of personnel selection there is a maxim: if you know how to select, you have licked 50 percent of the problem. And the problem, of course, is to *prevent* mismatches between person and task, mismatches upsetting to individuals and organization, mismatches that require repair that are psychologically difficult and fiscally costly. (If you think about marriage from the standpoint of "personnel selection," the escalating divorce rate is understandable.) Flexner knew all this, which is why he concluded that his recommendations would, over time, dramatically reduce the number of students who lacked the qualities subsumed under the rubric of the "educated man." He was clear about what the new selection process should prevent. What he offered as a kind of primary prevention turned out to be inadequate.

If there has been increasing concern about the lack of caring and compassion in physicians, let us note that there is nothing today in the selection of medical students that is at all related to the attributes of caring and compassion. A colleague of mine, Leland Wilkinson, was asked by a medical school to do an exhaustive statistical study to determine which factors best predicted who would be selected for admission. The selection process was very costly in terms of the number of faculty who interviewed candidates, the quantity of ratings that were made, the group meetings required, and so on. Wilkinson's results were stark: if you went only on the basis of college grades and scores on the medical aptitude test, you would make very few predictive errors. The correlation between college grades and test scores, on the one hand, and the attributes of caring and compassion, on the other hand, is unknown. We may safely assume that it is not high. And we may safely assume that in the future as in the past, virtually none of the billions expended on medical research will address this problem. Not so incidentally, the medical school did not see fit to publish Wilkinson's findings and there is no indication that they have altered their selection process.

One of the virtues of the primary prevention approach is that it forces you not only to be clear about what it is you seek to prevent but also what you need to know to justify action. Nobody is against primary prevention. Nobody, I assume, would argue that you act only when you are *absolutely* sure that your actions will not contain some error. There is a difference between feeling secure and being certain. Nobody will opt for flying blind in fog over flying by instrument.

Let us recognize that in the selection of educational personnel, as in the case of medical students in regard to caring and compassion, we are flying blind and we refuse to recognize it. The situation is more serious in education because many preparatory programs are not in a position to select; that is, the pool of candidates, relatively speaking, is too small. Schools take what they can get because if they did not, the very existence of these programs would be in doubt, a situation which Flexner bitterly indicted in many of the medical schools of his day.

In the next chapter I take up two related questions. How might we increase the pool of people desirous of a career in education? How can we do this in ways that prevent mismatches between person and career? I do not ask these questions in regard to preparatory programs (that will come later) but in regard to undergraduate liberal arts programs where my suggestions in no way will concern *professional* preparation.

Chapter Seven

An Undergraduate Program for Liberal Arts Colleges

Two principal methods have been used to increase the number of people seeking a career in education. By far the most frequently employed has been to increase salaries. This incentive gained force in the late fifties and sixties when it seemed as if schools could not be built fast enough to accommodate the postwar baby boom. Personnel needs were one fact; scandalously low salaries were another. The second way was to waive the requirements for certification, allowing college graduates without formal credentials to start teaching and then to enter a preparatory program. Both ways to increase the pool were transiently successful. Beginning in the mid to late sixties, there was an almost continuous drop in the number of entering college students expressing an interest in a career in education.

Why the drop? Certainly one factor was the successes of the women's liberation movement. As opportunities for a career in all spheres of activity opened up for women, a career in education became less attractive, not only in terms of income but in terms of intellectual challenge and social status. Being a teacher had associated with it imagery that could not compete with that of being a lawyer, a physician, or a scientist or of climbing the corporate ladder.

For a few short years a number of graduates with liberal arts majors from prestigious colleges and universities entered teaching as an expression of a social consciousness so much a feature of the zeitgeist we call the sizzling sixties. Most of them were women. Most of them found the experience disillusioning. I say that on the basis of a fair amount of formal and informal

98

interaction with them during the years of the Yale Psycho-
Educational Clinic (Sarason and others, 1966). The sources of
their disillusionment were several but the most obvious and
potent was a general ignorance of what I call the culture of
schools. It is important to note that this ignorance was equally
as true for new teachers who had had a traditional preparation
as it was for those who lacked it. They came to teaching extraordinarily motivated, wide-eyed, eager to make a difference
in the lives of students.

Two aspects of the experience, one obvious and one subtle, bewildered them. The obvious was that they had neither
the knowledge nor skills to cope satisfactorily with all the problems of all the students, and there was little or nothing in their
schools to support or help them. They coped, they truly tried.
In general, they were a bright, resourceful cohort who did not
want to retreat into guilt-producing apathy, neglect, and defeat.
The more subtle aspect, derivable from the first, was the sense
of a lack of intellectual challenge or understanding. They were
faced with such a *personally* demanding task that there was little
time to *think,* to come up with an explanation that if not practically helpful, at least provided them insights, food for thought.
They were so busy reacting that thinking became a luxury. At
the end of each day they were drained, not a state conducive
to putting and explaining experience in a wider context. And
there was no forum in their schools to help them understand
the wider context.

Let us examine for a moment the popular imagery about
teachers. It is imagery about individuals, each of whom is in
an encapsulated place we call a classroom. It is not about a
school: how it is organized, the formal and informal relationships within it, its decision-making processes, its resources and
their allocation, and how these and other factors affect teachers.
It is imagery about an individual, literally out of context. A more
obvious feature of the imagery is that the teacher, like a parent, manages, controls, informs, passes judgment, praises and
punishes, and motivates children — all in an encapsulated place
that presumably is minimally connected to anything or anyone
else. Imagery about teachers contains little recognition that

teaching is (or certainly should be) an intellectually demanding task, demanding not only high-level conceptualizations about children but also of the wider context of which students and teachers are a part. Understanding one's self as a teacher, no less than understanding the thinking and behavior of children, is a complicated intellectual affair not contained in imagery of the teacher as caretaker, information giver, and dispatcher. John Dewey once said that school teachers should receive the same salary as university professors. He did not say that to endear himself to teachers. He said it because teaching, whether with elementary or college students, is a very complicated intellectual affair, demanding an integration of all of one's personal and cognitive abilities. Neither the imagery or the preparation of educational personnel have been informed by such a view.

Given the situation today, our task is not only to increase the pool of people seeking careers in education but to do it so as to provide a degree of intellectual substance, respect, and breadth to the field it does not now have from the public generally and our undergraduate colleges in particular. And, as I shall soon make clear, when I say *undergraduate* I shall in no way be referring to education as a professional field. At the present time undergraduate programs in the arts and sciences do not, for all practical purposes, expose students to education as a social science, as a window through which one can better understand society and self. As a result, undergraduates are not provided an opportunity intellectually to comprehend the nature of a societal institution experienced by all of its citizens and considered by all as crucial for the public welfare, one that contains all the cross currents in the society, and in diverse ways plays a major role in shaping the personal, intellectual, vocational, and social features of those who pass through it. For undergraduates, education as an arena of inquiry and practice distinctively reflecting a distinctive society is a non-field. It is an arena only of practice, not one fit to be part of a liberal arts education.

Historically, the "liberal" arts are those that "liberate" the individual from narrowness of knowledge about past and present, from tunnel vision for what man has been, is, and can be, and from an imprisoning subjectivity. By its absence the undergraduate can only conclude — assuming that he or she ever gives it thought, which they do not — that education as the study of processes and institutions has no place in undergraduate, non-professional curricula. *And that absence is one of the subtle and potent factors determining who decides and on what basis to seek a career in education.* In attempting to increase the pool of future educators we can no longer ignore the fact that *self-selection* for any field begins before selection by professional programs. Is it any wonder that a small fraction of undergraduates completing a liberal arts program consider education as a career?

Let me now present an undergraduate liberal arts — social science proposal for the study of education. Let us postpone for the moment its justification as a primary prevention effort. My immediate aim is to concretize what I mean by an intellectually respectable demanding undergraduate experience in public education.

What I propose is *not* a course but a year-long field experience that could be called Schools and Society, or the Culture of Schools. Whatever the title, it should in no way suggest that it is a professionally oriented experience. Let me list some of the major experiences to which the undergraduate would be exposed.

1. Students would spend a good deal of time in classrooms at all grade levels, from kindergarten through high schools, including classrooms devoted to handicapped children.

2. During the year they would be apprenticed to or be in a position to observe and talk with principals, school psychologists, school social workers, and other individually oriented clinicians. To whatever extent feasible they would attend faculty meetings as well as those involving school personnel with parents and other community people.

3. They would spend time with the superintendent and his staff, and they would be required to attend board of education meetings. Not only would they attend those meetings but they would have the opportunity to get to know the members

so as to become knowledgeable about their background and educational perspectives.

4. Students would be expected to attend all meetings of local officialdom at which educational matters (for example, school budget) will be discussed and acted on.

5. If the school system has contractual relationships with teachers' and administrators' unions, it would be arranged for the students to meet and get to know their representatives and, again if possible, to observe the process whereby collective bargaining positions are formulated, and to observe collective bargaining sessions.

You do not just put students in the "field," tell them to observe this or that type of event, to spend time with this or that type of person, and expect them to have the conceptual wherewithal to make appropriate sense of their experiences. That is why the year-long experience would also include seminars by an anthropologist, a psychologist, a sociologist, a political scientist, an economist, and a historian — each with expertise about education or at least a developing interest in the field. A major focus of each seminar would be not only providing and discussing what each of these fields has learned about education but testing that learning in relation to a particular school system, community, and state. The major responsibility of these faculty members would be to provide intellectual, substantive direction to what the students observe and do "in the field."

The year-long experience, for which the students will get full college credit, would be intellectually and personally demanding. To understand schools from the several perspectives — derived as that understanding would be from being in "real" schools with all that subsumes — would be no easy task. Indeed, some would say that what I have proposed in outline is too tall an order for one year. The merits of that objection, like the merits of my proposal, cannot be judged by any existing experience. The details of my proposal are, at this point, less important than its intellectual-educational goal: to provide undergraduates with conceptual frameworks and "live" experience for the purpose of enlarging and deepening their knowledge of and outlook on self, schools, and society. There are thorny problems with my proposal but before discussing them I want to draw on some personal experiences and observations which suggest that more than a few students would be eager to participate in what would be an elective experience.

For the past three decades I and my colleagues, at Yale and elsewhere, have taught courses under the rubric of community psychology. As in the proposal I outlined above, these courses require students to spend a good deal of time observing *and* participating in the activities of diverse community settings. Students are not only helped to understand these settings but to carry out a research project that interests them and could be related to the existing literature. Before being permitted to enroll in these courses, students are explicitly told what the time and intellectual demands on them would be. What surprised me was how many students were willing to commit themselves to these demands. I am sure that there is a self-selective factor in who chooses to engage in the experience. But that is precisely the point: we underestimate the number of undergraduates eager for what some of them call a "hands-on" experience that is personally and intellectually stimulating.

During the sixties, of course, there was no problem attracting students. In recent years, we are told, students are more socially apathetic and only a minuscule number are motivated to engage in, to seek to understand, or to change some aspect of the "real world." That judgment is valid but only if you go by surface appearances. From my discussions with undergraduates, once you go beyond appearances you find concern, bewilderment, anger, and even anxiety about what they see as a crazy, immoral, disorganized, and disorganizing world. They do not want to be intellectually and socially passive. They desire more than facts and knowledge. They want to understand more and feel they can make a difference. They are far from satisfied with the role of the passive, knowledge accumulating, knowledge regurgitating student. They would like to experience the "real world" problems and settings in ways that would give them a sense of personal and intellectual growth. But there are few opportunities that would permit them to have such experiences with the stimulation, support, and guidance of committed faculty.

I do not want to exaggerate what is below the surface of what has been called the "me generation." But neither do I want to leave unchallenged the view that undergraduates today are dramatically less çoncerned with social issues and disinterested in engaging, personally and intellectually, in settings where those issues are manifest. We can, as we usually do, make the mistake we make with public school students: underestimating the nature, sources, and force of a passionate curiosity to understand self, others, and their social world. In our laudable but misdirected effort to hone skills and pour knowledge into students, curiosity becomes the seed beneath the snow awaiting a change in climatic conditions, a change that may or may not come. *Indeed, one of the goals of my proposal is to enable undergraduates to begin to comprehend the difference between passive and active learning, a difference no less relevant for children in a classroom than for college undergraduates.*

Now for the Achilles heel of my proposal. I know of no undergraduate college — or for that matter any comprehensive university — that has the faculty to implement my proposal. Education as a field of intellectual and social inquiry is far from the mainstream of the social sciences. As a field of inquiry, education commands neither respect nor support. During the sixties and seventies I came to know a number of young, brilliant social scientists whose interests and research were in education. Even though their sparkling abilities gained them respect from their colleagues, they did not obtain positions in colleges or universities of the caliber they deserved. Some left their fields.

Educational processes and institutions will not be productively comprehensible unless viewed from the perspectives of the several social sciences. This does not mean, I hasten to add, that at the present time the social sciences are sitting, so to speak, on a gold mine of knowledge directly relevant to matters educational. That is not the case, unfortunately. What is the case is that each of these disciplines has a distinctive perspective and methodologies which when applied to education would be as illuminating as when they have been applied to other facets of societal functioning. Sociologists have done some of the most penetrating studies of hospitals. Political scientists have contributed mightily to our understanding of power relationships in governments, national, state, and local. Anthropologists have made us aware not only about the nature and force of culture in diverse societies but of the practical import of that diversity for our foreign policies. Developmental psychologists have shed much light on the course and vicissitudes of personal, cognitive, and social development. And if you regard history, as I do, as a social science, who would deny the significance of what historians have told us about our past and present.

Potentially, the social sciences can make a distinctive contribution to our understanding of schools and school systems that not only express crucial features of our society but impact on our society in intended and unintended, desirable and undesirable, ways. But for that potential to be realized the social sciences would have to focus on educational policies, practices, and institutions, that is, to begin to look at them, to be in them, to comprehend them with the same searching seriousness with which an anthropologist approaches a foreign culture; a sociologist, a gang, neighborhood, a hospital, a social class grouping; an economist, the stock market, financial institutions, the budget process; a psychologist observing and studying problem-solving behavior, motivation, and change in children.

What I have just said is not based only on hope and faith. John Dewey was, among other things, a psychologist. Willard Waller wrote his classic book on the sociology of schools in the thirties. In the post–World War II era there have been a dozen or so social scientists (mostly anthropologists, political scientists, sociologists) whose writings have influenced and changed how we think about schools, educational personnel, and educational policy.[1]

So what do we do? I have gotten several answers to the

[1]The most recent example is a book *Who Will Teach? Policies That Matter* by Murnane and others (1991). It analyzes the factors affecting teacher supply and offers conclusions disconfirming conventional wisdom.

question. The first goes like this: if you are correct about your assessments of the potential of the social sciences, it is clear that it will be years before that potential will be helpful either to our understanding or practice. Given the enormity of the problems we face, we have to act *now*, we cannot sit back and wait. To this I reply that, of course, we have to act now but let us admit that in so doing we have no basis whatsoever for believing that our efforts will be more successful than they have been in the past. If we have the moral courage to admit that, should we not also have the moral courage to take the long-term view, to initiate and support efforts that are promising, albeit uncertain about if, when, and how we will be able to pick the fruits of those efforts? Why are you so ready to eschew the long-term view about educational problems at the same time that you would not think of eschewing that view in regard to the study of fatal or debilitating diseases? Yes, we must act now but let us realize that we are doing it from necessity and social pressure and not from a track record of which anyone is proud.

A second reaction is, on the surface at least, more telling: if our track record for changing schools is on the dismal side, is that not also true for changing departments in the university? If we know anything about academic departments, it is their bottomless capacity to resist efforts to change their priorities in regard to what they consider important problems. I know you know that in the university the status of the field of education is somewhat below the level of a second-class citizen. What makes you think that you can elevate the status of departments and schools of education *and* get social science departments will-

---

Murnane, the senior author, is an economist who was a public school teacher before he did his graduate work in economics. Still another example is a fascinating book by Pauly, *The Classroom Crucible* (1991), on the dynamics of power in the classroom.

Still another example is a 1984 paper by Henry Levin, an economist, on the seemingly universally held assumption that the amount of time one is exposed to instruction or engaged in learning *must* bear some relation to what is learned. Levin demonstrates that the validity of that assumption depends on variables ignored by those who prefer simple but misleading assumptions. The wisdom in his paper has yet to be taken seriously.

ingly to give attention to problems in education? How masochistic can you get?

There are several parts to my reply. The first is an expression of thanks for recognizing what public officialdom and educational reformers (and, therefore, the general public) are unable to face: changing *any* complicated, traditional institution—be it a school, school system, university, church, or large corporation—is extraordinarily difficult and problematic. And when I say difficult and problematic I refer not only to implementation but also to attaining conceptual clarity about the complexity of the issues you will confront. Failures in implementation are almost always failures of one's guiding conceptualizations and theories.

The second part of my reply to my realistic and pessimistic critic is that she is both right and wrong. She is right in the sense that resistance to change will be the order of the day and wrong in the sense of ignoring that universities have changed when certain conditions obtained. These conditions are recognition by the public and socially-politically influential groups that a set of interrelated problems is adversely affecting societal stability or health or values; a similar recognition by significant individuals and groups within the university; the willingness of public and private agencies to help fund the changes; and, often overlooked, the perceived leadership of prestigious universities that appear to be accepting of the change. The last point deserves emphasis if only because in the community of universities a very small number play a large role in shaping opinion. In earlier days we heard that Macy's does not tell Gimbels. That is by no means been true among universities.

Medical education is one example of how universities changed. Who will deny that universities are different—academically, administratively, demographically—as a consequence of racial injustice, the women's liberation movement, and the civil rights movement? Many universities have departments and programs and altered procedures for selecting faculty and students that were not dreamed of thirty years ago. The university was never an ivory tower unconnected to the societal surround. It changes in response to the interaction of internal and external forces.

There is one difference in the university that is most instructive in regard to my proposal for undergraduates. Although it started in graduate education, it has had percolating effects in undergraduate programs. It was a change I witnessed and in which I played a very minor role. I am referring to the emergence of modern clinical psychology after World War II. Briefly, the story goes like this:[2]

- Approximately seventeen million women and men passed through the armed services during World War II.
- Almost from the day we entered the war it was obvious that the number of medical and psychiatric casualties would be overwhelmingly beyond the existing resources of the Veterans Administration (VA).
- Before World War II, hospital and allied facilities administered by the VA were understaffed, of poor quality, and usually located in the middle of nowhere, unconnected with medical schools, the university, or anything else. (Shades of many of the medical schools Flexner castigated!)
- It was obvious that an enormous increase would be required in a wide variety of personnel and in new hospital and clinical facilities.
- The new facilities were to be administratively connected to universities and to be built as nearly adjacent to them as possible. Universities were to be given funding to increase the number of specialized personnel whose training would largely take place in these facilities under the supervision of an increased university faculty.
- Several thousand clinical psychologists would be needed. Before World War II clinical psychology did not exist as part of graduate education in psychology. When the war started there may have been a couple of hundred doctoral level psychologists who had become clinicians because they could not get jobs in the university during the Great Depression or

[2]The reader who wishes a more detailed story may wish to read my autobiography *The Making of an American Psychologist* (1988) in which I devote a long chapter to the emergence of this new academic field. Bear in mind that not only psychology but other parts of the university also changed as a result of the war.

because of gender or religious (Jewish) prejudice. Before the war, clinical psychology was pejoratively viewed as an arena of applied psychology by no means central to the development of psychology as a science and, therefore, not deserving of formal inclusion in graduate education. Psychology regarded clinical psychology the way it and the rest of the university regarded the preparation of educators. Enough said.

• It would be wrong to say that psychology embraced clinical psychology with enthusiasm. Indeed, some universities would have no part in introducing the new field into its graduate curriculum. Almost all the prestigious universities did accept the new field. If they did so in some cases without enthusiasm, they did it, in part, on moral grounds. Just as a grateful society wished to provide the best care and treatment for veterans whose capacity for normal living had been impaired, psychology could not or should not ignore a societal problem of staggering dimensions. Clinical psychology became part of graduate education in psychology.

Today, in regard to education we are in an analogous situation. In some ways it is a more serious situation than how to provide for returning veterans. With the veterans we felt secure about knowing what needed to be done. For some of their conditions existing knowledge was shaky or inadequate but at least we felt we knew what humane care meant. For many other conditions existing knowledge was a secure base for treatment and even cure. The problem was to train enough personnel to apply what we knew to be effective.

In regard to education, as in the case of the returning veterans, no one needs to be persuaded that we are dealing with problems we cannot ignore. And few need to be persuaded — just as few needed to be persuaded that the prewar VA program was semiscandalously inadequate — that we cannot continue doing what we have done, that what we have done simply has been feckless. We poured scores of billions of dollars into the new VA program and I have heard no knowledgeable person say it has been a failure. We have also spent billions on improving education but I have heard no one say, as a Vermont senator said about the Vietnam War, that we should declare victory and leave.

Where the analogy breaks down is in regard to the diversity of fields relevant to the problems we face. What the VA sought was to increase and integrate the variety of fields (that is, not only medical ones) that had something to contribute to the substance, organization, and evaluation of the postwar programs. In some VA medical centers, anthropologists, social psychologists, sociologists, and philosophers were given staff positions. Even if this catholicity was not, in practice, a prominent feature of programs, the vision and wisdom underlying the new articulated VA rationale should not go unnoticed. Indeed, the later deterioration of the quality of VA programs and facilities is, in part, a consequence of the allocation of resources primarily to the traditional medical fields. Primary or secondary prevention went by the boards. Parochialism of outlook won out. For example, there were some VA personnel, none of them medical, who early on pointed out that young veterans would become aging ones and the VA should begin to plan for a future when it would be responsible for more aged people than any other agency in the country, and perhaps the world. No one heeded that warning. As a result, when in recent years the VA woke up to the obvious, it was unprepared to deal with the problem. In any field, the long-term view is not a luxury. It is very practical.

We should no longer tolerate the present situation in which education is, for all practical purposes, unconnected to the social sciences. Someone said that war is too important to be left to the generals. Education is too important to be left to professional educators. Generals *are* important, and professional educators *are* important. But educators, like generals, have to recognize that their understandings and proposals for action and practice have to take into account perspectives missing or minimized in their educational background. But this point meets far less resistance from educators than from social scientists. It is not that social scientists resist getting meaningfully involved in educational matters and institutions but rather that they are so disinterested in education. They are content to leave the field to the generals, and then they criticize what they say and do. It is true that your inability to lay an egg should not prevent you from passing judgment on its edibility, but when, so to speak, the inedibility of eggs threatens the health of the social fabric, passing judgment is not enough. Should we not go beyond judgment and ask: what can, what should, we do?

My undergraduate proposal attempts to address this question. More correctly, it is an attempt to give force to the question. My concern is not only to increase the pool of people who would seek careers in education but to do this in a way that would be personally and intellectually respectable and demanding, and, in addition, would increase the number of social scientists who could use their different perspectives to broaden and deepen their and our understanding of schools and society. At the present time this is a non-issue. Not from our national leadership, or the social sciences, or the scores of intellectually pitiful, repair-riveted, quick-fix, short-term-oriented presidential, state, or foundation reports is there any sign of recognition that we have truly left education to the generals, that our existing knowledge is fatefully parochial, that truly radical changes are needed in regard to the ways we customarily think about educational practices, organization, and roles, or that the long-term view is not an exercise in fantasy.

Let us not lose sight of a primary significance of the Flexner report and the revolutionary change in VA policy. This was the assumption that to the degree that over time the university became seriously connected to certain pressing social problems, we stood a better chance of dealing more effectively with those problems both in terms of repair and prevention. That was both an assumption and a hope. On balance, it paid off. In the case of Flexner and the VA there was not only public support and funding but an intellectual and moral vision of what needed to be done. The old order had to change. That belief is lacking in regard to education.

One criticism of my argument is that I am making the same mistake we make in regard to our schools: if there is a social problem — teenage pregnancy, reckless drivers, use of addictive drugs, smoking — we ask the schools to "solve" the problem. Schools, these critics say, have become human service settings where we are supposed to save souls and, if we have time and energy, to enrich minds. What the "real world" fails to do schools are supposed to remedy. There is, of course, some truth to this allocation of social responsibility.

My critic, however, is quite wrong. True, schools were not conceived as clinical and social service agencies, but the social sciences were conceived as disciplines for the study of people, institutions, and society. The adjective *social* was not chosen at random. And it has not been the case that the social sciences, like the natural sciences, justify their existence only on the basis of contributing to knowledge. Undergirding the social sciences is the belief that enlarging our fund of knowledge contributes, directly or indirectly, to the public welfare. And there is another belief: to contribute to our understanding of people, institutions, and society requires transaction with them. No, the rationale for the social sciences makes inexplicable and inexcusable their disinterest in education, especially today when the inadequacies of our educational system are seen as threatening our *social* systems.

In taking this stance I do not wish to convey the impression that if the social sciences became more interested in matters educational, the dusk-like quality of our understandings would quickly take on the luster of sunlight. But my respect for the problems social science has illuminated convinces me that over time their contribution to educational matters will be both theoretically and practically significant. Before World War II anthropology was a very small field and academic discipline, one that seemed to have little of practical import for or use by our society. Then came World War II and its immediate aftermath. The United States became a global power responsible administratively for diverse, so-called primitive societies and, in addition, having to deal in all kinds of ways with countries whose cultures we hardly understood. Almost overnight government and other funding sources came to see anthropology as important to our national interests and security. When will we all realize that it is in our national interest to stimulate atten tion to education in fields that can alter education in fundamental ways?

Let me return to where we started in this chapter: the relation between primary prevention and my undergraduate proposal. We do not need any more studies to inform us that for most teachers — and I would say for *all* who begin in an urban school — their initial year or so is an unsettling experience during which idealism succumbs to the realities of the school culture.[3] That unsettling, and frequently destabilizing, process has many sources, all of which can be subsumed under "I never really knew that this is the way things would be." These teachers feel alone, bewildered, inadequate, resentful, oscillating between self-blame, castigating the "system," and blaming the irrelevance of much that they had experienced and been told in their preparatory programs. This is not to say that their experience is without any satisfaction or accomplishment or that they are eager to get on the psychoanalytic couch. But they have been shocked by the disjunction between what they are faced with and what they expected to be faced with.

It is not that they were misled but that they were not provided with ways of understanding the culture of classrooms, schools, and school systems. And by understanding I mean pos-

---

[3]The most recent study was sponsored by the Metropolitan Life Insurance Company (1991) and focuses on the reactions of teachers to and after their first year of teaching. The findings are, expectedly, quite sobering, especially in regard to the perceptions of teachers that their preparation for teaching was inadequate for what they encountered and, no less important, that the culture of schools was no support to their feelings of aloneness and desire for help. The findings paint a somewhat less unpleasant picture than I have stated above. That may be due to two factors. The Metropolitan Life study was conducted by telephone by the Louis Harris organization and my conclusions stem from extended personal discussions with individual teachers and groups of teachers. In my experience teachers do not find it easy to reveal their feelings and attitudes for fear of reinforcing what they view as a lack of respect on the part of the general public for teachers, a view confirmed by the Harris survey. A second factor may be that my conclusions derive from talking not only to first-year teachers but also from those in their second and third years when the collision between idealism and reality has taken on a disrupting force. I urge the reader to consult Farber's recent book *Crisis in Education: Stress and Burnout in the American Teacher* (1991). Farber has not only creatively brought together the literature but also pinpoints the importance of the preventive orientation.

sessing conceptualizations, rooted in experience, that sensitize you to what your future experiences will likely be and the ways by which you can cope with predictable problems. The new teacher, for example, is surprised and disappointed by the feeling of aloneness, the lack of collegiality, an unwanted social and intellectual privacy, but he or she has also not been provided with possible ways to cope with, to change, to ameliorate the untoward consequences of such alienation. Indeed, it has not been instilled in teachers that it is their professional and ethical *responsibility* to forge a collegiality productive for their and their students' personal, social, and intellectual development. The preparation of teachers is exclusively concerned with their responsibility to students, not with the responsibility of teachers to themselves and their colleagues. That omission is obviously not helped any by the preparation of educational administrators whose view of collegiality is as superficial as it is self-defeating. *If the collegial conditions do not exist wherein teachers can learn, change, and grow, they cannot create and sustain those conditions for productive learning in their students.*

My undergraduate proposal is not intended to be part of a preparatory program for educators. It is intended to give the students an intensive, demanding experience with the goal of providing perspectives that will add to and round out their comprehension of the complexity we call a school system. If we learn how to provide such an experience consistent with its overarching goal, we can help students toward more than a superficial understanding of what I call the culture of schools and school systems. I emphasize *understanding* as an antidote to adherence to misleading stereotypes, to unreflective indulgence of premature judgments, to simplemindedness at the expense of thinking, to a focus on deficits and inadequacies that ignores opportunities and potential assets, to the potent tendency to miss the forest for the trees, to the confusion between what is and what might or should be. Rushing to judgment is easy. Understanding is hard to attain, *especially in regard to a setting that influenced you in diverse ways and toward which you have attitudes you absorbed, not attitudes you thought through.*

I would expect that some, perhaps many, of those who elect to have such an experience will have given some thought to the possibility of a career in education. The experience could provide these students with a far more realistic basis for making a career decision than is now the case. They would not later enter a professional program ignorant of schools, uncritically hospitable to whatever they are told, eager more to be trained than to be educated. I have had fairly extensive experience with students in teacher preparation programs. Foremost among the conclusions I came to were, first, how narrow their understanding was of the school culture, and second, how much of their interest and training were in and about the encapsulated classroom. They were almost completely ignorant of how and why schools and school systems are organized and administered as they are, the nature and variety of decision-making processes and forums, the opportunities for and obstacles to change and innovation, the functions, status, and power of specialized nonteaching personnel, and issues of formal and informal power. Stated another way, they are, for all practical purposes, unequipped or not required to think about almost all the factors that will impinge on them, shape them as persons and professionals, determine their self-esteem or personal worth, and stimulate or inhibit their creativity and intellectual growth. My undergraduate proposal is intended to prevent, to some degree, the unfortunate consequences of an uninformed career choice and a stance toward professional preparation that results in tunnel vision.

One might argue that an unintended consequence of my proposal is to discourage people from seeking a career in education by exposing them to the unpleasant realities of what schools are and the seemingly overwhelming problems confronting them. That would happen only if the undergraduate experience concentrated more on inadequacies of schools than on their assets and opportunities, if it focused on what is and not what could be, if it did not provide a vision based on an understanding of institutional and societal change, and if that understanding did not provide a basis for realistic courses of action.

Let us take the extreme case where no student decides to seek a career in education. That, from my standpoint, would be disappointing but would by no means invalidate the major purposes of the proposal: to provide undergraduates an intellectually respectable, personally demanding exposure to settings vital for the social health of our society and to engender interest and commitment from fields that can potentially contribute to our understanding of these settings. Undergraduates are no minuscule fraction of what we call the general public. They become parents, legislators, and members of boards of education. They vote on matters educational; their comprehension of these matters, generally speaking, is at best superficial and at worst unwittingly destructive. The surprise would be for the situation to be otherwise. What in their experience permits them to take distance from, to reexamine, to *reexperience* settings in which they spent years, to see these settings not as bounded, walled-off oases but as reflections of a distinctive society with its own history and traditions? What we call the liberal arts are fields of thought and inquiry explicitly intended to liberate students from a subjectivity and a parochialism in which the present blots out the past, ideas such as the world was born yesterday, what people created and did in the past are of no import for how we should think and act in a present from which a variety of futures are possible.

My proposal takes on significance only if you believe that the present state of our educational systems has become the Achilles heel in our social body. If you so believe, it follows that our young people should no longer remain ignorant of the nature of these systems, and that is what informs my proposal. I do not present it as a panacea, and it certainly is not in the category of quick fixes. We have had a surfeit of quick-fix proposals and a virtual absence of courses of action based on a long-term, prevention-oriented perspective. As I read history, among the truly potent factors that transform any societal institution are demographic changes with which are associated new attitudes, outlooks, values, and courses of action. That is why wars transform societies. That is why other national catastrophies — the Great Depression of the thirties, the current economic recession, racial strife, assassination of public figures — have differential effects on diverse groups, produce generational gaps and conflicts, and can influence such social barometers as birth rate, living styles, voting behavior, career choice, and more.

No reader of this book has to be persuaded that our schools

are not understandable apart from demographic-cultural changes in the post–World War II era. Such changes have always been a feature of our schools. It used to be that the consequences of these shifts would come into national awareness every ten years or so; proposals for remediation of problems would be broadcast, followed relatively quickly by a pervasive amnesia. What is distinctive in the post–World War II era is that amnesia is no longer possible. Daily we are reminded that our educational system has to be altered and improved. Unfortunately, we are not also reminded that our past efforts at improvement have not worked and that those now being proposed are old wine in new bottles. We are not told that we have to adopt a long-term, preventive strategy. Even when that strategy is proclaimed in the abstract, one is left with the question: where is the beef?

A local chain of clothing stores advertises, "An educated consumer is our best customer." That logo undergirds my proposal. To the extent that we seriously and meaningfully expose young college students to what we call education and schools, we stand a chance of getting more sophisticated consumers of public education.

My proposal will require an articulated national public policy affirming the importance of providing college students the opportunity to participate in the program I have sketched. It will also require affirmation of the importance of gaining the interest and commitment of the social science disciplines. This, I must emphasize, would not be the first time that the federal government, in the face of a national problem or crisis, has proclaimed a policy and received legislative approval explicitly intended to alter in some way the priorities of this or that part of our colleges and universities. Indeed, beginning with our entry into World War II, and with increasing frequency in the postwar decades, higher education has been transformed by public policies affecting the selection and support of students and faculty, and the creation of new programs and even fields.[4]

[4]On the very day (November 12, 1991) that I completed this chapter I turned on my TV to C-Span, which was televising a discussion in the House of Representatives on a bill (H.R. 3508) intended to stimulate and support medical schools to develop programs for the preparation of physicians who would practice in underserved, or rural, or inner-city areas. As several representatives said, medical

In regard to my proposal the question will be this: under what conditions and with what incentives would social science departments be willing to participate in such an undergraduate program? And by participate I do not mean token gestures, especially since schools and school systems have not been anywhere near the mainstream of these fields. We are faced with the chicken and egg problem in that my proposal requires changes in both students and faculty. I would argue that the quality of the program — the intellectual and personal fires it lights in students — will reflect the glow of the fires lit in faculty by what for them will be a new intellectual, hands-on experience. What that faculty can count on is the burning desire of young people who, surface appearances notwithstanding, long for experience that will be intellectually stimulating, engender a sense of personal growth, and enlarge their understanding of the world they live in. That, of course, is what faculty want for themselves. *And, I cannot refrain from adding, the faculty who become part of this new venture will soon find that what they want for themselves, and what they want their students to want, is what the bulk of children in our schools want but rarely experience.* That would be the beginning of wisdom and the spur to change. The more people who attain that wisdom, the more we stand a chance of seeing and acting on the difference between reform and prevention, between the short- and long-term perspective.

---

schools value specialty training far more than training in primary care or family medicine, even though the need for primary care physicians becomes more pressing with each passing year. It is unlikely that very many medical schools will take advantage of the incentives the bill provides. Some will, and if their numbers will be fewer than the problem requires, we should be thankful for small favors. My undergraduate proposal would meet the same fate, assuming, of course, that the problem my proposal addresses ever gets recognized as a problem. Quite an assumption, I know. But my point here is not the degree of acceptance or the outcomes of such efforts but the fact that universities are subject to pressures for change and do change, however slowly or grudgingly. I venture the prediction that unless universities more quickly, more willingly, and more creatively change in regard to the preparation of medical and educational personnel, the time will come when they will be forced to change. At present, they have options. If in the future they are forced to change, it will be another instance of substituting one set of intractable problems for another.

My proposal will cost money. I am not advocating that we get that money by reducing support for programs, which, however they have the features of a band-aid, will in no way alter the incidence of problems. I am not an advocate for malign neglect. You do not walk away from these problems. In the best clinical tradition, you do the best you can on the basis of what you think will be helpful to problem children and schools. That our best has not been helpful, that what we think we know is riddled with unexamined and faulty assumptions, I have discussed in previous books. But I recognize and understand that when you are on the firing line, all the pressures are on you to act, to do something, even if that something is based largely on hope, prayer, and ignorance of similar past efforts. But to understand all is not to forgive all. At some point, those pressures to act *now* should not blind us to the obvious: reform, even secondary prevention, is second best to primary prevention. If you accept that obvious fact, then you are required to focus on how educational personnel are attracted to, selected for, and prepared for careers in education. My undergraduate proposal addresses those issues only in part because its overarching goal is to broaden and deepen the perspectives of a crucial segment of our population who are currently or will be uneducated consumers of education.

In subsequent chapters I discuss the selection and preparation of educational personnel, not in terms of existing programs but rather in terms of a fantasy: I have been told that I can develop preparatory programs for educational personnel any way I wish, with the explicit "restriction" that it must hold out the promise that over time the incidence of problems (individual and institutional) will be decreased, that is, it will be an example of applying existing knowledge for the purposes of primary prevention. That is a very tall order and inevitably many readers will find me unpersuasive, impractical, or even utopian. I am used to that reaction; this is not to say that I have cornered the market on truth, but no one shops in that market. The issues are too complex, too interrelated to problems and processes that impinge on but are not under the control of educators, too challenging to too many different values and vested interests to let me expect that what I shall recommend will be warmly embraced. It is realistic modesty on my part to expect that in tackling these issues, I shall fall short of the mark. What I owe myself and the reader is to gain clarity about what the mark is.

And what is the mark? It is to prepare educators for the realities of schools and school systems, and how they transact with the dynamics of other parts of our social system, and to do this in ways that instill in educators a proactive rather than a reactive stance to change and innovation. Such a stance is the polar opposite of an intellectual and professional passivity guaranteed to produce a sense of victimization, powerlessness, and resignation. You cannot be fully professional unless you have a secure basis for "professing," for advocating, for acting, for having weapons for engaging in the predictable battles about what schools are for, that is, who "owns" them, and by what criteria outcomes and personnel should be judged.

Several decades ago, Kenneth Davidson, Burton Blatt, and I wrote a small book titled *The Preparation of Teachers: An Unstudied Problem in Education* (1989 [1962]). That book went out of print and mind very quickly. Its central point was that the preparation of educators ill prepared them for the realities they would encounter in the "real world," and that gulf could and should no longer be tolerated. Subsequent years have proved us right, a conclusion some reviewers shared when a somewhat enlarged version of the book was republished in 1989. Even so, in every sleep-producing report I have read on school reform the problem of preparation of educators has, for all practical purposes, been ignored. That I continue to pursue and agonize about the problem may be viewed by some as manifestation of a pathological repetition-compulsion on my part. To such a diagnosis I can only say that what I advocate has rarely met with disagreement from educators on the firing line. These educators are far more aware of the problem than any other group with whom I have discussed the issues.

In 1903 John Dewey wrote an article "Democracy in Education," published in *The Elementary School Teacher*. (I am indebted to Ray Budde for reminding me of that article which was reprinted in *Progressive Education*, 1931, *8*(3), 216–218, and again in *Education Today* in 1940, a book edited by Joseph Ratner.) That article should be read in its entirety. For my present purposes it is sufficient to present a condensation of the article, which Budde sent me together with a copy of the original piece. I am grateful for his permission to use his condensation.

Until the public-school system is organized in such a way that every teacher has some regular and representative way in which he or she can register judgment upon matters of educational importance, with the assurance that this judgment will somehow affect the school system, the assertion that the present system is not, from the internal standpoint, democratic seems to be justified.

What does democracy mean save that the individual is to have a share in determining the conditions and the aims of his own work and that on the whole, through the free and mutual harmonizing of different individuals, the work of the world is better done than when planned, arranged, and directed by a few, no matter how wise or of how good intent that few? How can we justify our belief in the democratic principle elsewhere, and then go back entirely upon it when we come to education?

If the teaching force is inept and unintelligent and irresponsible, surely the primary problem is that of their improvement. Only by sharing in some responsible task does there come a fitness to share in it. The argument that we must wait until men and women are fully ready to assume intellectual and social responsibilities would have defeated every step in the democratic direction that has ever been taken. The prevalence of methods of authority and of external dictation and direction tends automatically to perpetuate the very condition of inefficiency, lack of interest, inability to assume positions of self-determination, which constitute the reasons that are depended upon to justify the regime of authority.

All other reforms are conditioned upon reform

in the quality and character of those who engage in the teaching profession. Just because education is the most personal, the most intimate, of all human affairs, there more than anywhere else, the sole ultimate reliance and final source of power are in the training, character, and intelligence of the individual. But as long as a school organization which is undemocratic in principle tends to repel from all but the higher portions of the school system those of independent force, of intellectual initiative, and of inventive ability, or tends to hamper them in their work after they find their way into the schoolroom, so long all other reforms are compromised at their source and postponed indefinitely for fruition.

Dewey was absolutely correct in describing what schools can do to teachers and others. Can we prepare educators to understand and cope better with the realities and organization of schools so that they can play a more proactive role in changing the existing scheme of things? We had better try. The stakes are higher than ever before. If, as Dewey said, we wait until we are certain about what will happen, we will prove that the more things change the more they will remain the same. The quest for certainty (the title of one of Dewey's greatest books) is an invitation to defeat.

Chapter Eight

Again:
Teaching Children,
Not Subject Matter

One of the ways we think about college or university programs is in terms of course titles, that is, their subject matter, duration, and prerequisites. In this and subsequent chapters I shall not be concerned with these matters. I quite agree with Goodlad who said, in regard to his *Teachers for Our Nation's Schools* (1990):

> We are once again embarked on a reform era that assumes that broken educational machines need new parts. Virtually all the research on change since the previous era of such folly points to the power of *school-based* groups engaged in a process of renewal that is characterized by dialogue based on relevant data, decisions stemming from such dialogue, the implementation of the decisions, their subsequent evaluation, and the continuation of the dialogue. Such groups can reach out to draw on the research-based models of others. Moreover, this process is as relevant to curriculum planning in teacher education as it is in elementary and secondary schools.
>
> Had I recommended a specific curriculum, critics (and virtually everyone in teacher education is a critic in this area) would have focused on this and little more. The malaise in teacher education runs deeper and is far more complex than problems with the curriculum. It will not be cured by agreement on a remedial curriculum package, even though renewal

of curricula must be a central component of any reform [p. 5].

My aim is to indicate topics and issues that are relatively
easy to formulate but which, to be understood and absorbed,
require discussion, observation, and, wherever possible, hands-
on experience. It is one thing to accept the validity of a principle because it rings true and you are able conceptually to defend it; it is quite another to accept and defend it because you
have experienced that principle in concrete observation and action. Every educator, for example, will nod assent to the maxim
that you should never forget a teacher's primary obligation is
to teach children, not subject matter. This means that if you
do not take into account the interests and characteristics of a
child, his or her individual peculiarities and learning style, that
child's understanding of subject matter will not be productive
of development in the domain of that subject matter. The child
who has to fall back on rote memory, who does not comprehend the structure and rationale of a particular subject matter,
who literally gives up trying to understand why the subject matter has the rationale it does, is a child who has been taught but
not educated in the root sense of education: to lead forth, to
get from the child, those psychological features that make understanding possible and consequential. Education, we all agree,
is not a pouring in of subject matter.

It is easy to state that maxim and we can assume that
our would-be educator will be in full agreement. But we cannot assume that that candidate can distinguish on the level of
observation between instances of teaching subject matter and
teaching children. And we certainly cannot assume that when
given the opportunity to teach something to a particular child,
what that candidate does will be consistent with the maxim.
What we can assume, what indeed we know, is that *we* have
to adapt *our* supervisory strategies with these candidates to what
we know about their individual differences in personality, knowledge, and observational sensitivity. *Consistency with the maxim is
no less an obligation of the educator of educators than it is of a classroom
teacher and his or her pupils.*

A colleague, Alice Carter, related to me the following requirement she had to fulfill in a graduate course in child development. Students were asked to observe a classroom, then each chose a child for whom the student had to invent a toy that would be of special interest. The students had to justify the basis for their invention, present it to the child, and interact with the child. That requirement is a good example of taking the maxim seriously, of alerting the student to what is involved in thinking about and trying to act consistently with the maxim.

For any of the maxims and principles I shall discuss there are numerous ways they can meaningfully become a part of a lived experience. It would be a source of distraction and obfuscation if I discussed any of these principles in terms of courses and their sequences. The structure of a preparatory program should derive from an agreed-on set of principles and the kind of experiences they dictate. There is no one correct way of structuring the program, a fact that will trouble those used to thinking in terms of course titles. I have no objection in principle to courses and their titles. But, more often than not, course titles do not live up to expectations.

The maxim I have used for purposes of introduction was not chosen at random. It brings to the fore the obstacles to its application in real classrooms in real schools where class size is frequently large and the pressures to complete a curriculum are real, however self-defeating. In the modal classroom it is virtually impossible to take into account individual differences in personal and cognitive styles. That impossibility has to be understood and confronted by would-be educators *before* they become independent practitioners, if only to make them aware of the gulf between theory and practice and to prevent or dilute the tendency to blame themselves, to feel defeated, and to retreat to a routine that is "safe" but guilt producing. If the task is impossible in practice, it does not mean that there are no opportunities to act on the maxim. Take, for example, a practice I have seen only one teacher employ. At the beginning of the school year she told her students that in each month each child would have a "day" during which all of the teacher's free time would be "owned" by the child to meet with her with no predetermined agenda. How the child wished to use the teacher in that time was left to the student; this condition did not mean that the teacher felt no obligation to raise questions and issues. What was so refreshing to observe was how the class respected that teacher-child interaction, even "protecting" it from interference. Children looked forward to their day. For the teacher it was a way to learn something about each of her pupils.

It was not a practice the teacher had learned in her preparation. But she was a teacher — better yet, a person — who somewhere somehow had concluded that she had to know something about a child's individuality, and that whatever that something was would be helpful to her in teaching that child. I asked her this question: if you were required to justify the practice by "outcomes," what would you say? She looked at me quizzically as if to say: 'Why does it need justification, it is all so obvious?" I pressed on. Her answer was in three parts: she felt a need to know each child somewhat better, that is, she had to satisfy *her* curiosity; she wanted a child to feel that there was a time when that child "owned" (her word) the teacher; and in some instances it served the purpose of diluting or preventing a problem.

There are teachers, albeit too few, who have devised other ways of acting on the maxim, however short those ways are from the ideal. If their numbers are few, it is not because teachers generally lack imagination. It is largely because they have not been prepared to think about how they might handle the predictable and upsetting gulf between an abstract maxim and the realities of classrooms.[1] I do assume that the more would-be

---

[1] In a fascinating article, "How Asian Teachers Polish Each Lesson to Perfection," Stigler and Stevenson (1991) call into question large classes as inherently anti-educational. This article is one of the very few cross-cultural studies of pedagogy which made practical sense to me; it goes beyond mindless statistical comparisons to describe and illuminate what goes on and why in Chinese and Japanese classrooms. It pulls the rug from under stereotypes about the autocratic, semi-military, memory-emphasizing Asian classrooms. For my purposes, what Stigler and Stevenson say about our preparatory programs for educators in every respect confirms what I say in these pages. I consider their article must reading, as I do their book (Stevenson and Stigler, 1991). Fairness requires me to note that there have been other observers and writers who describe Japanese classrooms and schools in far more negative terms and conclude that American schools

teachers know and understand the dilemmas of that gulf, the more adequate will be their coping with it. The less they know, the more vulnerable they are to personal problems and professional stagnation. There is no way you can prepare any human services professional that will eliminate the Sturm und Drang of baptism for independent practice. If you cannot eliminate it, that is no reason for not dealing directly with it in preparatory programs in ways that dilute the worst features of that baptism.

There is another reason I have used the maxim for illustrative purposes: to instill in teachers the moral responsibility to advocate changes in schools where now to act on the maxim is so difficult—indeed, where even thinking about it is an indulgence of wasteful fantasy. By moral responsibility I mean more than responsibility for improving the education of children. Teachers should feel a responsibility for themselves and their personal and professional development. To the extent that the maxim is empty rhetoric—piously proclaimed, universally agreed on, and denied in practice—teachers, no less than children, are victims. It implies that what teachers *ought* to do, a moral imperative, is vital for *them,* not only for children. I would consider it the most successful of outcomes if over time increasing numbers of educators would be able to say that the conditions for taking the maxim seriously simply do not exist and to hold otherwise is to sustain a moral charade. What I find both discouraging and appalling is how educators at all levels of responsibility assert agreement with the goal of "helping each child realize his full potential" and then say nothing about how the organization and culture of schools undercut that goal, about how teaching children, not subject matter, is made impossible.

I am not advocating that teachers become agents of social change. I am advocating that they become agents of *school*

---

are more humane and successful than those in Japan. The conclusions of Stevenson and Stigler may be based on an atypical sample; this requires further study. Respectful as I am of Harold Stevenson's past track record as observer and researcher, I go on the assumption that his recent studies with Stigler have to be taken very seriously, that is, they are not off the mark to the degree some people have said.

change, that they not see themselves as powerless victims of an uncomprehending public. If the reader thinks I ask too much of educators, or am unrealistic about the obstacles they will confront, or overestimate the courage of which educators are potentially capable (overestimating their assets and underestimating their deficits), I have two answers. The first is that there are schools, admittedly too few, where teachers have sought and achieved changes in line with the maxim. This came about not because of their preparation but despite it. The significance of these instances has not yet seeped into the substance and direction of preparatory programs. The second answer is that *all the arguments that can be directed to preparing teachers as agents of school change were in almost all respects directed to the feasibility of the unionization of teachers.* Someone said the unionization of teachers came about only after teachers no longer could tolerate being hit over the head; treated as no different from laborers; viewed as semi-professionals, a proletariat, deservedly at the bottom of the mountain on top of which were the sophisticates, the powerful, in Kafka's castle. Someone else said that teachers came ambivalently, kicking and screaming, to unionization. If unionization has demonstrated anything, it is that the powerful depend on the powerless to see themselves that way, and when they see themselves otherwise the "revolution" has begun.

Unionization, however, was about bread and butter issues, not educational ones. Granted that these issues have consequences, always indirect, for educational issues, the fact is that the two major teacher unions, and those for administrators, stay within the confines of the trade union tradition, which means that important educational issues are off limits. Nevertheless, the success and strength of these unions illustrate the obvious: the potential power of teachers to bring about school improvement is no pie-in-the-sky possibility. But that potential will remain unfulfilled as long as the preparation of educators does not provide them a clear and compelling, non-self-serving rationale obligating them to take actions consistent with that rationale.

What do educators stand for? My experience has led me

to the conclusion that educators, no more or less than the general public, answer that question with clichés and rhetoric with which no one will disagree; too few, however, are capable of examining the implications of these clichés, for current practice. We use the word *cliché* as a pejorative because the kernel of truth it contains tells us nothing about what it means or how it should be applied in real life. Teach children, not subject matter! What do we want people to understand by that? What does it mean for current practice? What changes would we have to consider if we took its implications seriously? Do we not have an intellectual *and* moral obligation to go beyond uttering the cliché? And if we do not discharge that obligation in the preparation of educators, why should we expect the general public to begin to understand that current practice is at variance from what we know and believe? Why should they understand that that variance is a source of problems and that reducing that variance will prevent problems, to a discernible degree at least?

The preparation of educators should have two related, difficult, and even conflicting goals: to prepare people for the realities of schooling, and to provide them with a conceptual and attitudinal basis for coping with and seeking to alter those realities in ways consistent with what we think we know and believe.[2] To be a professional means, among other things, that you have something "to profess" and that something rests on experience, tested knowledge, and values. We expect a professional to have technical knowledge and skill, but we expect that person to apply that knowledge and skill in ways and for pur-

---

[2]In the past decade I have yet to talk with a newly trained teacher or administrator who was knowledgeable about the Rand Corporation's comprehensive studies of school change, spearheaded by Paul Berman and Milbrey McLaughlin. I refer especially to Volumes 7–8 by McLaughlin (1977a, 1977b). At the least, if they were knowledgeable about McLaughlin's writings they would have some basis for "professing" in regard to what has worked and not worked (and why) in efforts at school improvement. Is not such knowledge crucial for educators who, in one or another way, will be involved in some school improvement effort? McLaughlin's (1990) recent revisiting of the Rand studies is a most instructive example of gaining new and important knowledge, that is, which conclusions have held up and which need to be revised.

poses that go beyond the technical. It has been decades since my cardiologist personally took my cardiogram, a technical skill he possesses but relegates to a technician. What I pay him for is *to read* the cardiogram, to read it in the context of all he has learned about *me,* to tell me what it means for *me,* and to do this in a caring and compassionate way. My previous cardiologist, no less technically sophisticated, was the polar opposite and caused me unnecessary suffering. As I have discussed in a previous book (Sarason, 1985) no physician would quarrel with the assertion that he or she should be caring and compassionate. And I have never met a physician who did not *want* to be caring and compassionate and did not regard him- or herself as such. The general public, however, is far from convinced. What they do not know is that the preparation of physicians pays only lip service to what these characteristics mean and require. Their preparation is not for but against understanding what caring and compassion require. I need not elaborate on what such issues suggest about the preparation of educators.

In this chapter I have used one maxim or principle to illustrate how we might look at any aspect of the preparation of educators. If I had to put it in a general but succinct form it would be that *abstract* knowledge and *concrete* experience should always be seen in relation to each other. In what one does and how one does it, there is always the possibility of inconsistency between abstract principles and actions. In the context of a preparatory program those inconsistencies are predictable; indeed, they are productive opportunities for understanding better the relationship between principles and actions. The would-be educator cannot do this on his or her own. It requires someone who has *super*vision. It also requires forums in which they come to understand that what they have learned will not be easily applied or even warmly welcomed in the real schools in which they will start their independent, professional careers. This difficulty of application is and will be a problem they cannot avoid. It is their obligation to children *and* themselves to devise ways, however modest, to prevent rather than manufacture problems.

Routinization, passive uniformity, humiliating powerlessness, the extinction of self-esteem, the sense of unwanted privacy and isolation, the absence of learning and growth—these too frequent outcomes in education careers will not be prevented *in any degree* by preparatory programs that ignore or ill prepare educators for the real world of schools. It is indefensible to expect educators to dramatically transform schools independent of other changes in the larger society, but that does not mean they are powerless to change anything. Generally, they feel powerless and victimized, and these feelings lead them to look for saviors beyond their clan, for a societal transformation that will never come. Their sense of powerlessness is so deep that they see themselves as totally without assets in regard to power. That is a very effective defense against thinking and acting. It is a defense that cannot remain ignored or unanalyzed in programs that prepare educators. One of the most important obligations of such programs is to provide its candidates with a secure intellectual and personal basis for "professing."

What I have said or implied in this brief chapter has been said more fully and persuasively by John Goodlad who has done the most heroic, comprehensive, and systematic study of the preparation of teachers. Anyone who is at all serious about the preparation of educational personnel must read his *Teachers for Our Nation's Schools* (1990), *The Moral Dimensions of Teaching* (1990a), and *Places Where Teachers Are Taught* (1990b), edited in 1990 by him, Soder, and Sirotnik. The conceptual guts of Goodlad's conclusions are well summarized by him in an article with the appropriate title "Why We Need a Complete Redesign of Teacher Education" (1991b). In reading it, the reader must keep in mind that Goodlad is literally in a class by himself in describing, analyzing, and critiquing teacher education programs. The following excerpt from an interview of Goodlad by Ron Brandt is informative (1991, pp. 11–12):

Brandt: The studies you've done paint a very negative, discouraging picture of American education. A lot of elementary and secondary educators argued with the descriptions of typical classrooms in *A Place Called School,* saying that not all schools are the boring, joyless places the book describes. Have some teacher educators objected to your book, claiming that you didn't pay enough attention to innovative education programs?

Goodlad: Yes, a couple of the reviews said that. One reviewer writes that he's been traveling around the United States and has seen all kinds of exciting things. I think it's alarming that someone's casual travel would be used to refute the most careful, comprehensive study ever done on the subject. We have 1,800 hours of interviews. We have observations, we've analyzed documents.

And it's interesting that you mention people saying that about *A Place Called School.* Out of the hundreds and hundreds of letters I received following publication of that book, only one said, "You've got it wrong."

With respect to the new book, I so far have none. The responses I've been getting are like one last week from a Missouri professor who said, "You didn't visit our place, but I'd swear you did." Or Dick Andrews, the dean at Wyoming, who told me he kept his wife awake reading in bed one night, laughing because "You weren't here but everything you said is here."

Of course there are some good things going on here and there, but nobody's put it all together.

I predict that Goodlad's *A Place Called School* (1984) will come to be regarded as a classic in the research literature in education. Unfortunately, the respect for classics too frequently is manifested only in the large number of times they are cited by others, not in their impact on practice and policy. The following excerpt from Goodlad's (1991b) article further demonstrates his grasp of the problems in teacher preparation:

> During the 1980s, policymakers trotted out virtually every panacea for school reform ever recommended. Large numbers of educators criticized most of these recommendations as superficial and inadequate. But, by the end of the decade, policymakers and educators were close to agreement on an important concept: The individual school is a natural and most promising focus for effecting significant improvement.

The idea that school-based educational reform requires the empowerment of principals and teachers opens the way for serious consideration of the charge that the educational bureaucracy is the villain and that decentralized "schools of choice" are the hope of the future. But regardless of how far one takes the concept of decentralizing educational authority, the idea of "the school as a center of change" conjures up a vision of principals and teachers as change-oriented stewards of schools.

An accompanying question, however, one that up to now has been on the periphery of discourse, is: Are a large percentage of these educators thoroughly grounded in the knowledge and skills required to bring about meaningful change? Judging from research my colleagues and I conducted several years ago on the nature of inservice education in school districts, the answer is no. My recent informal forays into staff development lead to the same negative conclusion: The primary focus of district-driven staff development remains teachers' individual teaching competencies, not the capability of an entire staff to renew the school. The conventional paradigm of staff development lags far behind the contemporary perception of school renewal.

What about new teachers? Are they coming out of enlightened teacher education program with the skills to manage classrooms as well as the ability to address the total array of problems and issues they will likely face in school renewal? Again, the answer from our recent research is a resounding no.

As a matter of strange and puzzling fact, educators throughout this century have failed to join the reform of schools and that of teacher education conceptually, never mind in policy and practice. Only in recent years have educational reform reports addressed the connection between the way we prepare teachers and the needs of the schools. And even with

that, teacher education programs still need a mission
tied to a reasonably explicit concept of what teachers
do and should ideally do [Goodlad, 1991b, p. 6].

There are good, empirical reasons why Goodlad calls for a complete redesign of preparatory programs. It is to that call that
I am responding in this book. So, let us go on to some other
major principles or issues — call them what you will — which will
not gain clarity by talking in terms of courses and course titles.

Chapter Nine

Teaching Teachers and Teaching Children: Ignorance Assumed and Assets Unmined

Teaching teachers, like teaching children, is not a morally neutral affair. It is the discharging and instilling of obligations, the primary one of which is the sense of discovery and growth in what may be termed the learning process. It is not an aim only for pupils. It is also one for the teacher for whom, no less than for pupils, that sense is the sole antidote to mindless routinization of thought and action. What we owe children we owe teachers. No one will say that teachers are only or primarily conduits for information and the articulation of abstract principles. We expect more of teachers and that more is that they have identified in their own experience the nature and context of productive learning and have taken on the obligation to create similar conditions for pupils. This ideal holds for the teacher of teachers and the teacher of children. Even though it is an ideal impossible to attain, or if attained impossible to sustain, it is one by which we should judge any teacher. The realities of classrooms and schools are obstacles to approximating the ideal, but that is no excuse for forgetting it. We know that "love thy neighbor" is a statement of an ideal our world and our frailties seem intent to subvert but we also know that it is a statement by which we should judge ourselves and others. In the quiet of the night we know we should expect more of ourselves and others. Ideals are double-edged swords: they tell us what we should be even though we know at best we will be only partially successful in attaining them.

I have said that the primary aim of education is fostering the sense of discovery and growth in the learning process of teachers and students. The learning process in the world of real classrooms involves more than what we conventionally call subject matter. In the course of any one day things happen in a classroom for which that aim is as relevant as it is for learning to read or write; it requires an understanding and a course of action consistent with the primary aim. For example, a teacher discovers that a child has lied or cheated. How would we want the teacher to understand and respond to that knowledge? We would, I assume, not be satisfied if the teacher only punished the child: break the law, pay the penalty. That would bother us for the same reason that we feel if a child got all or mostly wrong answers on an arithmetic test, the teacher should go well beyond merely indicating that the answers are wrong. We expect the teacher to seek to discover why the child performed so poorly. Of course the child has "a problem" but so does the teacher. Indeed, the teacher has two problems: to reexamine her way of teaching that child and to determine what other factors may be at work. *For any untoward event in a classroom the teacher, consistent with the primary aim, has to look both inward and outward, a stance that makes discovery and growth possible.* It is also a stance that makes discovery and growth possible for the child. In the case of the child who lied or cheated I am not one who believes that punishment is unnecessary or undesirable. But before punishment is pronounced is it not the obligation of the teacher to try to understand the lying and cheating and to help the child in ways that might prevent such occurrences in the future?

We hear much today about the teaching of values. What we do not hear is that in the course of one day a teacher inevitably faces and has to deal with value issues arising from or impacting on the learning process. Is it not likely that our dissatisfaction with educational outcomes, deriving as those outcomes do from teaching subject matter and not children, is what makes the "clarification of values" a matter of chance in the modal classroom? I cannot refrain from saying that we need a curriculum for values like we need a hole in our heads. If you think that statement is unwarranted, then I suggest that you sit in any classroom for a day and note the number of times moral and ethical issues, implicit or explicit, arise and are ignored, glossed over, superficially discussed, or handled in counter-productive ways.

Years ago I had several colleagues sit every day for a month in elementary school classrooms and note each time something occurred that was relevant to and illuminated the "constitution" of that classroom, that is, the "values" without which what went on in the classroom was inexplicable, and who "wrote" that constitution which said, so to speak, what the rights, duties, and obligations of students *and* teacher were—what the "laws" were. The occurrences were many. In each classroom, however, the constitution was "written," proclaimed, and enforced by the one adult. If some of the laws you will note lack the specificity of the ten commandments, from the standpoint of the children the teacher was, like Moses, confronted by pagans who did not know right from wrong, who needed to be subdued. I am not an advocate for participatory democracy in which everyone's opinion should have equal weight, but if you are to be consistent with the primary aim, then how the constitution of a classroom is forged has a pervasive effect on learning subject matter and assimilating values. To set the teaching of values apart from the teaching of subject matter makes as much sense as separating the teaching of subject matter from the teaching of children. It makes less sense in that it belies ignorance or insensitivity to what life is like in the classroom.

The preparation of educational personnel inadequately prepares them for what life is like in real classrooms in real schools and leaves them unable to capitalize on opportunities to be consistent with the primary aim. The preparation of such personnel should begin not with theory or history or research findings or pedagogical technique but with concrete issues of classroom life: the practical, inevitable, action-requiring issues on the basis of which the would-be teacher can judge and utilize theory and research.

It apparently is easy for the teacher of teachers to forget that the would-be teacher is not without experience or assets. That individual has been a student for years and can identify those contexts in which he or she experienced discovery and growth, the difference between values espoused and values practiced, the teachers whom he or she trusted and the ones who were feared, and the difference between having one's feelings sought and understood and having them ignored or misunderstood. *Far from being without assets, the would-be teacher has loads of assets that the teacher or teachers should help the student recognize, mine, articulate, and apply.*

It is not only the teacher of teachers who sees the student as having no assets, however. That is the way most students see themselves: empty vessels possessing the understandable "deficit" of ignorance and inexperience, waiting to be filled with facts, knowledge, wisdom, and technical skills. Getting students to see themselves otherwise is, will, and should be no easy task, and that also holds for the teachers of teachers who have to change their attitudes about the assets of the would-be teacher. None of this can be accomplished quickly and none of this can be learned in a "once and for all way." It is something we have to learn again and again in relation to the myriad happenings in classroom life. It is not a stance or habit you can learn in a single course or in regard to a particular subject matter. It is a stance that, among other things, should be the object of inquiry and use throughout the preparatory process.

What I have said thus far in this chapter has been by way or prologue to discussion of more conventionally labeled topics. It is a prologue that contained three assertions:

- The primary aim of education is to nurture the sense of discovery and growth in students and teacher. If educational personnel are not committed to that ideal (or to a similar one couched in different language), if for whatever reason they forget or ignore that ideal, their role is robbed of moral justification.
- The arena of classrooms and schools contains mammoth obstacles to actions consistent with the primary aim. That, today, is a given, a glimpse of the obvious, that has numerous sources one of which (and *only* one of which) is how educational personnel are inadequately prepared for what they will confront — conceptually, personally, interpersonally, morally — as independent practitioners. Unless and until the

preparation of educational personnel deals directly with those confrontations and enables candidates to see that there are ways of thinking and acting consistent with the primary aim, those personnel will remain *one* of the sources of inadequacies in our schools.

- Those who seek to become educators have a major asset: they have spent years as "learners" in classrooms. The asset consists not in sheer experience, or the validity or invalidity of whatever conclusions they may have come to, but in the potential that asset has for intellectually and personally grasping the nature and practical consequences of the primary aim.

I anticipate several critical reactions to these assertions and others that will follow. Let me deal with them here so as not to have to repeat them later. The first is this: "What you state as the ideal, the primary aim, sounds like the musings of a university professor who believes that each child is capable of becoming an intellectual, a devotee of the life of the mind." My critic will be surprised to learn that he is partly right in that I believe Piaget and Freud were absolutely correct that from its earliest days each child is a question-asking, answer-seeking organism trying to make sense of self and the world, a budding "intellectual" already containing the seeds of complex thinking: asking questions, arriving at answers (more often than not invalid), experimenting in the sense of trying things out, and knowing in inchoate ways the sense of and the satisfactions from discovery and growth. When I state the primary aim I am saying that our task as educators is to recognize and nurture features already characteristic of the child.

Lest you think that I regard the preschool child in narrow intellectual or cognitive terms, I must refer you to my book *The Challenge of Art to Psychology* (1990a). That book deals with this question: the observational and research evidence is overwhelming that young children everywhere seek and engage in creative, artistic activity, so why *in our society* does that activity virtually disappear as a self-initiated activity when they begin formal schooling? No, my primary aim in no way implies or assumes that all children are capable of becoming committed intellectuals, let alone university professors. It does imply that our obligation is to foster the sense of discovery and growth about self and the world in whatever ways we can (subject matter being but one), knowing that the outcomes of our efforts are far from predictable. Regardless of what a child appears to be, the primary aim dictates that you begin by giving the child the benefit of any doubt you may have.

The second critical reaction is in principle similar to the first, except now it concerns my expectations of teachers: "You, like many others, have commented on the number of different roles society asks teachers to adopt, for example, parent, social worker, policeman, psychiatrist. You now seem to be adding the role of psychologist, and a very sensitive and astute one at that. Not any kind of psychologist but one who can identify and understand and appropriately react to a wide variety of behaviors, feelings, and events. Apart from what that role requires in terms of classroom time, why do you assume that most of those who seek careers in education are capable of becoming effective in that role?"

My answer is in several parts. The first is that teachers have always operated as psychologists. They, like the rest of us, have a "psychology" that informs their thinking and actions. What we are dissatisfied with is that their psychology is inadequate in regard to recognizing and preventing problems. Put in another way, their thinking and actions violate the maxim that you teach children, not subject matter, that there are myriad non–subject matter opportunities to further discovery and growth. Once you take the maxim seriously you are, so to speak, hoist with your own petard: the psychology of the teacher takes center stage in regard to subject matter and other things. Better *not* to take it seriously than to mouth it and then ignore it, to reinforce the charade in which the utterance of truths remains on the level of cliché.

The second part of my answer is that if my critic does not view favorably the capabilities of those who seek a career in education, then my critic is raising two very important questions: how do we get to the point where preparatory programs can *select* appropriate candidates rather than having to take whoever comes through the doors? And what do we know on the basis of systematic experience or research about the criteria for selection we should employ? The second question is, unfortunately, easy to answer: we know precious little, and that may be an overstatement. Implied in my critic's reaction is the assumption that because those who seek a career in education have, on average, discernibly lower scores on intelligence and aptitude tests than those in the more prestigious professions, it is asking too much of them to expect them to become psychologically sophisticated.

Studies on this point are very few but they confirm the conclusion from my own experience that the correlation between intelligence test scores and the grasp and application of psychologic principles is not far from zero. Future research — assuming that an important problem like this gets the attention and study it deserves, an unlikely assumption — may demonstrate otherwise. So I have to say to my critic that in redesigning preparatory programs we have no alternative but to assume that teachers are capable of becoming better psychologists. To assume otherwise is to indulge the self-fulfilling prophecy, which is what too many teachers indulge with their students.

The third critical reaction goes like this: "If teachers become better psychologists and appropriately take advantage of the many opportunities in the classroom to nurture the sense of discovery and growth in students, would that not cut into the time teachers allot to learning subject matter? Given the brute fact that teachers are under increasing pressure to complete the curriculum in ways that get reflected in achievement test scores, how much time could or should a teacher devote to other aspects of a child's development?" My critic is getting at the heart of the matter which is how long we will continue to require teachers and students to adhere to and meet criteria in ways that are ultimately self-defeating of the productive development both of teachers and students. The issue is not subject matter. The issue is the assimilation of subject matter in ways that capitalize on, stimulate, and reinforce the sense of discovery and growth in regard to self and the world. Subject matter, any formal subject matter, is taught in a social context in which diverse factors have consequences for how that subject matter will be approached, judged, and learned. Subject matter is crucial, so crucial for life that we cannot be other than aghast that most students experience learning of subject matter as a form of harassment and child abuse. Implied in the primary aim is that students should *want* to learn subject matter, not to feel that it is an exercise that an uncomprehending adult world foists on them, an exercise quickly forgotten when the curriculum has been completed.

Of course what I am suggesting may well cut into the time allotted to formal subject matter. But should we not realize that increasing the time devoted (in the most narrow ways) to subject matter has been either fruitless, or has raised test scores to a minuscule degree, or has had the counterproductive effect of guaranteeing that in the development of children subject matter has no personal or intellectual significance for them? Subject matter is too important to be learned but not assimilated, to suffer the fate of enthusiastically motivated memory loss. Yes, I expect a lot from and for teachers and students. And if those expectations require changes in classrooms and schools, the preparation of educational personnel cannot remain what it is.

As I look back at the reform efforts in the post–World War II era, it is truly remarkable how cosmetic the changes have been in the preparation of educational personnel, amounting to little more than add-ons to conformity-reinforcing programs. So, for example, we have been told that teachers should be far more steeped in the subject matters they teach. How can you quarrel with that cliché? How can you be against virtue and motherhood? But how can you ignore the fact that the preparation of educational personnel ill prepares them to make subject matter intellectually and personally meaningful to students? How do you get would-be educators to recognize and act on what they know *before* they enter a preparatory program: the differences between productive and mind-stultifying learning experiences. And how do we discharge our moral obligation to the would-be educators to make them knowledgeable about the obstacles they will confront when they become independent practitioners in schools where trying to act consistently in regard to what they know will be so difficult? Do we have a viable alternative that holds promise for preventing, to a degree at least, disillusionment, burnout, ritualization, and retreat into routine on the part of teachers and, therefore, intellectual passivity in students?

Changes in any traditional, complicated type of organization do not derive from one source. Changes always have internal and external sources that are not always compatible with each other. What I have said and will say suggests changes for which the general public is not prepared. For too long it has been given superficial, issue-avoiding "solutions" that turned out to be failures. Although I do not expect the educational community warmly to embrace my proposals, there are two things about which I am certain. The first is that that community does not need to be persuaded that the current situation is either desirable or to be tolerated. The second is that a surprising number of educators (among those who write) have been saying what I have said. If our rationales and proposals are not identical, the most informed critiques of the way things are have come from within the educational community. I do not believe that I have a corner on the truth. I justify this book on the basis of two facts and one belief. The first fact is that for the past thirty years I have been correct in predicting that reform efforts will fail. It could be that I was right for the wrong reasons, but I obviously prefer another explanation! The second fact is that the reform efforts have, for all practical purposes, ignored preparatory programs. My belief, like that of Goodlad's, is that these programs need to be completely rethought and redesigned and that if over time those programs do change, they will serve better the purposes of primary prevention.

I have described a stance that should undergird the approach of teachers of teachers in every aspect of the preparatory program. Let me illustrate this further by two questions with which the would-be teacher should be presented. The first question is this: what will be the thoughts, feelings, and expectations of the would-be teacher on his or her first day of teaching, be it the first day of practice teaching or the first day as

an independent practitioner? That question is a concrete instance
of a more general question: what goes through the mind of anyone who has to demonstrate competence in a new role or task
before some kind of a judging public? Long before the would-
be teacher entered a preparatory program he or she has had
many "audition" experiences, which is to say that the would-be
teacher is not devoid of any experiential assets when asked to
think about the first day of teaching. In any event, what would
we want the would-be teacher to become aware of? What should
that person know about an event that will inevitably be challenging? How can we prevent its more destabilizing consequences?
Let me briefly list some of the thoughts that run through the
mind of that teacher:

- Will I be adequate or competent?
- Will I be liked and respected?
- What will I do if a child challenges what I say or do? Will
  I be able to do what I know I should do if a child does something flagrantly wrong?
- Will the principal and other teachers show they understand
  how I feel, that I may screw up, that they want to be helpful?
- What if a child asks me a question I can't answer? Will I
  be able to say I don't know, I want to think about it?
- What if I do something wrong? Will I be able to say out
  loud I made a mistake, and that I, like my students, have
  to learn from my mistakes? Will I have enough control and
  self-confidence to be consistent with the principle that *I* am
  a model of how *they* should think and act?

The reader, educator or not, will have no difficulty comprehending the phenomenology of the beginning teacher. Others may
employ a different phraseology or come up with a longer list,
but every list will reflect one common theme: the beginning
teacher is an anxiously curious individual, curious about self,
others, and social context. That individual is no different from
an actor on opening night, a lawyer trying his first case, or a
surgeon performing her first operation.

Now for the second question we ask the would-be teacher

to ponder: what are children curious about on the first day of school? Let me list a few of the questions that will occupy the student, putting them in adult language.

- What kind of a person does my teacher appear to be? Should I, will I, like her, trust her? Will she like me?
- Is he going to be fair and consistent? How will he react if I get wrong answers or I do something he thinks is not right?
- Will I be one of the smart ones or one who doesn't catch on quickly? If I don't understand what she asks the class to do, will she help me, talk to me, or make me look dumb in front of the class?
- Will I get up in the morning eager to go to school? Will school be interesting?

The phenomenology of the teacher and student is, in principle, virtually identical. I have yet to meet a beginning teacher who had been prepared to be sensitive to and act on that identity. It is understandable if the teacher is self-absorbed, but when that self-absorption, as is too frequently the case, renders her insensitive to what children are feeling and asking themselves, it can initiate a dynamic not conducive to a context of discovery and growth. I am *not* saying that what happens on the first day or days is fateful for all days thereafter, but my experience has forced me to conclude that those very early days are, unfortunately, representative of the substance and level of many teachers' understanding of "where children are coming from." Teachers have two theories of learning: one for them (adults) and one for students. That, of course, is theoretical nonsense, just as it would be nonsense to say that we need one theory for the oxygen atom and another for the hydrogen atom.

Children are not adults, but that does not mean that their needs are totally different or that faced with similar situations, their reactions will in no way be similar. I am reminded here of a teacher whose understanding and handling of students I had to regard as inadequate and insensitive. One day the principal appeared, whispered something to the teacher, and then left. The teacher then told the class to continue with their seat assignments because she wanted to talk with Kenneth Stone at her desk. I was seated in the back of the room and could only see their interaction. What I saw was a woman tenderly talking to a child in tears, one of her arms around his shoulders as if she was going to embrace him, the hand of her other arm cupped gently under his chin so that eye contact was unavoidable, tears were streaming down his face, she then kissed him on the forehead, turned to the class and said she would be back in a few minutes, and left with the boy. I, like the children in the class, watched the interaction with fascination. When the teacher returned, she immediately assumed her "role" of teacher: the "lesson" continued.

Two things were remarkable about this incident. The principal had told the teacher that the boy's mother had been in an auto accident, was in the hospital, the boy's father was coming to pick him up, and the principal had asked the teacher to talk briefly with the boy and then bring him to the office. What was more remarkable to me than the "out of role" behavior of the teacher with the boy was her volunteered explanation to me of what crossed her mind when the principal relayed the news: "I remembered how I felt when I was in the sixth grade and my mother came to school to tell me that my father had died. My heart went out to Kenneth." The second remarkable thing was that her interaction with the boy, on which everybody's eyes had been rivetted, was never discussed in that class, except to inform them that someone in the boy's family was ill.

The point of this anecdote is that in the course of a day the behavior of this teacher seemed to be based on the assumption that there was nothing in her experience as a student relevant to her understanding and managing of her students. Her experience was unused and unusable. It took a fortuitous and unfortunate set of circumstances to allow her unreflectively, spontaneously, to use her experience to comfort the boy in the most exemplary way.

The reader should ponder this question: in what ways could a teacher capitalize on such an incident for *educational* purposes? I italicize the adjective *educational* in order to disabuse the reader of the impression that I am advocating using the incident only or mainly for therapeutic or cathartic purposes. One thing we know: the children (and I) saw something that was atypically moving and about which they (and I) were curious and full of questions. Who was ill in the family? What was the illness? Was that person going to die? Was the person in the hospital? When would Kenneth come back to school? How would he make up the lessons he would miss? How can we help him? There was one other thing I can assure the reader was true: for the rest of that morning the minds of those children were not on subject matter. And I confess that for the rest of that morning I was puzzling over the discrepancy between the usual and unusual behavior of this teacher.

I once discussed this incident with a group of teachers. Here are a few summary highlights of that discussion:

• By the end of a two-hour seminar class, there was general agreement that the teacher should have known the students would be preoccupied with questions when they saw her with tearful Kenneth. Those questions should have been discussed, if only because ignoring them interfered with learning the formal curriculum. Most of these teachers, however, felt that to call such surfacing and discussion *educational* was defining the word much too broadly. Granted that the children would learn something, the teachers still considered the discussion of Kenneth's problem something of an interference or luxury.

• There are countless times during a school year when things happen in and out of the classroom that arouse interest and questions in children. If a teacher were to respond, to try to capitalize on even a small number of these happenings, that would measurably cut into the time required to teach the formal curriculum. Also, to respond to these happenings "in the way you are suggesting requires a degree of psychological sophistication we don't have. We would like to have it, but we don't."

• One of the teachers taught math. "I'll tell you what I would have liked to have done but would not because of the time it would take. I would have asked the class if they were interested in these questions: How many auto accidents are there in one year? Do auto accidents happen more on certain days than on others, more on certain times of the day and night? Who gets in more accidents, men or women? Young people or old people? Do American cars stand up better in accidents than foreign cars? Do seat belts prevent serious injuries?" She must have reeled off a dozen or so questions. And then she said, "I would discuss with them how and where we could get answers, prepare tables and graphs, and do other things that require number concepts. Sure, you can, in your words, capitalize on the Kenneth incident for educational purposes but what if what they learn is not on the achievement tests they take in the spring?" That, I replied, was a legitimate question but I also regarded my answer as legitimate: learning arithmetic and math in ways and for purposes unrelated to the world of childrens' interests and activities has been an educational catastrophe.

One more example. President Kennedy was assassinated on a Friday. Schools in New Haven did not open until Wednesday, which was the day of the week I met with first-year teachers after school. When I walked into the conference room of the Yale Psycho-Educational Clinic, the twelve teachers were sharing a common experience: it had been next to impossible to get their pupils to attend to the lessons of the day. As one teacher put it, "This was not a day to teach children anything." The point of this anecdote is not only that there was a great deal that the children could have and wanted to learn, but that these teachers were so focused on subject matter that they could not respond to what was on minds of all pupils, indeed everyone in the country. These teachers were not unaware of what the children had experienced, nor were they unimaginative souls possessing no spark of creativity. In fact, all but three were recent graduates of prestigious liberal arts programs, they had all taken a couple of educational courses in a local teacher preparatory program the previous summer and were now taking more courses leading to a teaching certificate. And, yet, after three months of teaching they felt under pressure to stick to a prescribed curriculum, come what may.

I trust the reader will agree that the aim of preparing educational personnel is *not* to instill in them a conformity to the way things are. That does not mean that the aim is to prepare revolutionaries who will storm the barricades. But it does mean that they will be knowledgeable about and sensitive to the obstacles to taking seriously what we know about children and productive learning. More than that, they will feel more secure, intellectually and personally, in justifying their departures from the way things are and their obligation to seek to influence educational policy, never forgetting that what is at stake are their fates and those of their pupils. That, to some people, may seem to be asking too much of these personnel.

I find it ironic that this criticism has tended to come from people who indict teachers for not expecting enough from their students. Yes, I expect educational personnel not only to grasp the nature of the ideal but to strive for it even though that striving is an uphill battle. Preparatory programs that ignore or gloss over these issues contribute to the manufacture of problems both in educators and their students.

The principles educators need to grasp, the realities the implementation of those principles will encounter, cannot be learned only by reading or listening to lectures or observing the implementation of those principles by others. These are important modalities, but unless they are embedded in or accompanied by personal, hands-on supervised experience *throughout the preparatory process* — and I literally mean from day one — the chances are that the principles and the ideal will remain abstractions, lacking that sense of concrete experience that alone provides the basis for understanding the relations between ideas and actions. To wed thought and action requires that we overcome the too-frequent divorce between thought and action. At the present time preparatory programs are inadequate in two respects: the gulf between thought and action, principles and action, is very wide; the gulf between how educators are prepared and the realities they will encounter is no less wide. It is one thing to com-

prehend and explain those gulfs in light of the history, traditions, and formal laws and regulations which have shaped them.
It is quite another thing to excuse them. We are living at a time
in regard to matters educational when to understand all is no
warrant to forgive all. We are at a time for judgment.

It was to John Dewey a glimpse of the obvious that teachers are psychologists. He never advocated that educators should
"learn psychology" and *then* become educators, the kind of separation against which he was the most thoughtful critic. And
Dewey never expected or suggested that educators should become whatever is meant by a "sophisticated" psychologist. What
Dewey did advocate was that educators grasp and appropriately
implement psychological principles essential to their task as educators. Dewey stated explicitly that those who had the awesome
responsibility to prepare educators should be psychologically sophisticated, a kind of what he called a "middleman" who understood children, classrooms, schools, and the moral and intellectual purposes of education. In setting up his lab school at
the University of Chicago at the end of the nineteenth century,
Dewey was, of course, the model middleman. He was not on
an ego trip when he insisted that he would come to Chicago
only if he could head up a department of psychology and pedagogy. His insistence was not based solely on the signal contributions he had already made to the new field of psychology and
his desire to relate the potentials of that field to the educational
arena. Nor did it stem only from his extraordinary awareness
of the relation between social-economic inequities and their per-
petuation by educational practices of the time. Those background
factors were important but so was the fact that Dewey had been
a school teacher. Dewey's concept of the role of the middleman
did not come out of the blue.

Teaching teachers involves every psychological issue and
principle involved in teaching children. The would-be educators, like the pupils they will later teach, are not unformed, empty
vessels, devoid of knowledge, assets, interests, and experience
in matters educational. To ignore what the would-be teacher
knows and has experienced, what that teacher aspires to be and
achieve, is to seal off a gold mine in the face of poverty.

On several occasions I have presented the contents of this chapter to groups of teachers of teachers. Because I assume that their major reactions will be those of many readers of this book, or they are reactions that will be engendered by chapters that follow, I take them up here. The first reaction went like this: "It's hard to argue with the implications you draw from the maxim that you teach children, not subject matter. And we cannot quarrel with your suggestion that would-be teachers are not devoid of knowledge and experience about productive learning. But when you say that capitalizing on those assets and instilling in our students what the maxim means in practice should begin on day one and should be center stage throughout the program, *we* don't know what that means for *us* and the way our *programs* are structured. You say you are not opposed to courses but everything you say suggests a kind of one-on-one relationship that, you will have to admit, is quite impractical, even utopian. But let us assume that we decide to move in that direction, what kinds of facilities would we need, what kind of techniques could we employ, to make the relationship between principles and actions more meaningful and consistent?"

My answer is in several parts. The first is that form follows function; how you design a program depends on what you want to accomplish. If traditional courses and their sequencing are not accomplishing a stated purpose, then what will? It is true that I look with disfavor on a program that says you have to take this course and then that one, on the assumption that acquiring knowledge is a necessary and sufficient basis for applying that knowledge appropriately in a classroom. The knowledge acquired in course *x* or *y* may be valid in a scientific or consensual sense. For example, what is learned in a math, history, psychology, or methods course may be completely valid as sheer knowledge, but the students in these courses will be *practitioners* who are supposed to be able to make subject matter something of interest and curiosity in children, not things unrelated to their past, present, and future. Subject matter is not something to be delivered as we deliver mail but something that is willingly digested, intellectually and personally, and reinforces the sense of discovery and growth. The subject matter of any course takes on appropriate significance *for the practitioner* only if it provides a basis for creating the conditions that make the acquisition of that subject matter productive for students. Far too frequently, those who teach subject matter courses are partisans of subject matter, not of children in classrooms. Of course teachers should be steeped in subject matter, but they should no less be steeped in what makes that information digestible to children. It is this dual obligation that makes teaching as challenging as it is difficult. I am not opposed to courses. I am opposed to courses in which that dual obligation is ignored.

There is an irony here. University professors have been among the most vocal critics of teachers and our schools, especially in regard to teachers' superficial grounding in subject matter and, therefore, to the poor performance of their students. By whatever criteria you employ for "good" teaching, there is no evidence that the quality of college teaching is obviously better, on average, than that of school teachers. But it is my opinion — and it is no more than an opinion — that college students, again on average, gain more than school children from their courses. If that is true, it is not because (certainly not *only* because) college teaching is superior but in large part because college students have more opportunity to take courses that they think interest them, that is, they *want* to take those courses.

Often school children do not want to learn what is given them. That is not to say they do not want to learn a lot about a lot of things but rather that what they are asked (that is, forced) to learn has no special intellectual or personal significance. I could count on students wanting to take my courses. That kind of wanting, however, is rare in the modal school classroom with the modal teacher. The aim of a preparatory program is to nurture that kind of wanting, a wanting with which children started school but which went quickly underground.

The second part of my answer is that my hold on reality is not so shaky as to allow me to suggest a one-on-one relationship between instructor and student, although I am suggesting that such a relationship should be far more frequent than it is. There is no one way of acting on my suggestions. In this day of wondrous technologies there are myriad ways they can be used in preparatory programs. Let me give but one example that is directly relevant to something I discussed in an earlier chapter: how a teacher should relate to parents.

Decades ago I taught a seminar on educational issues for graduate students in clinical psychology. One segment concerned how to convey to a parent that his or her child was mentally retarded. I had a student from the drama school act the role of the parent telling him only that he would be in the role of a parent whose child had been failing in school and he had been called in to talk with the school psychologist. The student in my seminar was told: "You have observed the child, spoken to the teacher, tested the child, and the unambiguous conclusion is that the child has to be placed in a special class. Your job is to convey this information in a helpful way." Famous last words! The drama student made mincemeat of my would-be psychologist.

In the intervening decades I have taken advantage of every opportunity to try to convince educators and others to develop a series of films that could be used in preparatory programs to illustrate the difficult problems one encounters in interacting with parents — and I do not mean only "how to do it" films in which errors of omission and commission are left out. I also suggested that every would-be educator have the opportunity to be filmed in real or simulated conditions. (I also have tried to persuade people to consider films about how to think about and chair faculty meetings.) My powers of persuasion obviously leave much to be desired; to my knowledge, no one has taken the suggestion to heart or mind. The point here is that the technology exists whereby real and realistically simulated educational issues, events, *and* settings can be used in the preparation of educators. It is not a technology that should be employed so as put the student in the passive role of a viewer of films. As in the case of any subject matter, the task is to help students integrate attitudes, knowledge, and action in regard to events that will be central to their professional careers.

William James and John Dewey alerted us a century ago to the dangers of designing laboratory experiments that were unrelated to the real-world phenomena those studies were meant to illuminate. They were not opposed to rigorous research but rather to research which, by virtue of the conditions created, did not permit generalization to events outside the laboratory. The preparation of educators is not a formal experiment but the dangers James and Dewey articulated are, unfortunately, too characteristic of too many preparatory programs. The thrust of my entire argument in this book is that those dangers have to be confronted and overcome to whatever degree possible.

The third part of my answer to the reactions of teachers of teachers is that, like Goodlad, I am advocating a total redesigning of preparatory programs. I am not advocating add-ons or strengthening what now exists. Obviously, this redesigning will not, cannot, occur quickly. To redesign assumes that there is a new rationale, a new set of governing principles that have been thought through and accepted, that there is the courage to realize that one is setting sail on somewhat uncharted seas, and that the fear of failure works against change and creativity.

In the past few years we have begun to hear people, in and out of education, both plead and insist that we think more radically about changing educational policy, practices, and organization. The call for radicalization has often come from people who, in a narrow political sense, are the opposite of radicals. There is a desperate quality to these pleas, and even a willingness — in the private sector, foundations, and government — to come up with millions of dollars to stimulate and support radical changes. If only because I do not possess the corner on truth, I applaud these developments even though — as I argued in *The Predictable Failure of Educational Reform* (1990b) — they rest on the most dubious assumptions.

To these proponents of radical thinking I have to ask these questions. The first is why they have virtually nothing to say about the selection and preparation of educators? Why, when they say anything, is it about deepening teachers' understanding of subject matter, as conventional a recommendation as has ever been articulated, as if the unsatisfactory performance of students is a *direct* consequence of the teacher's grasp of subject matter? Are these pleaders prepared for the predictable: that implementing any truly radical change is an awesomely complex task that can fail because its conceptual underpinnings were wrong, or the problems of implementation were vastly underestimated, or the pressures from the calendar, the budget, and the need to succeed blot out the signals of failure? Will you regard failure, partial or total, the way you do medical research so much of which is not fruitful, or will you blame those who fail, creating grist for the mill of those who like to believe that educational theorists, researchers, innovators, and practitioners are a sorry intellectual lot?

I ask these questions, and I could have asked many more, because I do not want to be perceived as offering a blueprint for action, as if there is but one way of implementing my suggestions, as if I were to say: "Think the way I do and the clouds will part, the sun will come out, and enjoy." I, like the teachers of teachers with whom I talked, am quite aware of the changes my proposals explicitly require in their thinking and practices. More than that, if the proposals are taken seriously they will require a tremendous moral and institutional support. Those who plead for radicalization seem ignorant of the importance of such support.

Because this redesigning will require new facilities, equipment, and personnel, it cannot be done without additional funding. This is not to say that little or nothing can be done unless there is additional funding. That is not the case. If I had my own, well-heeled foundation, I would automatically reject any application that implicitly conveyed the message that without funding redesigning cannot occur. The reader will recall that in Chapter Four I discussed President Nixon's ill-fated Experimental Schools Program. I read many of the applications from schools seeking to put "everything together" in accord with the guidelines. In reading these applications one question kept intruding into my mind: *"Why are they asking for funding to do x and y when they could and should have done them without funding?"* It was obvious that the stimulus for change was the announcement that external funding was available and *not* the changes in thinking and action, however modest, they had experienced, initiated, or acted on. "Give us the money and we will do well what you want us to do." To this one can only reply, "What evidence can you present, modest but compelling, that what we want you to do, you have already started to do?"

As they now exist, preparatory programs — however they vary in size and resources — are not devoid of assets, actual or potential, for beginning the redesign process. Funding should serve as the *reinforcer* for initiating redesign, not as the stimulus for it. That was a principle that Flexner insisted on in 1910 when giving advice to foundations seeking to improve the education of physicians. They followed his advice.

The penultimate reaction of teachers of teachers to my position was, "The more you talk, the more examples you give of how teachers can take advantages of happenings (inside and outside the classroom), the more you seem to be saying that adhering to a formal curriculum is a mistake. If teachers did more of what you are suggesting, not only would the curriculum not be covered but different classrooms with same-age children would finish the year at different points in the formal curriculum.[1] That would mean that their teachers in the following year could not count on the previous year's curriculum having been covered." I shall not repeat here that this reaction speaks volumes of how imprisoned we are in a view of curriculum that says it must be covered if its intended intellectual and personal consequences are to be realized. I am not in principle opposed to predetermined formal curricula. I am opposed to adherence to a curriculum that results in student disinterest in subject matter.

The last group with whom I discussed this issue and from whom the reaction surfaced I met on the day after the ending of the West Palm Beach trial in which William Kennedy Smith was found not guilty of rape. That trial was, to indulge understatement, one of *the* media events of the decade. I am safe in assuming that most adults and many high school students watched or knew about the trial. Here is what I said to the group.

---

[1]This is the kind of argument *The Story of the Eight-Year Study* demolishes in regard to the relation between high schools and colleges. As I said in Chapter One, that story should be carefully read by everyone in education.

If I were principal of a high school, and let us assume that every classroom had a TV set, I would have canceled the "formal curriculum" for all juniors and seniors so that they and their teachers could watch and discuss the proceedings. And I would justify it on two grounds. The first is that we are all dissatisfied with what students know about our judicial system, its relation to our constitution, its rationale for safeguarding individual liberties, the goal of fairness and the rules of evidence, the role of judges and juries, why we have an adversarial relationship between those who represent accused and accuser, why certain information is deemed relevant or irrelevant, admissible or inadmissable, and much more.

As educators we are criticized for the abysmal ignorance of young people of why we have the constitution we do, why it shaped our judicial system as it did, and the differences in these respects between our countries and others. We teach civics, history, and social studies but is it not apparent that students are absorbing what we want them to know in order to be informed and responsible citizens. That trial contained more things relevant to crucial subject matter than is contained in our formal curricula. And it is embedded in an event of intrinsic interest and curiosity to our students.

To use that event for educational purposes requires that two conditions be met. The first is that teachers have to feel free to capitalize on the event, that is, it is *not* an intrusion or an interference with the learning of subject matter. The second is that teachers should know the subject matter to the degree that they feel intellectually and personally secure to handle discussion of the issues, to listen to, indeed to anticipate the questions and attitudes students are likely to verbalize.

Creating the conditions that instill in teachers the importance of capitalizing on unpredictable events

of interest to them and their students is one problem
a preparatory program cannot ignore or gloss over.
But it is no less important that when would-be teachers
are learning subject matter, *their* instructors will have
illustrated for them how ongoing, naturally occurring
events in the quotidian world can be used for educational purposes. It may well be that what students
learn from the Palm Beach trial will not be on their
achievement tests. But does anyone doubt that what
they will learn from such discussions will remain with
them longer and have more personal significance for
them than what they are now learning?

But what about the titillating sexual content of
the trial? How, some will say, can you justify on
educational grounds "exposing" students to such content? The obvious answer, of course, is that we are
exposing them to what they already know, or practice, or fantasize. Indeed, in many of our schools there
are curricula geared to provide information on sexual matters specifically and health matters in general.
I doubt that there are many junior and senior high
school students who don't know what a condom is or
have not engaged in one or another type of sexual activity. To assume otherwise is to deny the obvious.

What would we want students to learn from the
trial? The first is that there is a difference between
love and affection, on the one hand, and sex for the
sake of sex, on the other hand. That is not a moral
judgment. It is a fact that can have predictable and
unpredictable, desirable and undesirable consequences,
depending on one's sense of obligation to one's self and
one's health.

The second is that if you, married or not, in
love or not, engage in sexual intercourse *with no intention to have a child,* you jeopardize two lives if you
have not used condoms. Again, that is not a moral
judgment but a statement of possible factual consequences. I am aware, of course, that there are parents

utterly opposed to their children's engaging in sexual
intercourse before they are married. That is their
moral judgment and I respect it. Their children would
not be asked to participate.

The third thing I would want them to learn is
that rape, *or any other form of sexual harassment* is abhor-
rent, evil, and illegal. And the fourth thing I would
want them to learn is that in the Palm Beach trial the
accused was judged not guilty, which does not mean
he was innocent. What it does mean is that the prosecution did not prove its case beyond a reasonable
doubt. Nor does the verdict allow us to conclude that
the accuser lied. Whether she lied or consented we
will never know. All we know is that the prosecution
failed to prove its case. It was Justice Holmes who
said that courts exist to serve the law, which is not
the same as saying they exist to serve justice.

I did not say this to the group facetiously but rather as
an example of how one can capitalize on an event of which students are aware, about which they are very curious, for the purpose of helping them acquire subject matter — legal, historical,
cultural, health — vital to them as public and private citizens.
It is easy, I have learned, for people to interpret my emphasis
on teaching children, not subject matter, as a deemphasis on
subject matter, as a "touching-feeling" approach and mystique
subverting the "true" aims of education. That interpretation
could not be more wrong. What subverts these aims is the conventional approach that locks on to a predetermined agenda
(meaning curriculum) that eschews the concrete and stays on
the level of acontextual abstractions and rote memory, thereby
guaranteeing that whatever is "learned" will be intellectually non-
productive and quickly forgotten.

What I am suggesting requires casting the concept of *the*
curriculum in a new light. But that recasting will not take place
unless preparatory programs instill in their students the importance of feeling free to depart from the predetermined curriculum and, no less important, providing them in their exposure

to subject matter example after example of how they should seize those opportunities that take advantage of student interest and curiosity. This goal cannot be achieved only by reading or listening to lectures or by discussing examples, although each of these can be helpful. No less than the children they will someday teach, the would-be educators will have to be helped to experience for and by themselves what is involved in capitalizing on the kinds of events that have stimulated student interest and curiosity.

If the substance, procedures, and aims of preparatory programs were to be radically reformulated, would-be educators would not have an easy time when they become independent professionals in real classrooms in real schools. Schools as they are now will not roll out the welcome mat for teachers who do not conform to the traditional conception of *the* curriculum: its organization of time and the ways in which student achievement are evaluated. The pressures to conform are real and great. But two things are obvious: those pressures are part of the problem and not the solution, and it is the obligation of educators to seek to change what is a self-defeating set of conditions. I am not asking that educators change the world, and I am not suggesting that radically changing their preparation and, therefore, their conception of their professionalism will quickly produce a more satisfactory state of affairs. But I am asserting that as long as educators see themselves as lacking the power to change anything in a meaningful way — waiting, like Godot, for salvation from others somewhere in an uncomprehending world — they will remain part of the problem. On the very day I wrote these words I received a letter signed by eight experienced educators who had taken a seminar with Dale Brubaker of the University of North Carolina at Greensboro. He had asked them to read and discuss some of my writings. In light of their discussions Brubaker suggested they write to me. It is a long, thoughtful letter from which the following paragraphs are relevant to my present purposes:

> In your writing you highlighted the recent major
> changes in education as being initiated and mandated
> by the federal government. Is our society doomed to

educational changes only as dictated from above by the Washington power structure that contributes to needed change as well as unexpected outcomes? How can educational leaders who are encouraged to think globally and to act locally work passionately without burning out, all the while knowing that their innovative and progressive reforms will be predictably thrown out with the wash? How can power relationships or the total gestalt be changed in order to improve education, to create an affirming world where everyone can realize his talents, and to improve our economic base in the world's competitive marketplace? How can creative educational decision-making be shared not only within the educational community but also with the existing political-economic power structure that mistrusts educational leaders? Even if changes occur in power relationships, how can the unintended outcomes be minimized?

In private fields of business activity, important changes have resulted from trial and error experimentalism within an encouraging environment that allows for failure. How can a spirit of collegiality and experimentation be nurtured in education if governmental and private grants demand specific evaluations and guarantees for success without which the funding would never be awarded nor be renewed? Knowing that the nation's historical and cultural setting greatly influences the direction of education, how can we, as educational leaders, be pried from the safe, but rigid traditional approaches that have not worked and provide the moral, co-operative, and spirited leadership necessary to get the attention and support of funding agencies? Why aren't educational leaders and teachers paid to be risk takers? How can we be invited to the dance? What would it necessitate to change the gestalt?

This was not a letter from would-be educators. They have been in the game for many years. They were in a seminar on educational leadership, one in which, it is clear, that truly gut issues have surfaced and been discussed. What they articulate in the letter I have heard hundreds of times before, with one important exception: the educator as risk taker, a conception obviously emphasized by Brubaker. The sole reason I quoted from the letter is to make the point that "educator as risk taker" is a conception foreign to almost all preparation programs. It is a conception that was not instilled in teachers when they were in a preparatory program, and it is understandable if after years in schools they should be pessimistic about adapting a new stance and about the level of support they anticipate. *It is precisely to prevent, to whatever degree possible, such pessimism, despair, hopelessness, and sense of powerlessness that I have focused on preparatory programs.*

The questions asked in the letter are those that should never be far from center stage in these programs. To slight or ignore them is to contribute to the manufacture, not the prevention, of problems in educators, which then have adverse consequences for children. Educators are not powerful, but neither are they powerless. Many things have to happen for change to occur, in addition to redesigning preparatory programs. You start where you can, where you are obliged to start, where you can make some kind of difference, where there is reason to believe that your efforts will have percolating consequences.

Our nation was quite taken with President Kennedy's "Ask not what your country can do for you. Ask what you can do for your country." In regard to our dissatisfactions with our schools, educators should articulate what they feel our country should do for schools, children, and educators. Where they stand should not be kept private. *At the same time, however, they should be no less clear about what they can and should do for themselves.* If they ask of our country what they have asked in the past, it will reinforce a view of educators as self-serving, unimaginative, feckless conveyors of ideas and programs that have failed in the past. But if educators begin to convince the general public that what they advocate is not cosmetic, that they are willing and able to take responsibility for helping themselves, they will have started a change in how the general public will perceive educational issues. They can show their willingness to make radical changes in preparatory programs, to take primary prevention seriously, to act on what we know (and know well) about children, productive learning and productive contexts, and to be prepared to alter the relationships between teacher and child, between teachers and teachers, and between educators and communities.

How many preparatory programs have their students read and discuss David Hunt's aptly titled book *Starting with Ourselves* (1987)? Will preparatory programs continue to select and prepare educators who then will require all kinds of consultants and inservice programs to help them cope with problems, the benefits from which are at best far from robust and at worst useless? I am, of course, not opposed to consultants or inservice programs but rather to the lack of recognition that they do virtually nothing about what affects the incidence of problems, that is, the rate at which new problems occur. When repair is all we do and prevention is seen as a luxury, we are indeed in trouble.

In this chapter I have discussed some of the implications of the principle that you teach children, not subject matter. In the next chapter I discuss this question: What are the issues of governance in a classroom, a school, and school system with which a preparatory program should be concerned? As well as I have been able to determine over the years, those issues, so fateful for those seeking a career in education, are given short shrift in these programs.

Chapter Ten

Governance and
Issues of Power

Governance issues are political and moral — political in the sense
that they involve the allocation of power and moral in the sense
that they rest on "shoulds and oughts." So, it is a glimpse of
the obvious to say that a teacher has more power than his or
her students, a principal has more power than teachers, and
a superintendent more power than those lower in the hierarchy. But what do we mean by power? If we mean the degree
to which an individual can directly influence the lives of others,
one could argue that teachers exercise more power than principals or superintendents. In their own encapsulated classrooms
teachers have great latitude in how they choose to use their
power. They may be given all kinds of messages and directives
about what they should do but for all practical purposes there
is no meaningful follow-up to determine how the teacher inter-
prets and acts on those messages. A frequent teacher complaint
is that there are too many constraints on what they can do.
Whatever the validity of the complaint, the fact remains that
the teacher has a good deal of freedom in exercising power.

You could fill the shelf of a large library with books and
articles by and about teachers who, despite what they thought
their administrative superiors expected of them, did precisely
what they thought was more appropriate for children. In almost
all of these instances the writers never explained their departures from convention as a result of what they learned in preparatory programs. But these instances bring to the fore the obvious point that the political and moral features of governance
are undergirded by psychological conceptions of what children

164

are, what they are capable of, and what they should learn to be. Power for whom, for which purposes and why, are questions that get answered in terms of conceptions of people's capabilities, obligations, and needs. Over the millennia, dictatorships assumed that people needed and wanted to be told what to think, do, and say. That is one reason Periclean Athens continues to engender such interest and awe in us. In a world history in which dictatorship was and continues to be the most frequent form of governance, how do we explain how fifth-century B.C. Athens came to view people as it did?

The above is prologue to one fact and one question. The fact is that educators—not only teachers but all educators—vary dramatically in how they conceive of and use power in their relationships among themselves and with children, that is, how those conceptions determine or are the rationale for governance. The question is, how do we want people in a classroom and school to live with each other? More concretely, in regard to governance, to what do we want preparatory programs to expose their students and why?

Let us not forget that educators generally, and teachers in particular, complain bitterly about how they are governed. External critics of our schools are quite explicit in indicting the consequences of school governance, that is, decision-making processes, "stifling and ever increasing bureaucracies," accountability, and on and on. What these critics are less sensitive to is that no less than they, school personnel are very despairing critics of the way they are governed. That observation should occasion no surprise because no working person (and no child in school) is unaware that his or her personal outlook, stability, and self-esteem are very much affected by how he or she is governed.

Job satisfaction derives from several components and among them style of and rationale for governance are most important. At this point it is not necessary to examine the validity of the criticisms from within and without the educational arena. What is necessary is that we take seriously that the existing structures of governance are counterproductive to the achievement of stated educational goals. And "by taking seriously" I mean examining the relationship between the types of policies that derive from the "governors" and the *intractability* of schools to change and improve in accord with those policies. In *The Predictable Failure of Educational Reform* (1990b) I make several points:

- Schools have been consistently intractable to change in accord with policies emanating from anywhere in the governance structure (local, state, national). Any new policy that does not deal with that fact and its history is doomed, however well intentioned and even well supported.

- The "governors" of educational policy may adopt, proclaim, and take steps to implement a policy, but if that policy is not explicitly and directly geared to alter what goes on in the dynamics of life in the classroom — especially in regard to alteration in power relationships — the policy is an exercise either in futility or irrelevance, or both.

- Power — its allocation, uses, and vicissitudes — is a feature of every classroom, which, among other things, determines how children will view themselves, others, and subject matter. There are numerous beliefs representing a conventional wisdom that the research literature on cooperative learning has thoroughly undermined: the popular view that teachers are powerful and children are powerless, that learning is an individual and not a social phenomenon, that only teachers can teach and that children are unable to "teach" or "learn" from other children, that "control" of a classroom is the teacher's responsibility and not one that to any meaningful degree can be given to students. (Few educational ideas and practices have met the criterion of having been successfully replicated by different people in different places in this and other countries. Cooperative learning is one of them, which does not make it a panacea.)

Mine was not a scholarly book but rather a plea to the policymakers: when will you face up to the fact of intractability? What will it take to get you to see the obvious? When will you see that you have been and continue to be part of the problem and not of the solution?

A year after my book appeared, another book was published that provided substantial confirmation for what I had written. The book is *The Classroom Crucible* by Edward Pauly (1991). If I were setting up my own preparatory program, it is one of the books I would have would-be educators read. Its implications both for governance and policy are enormous and not because Pauly presents new data or observations. That point deserves emphasis because Pauly's contribution inheres in his taking seriously what has been known and is in the literature. But he brings this knowledge together in the most reasoned, compelling way and with conclusions that make understandable why those conclusions will not sit well with the proponents of conventional wisdom. Some of Pauly's major points along with my summary statements are presented below, although no summary can do justice to the way he marshals the evidence and logically arrives at his conclusions.

1. "The book argues that the success or failure of the schools depends on daily life in classrooms. Although it may seem hard to believe, education policy research has paid little attention to the influence of classrooms on education. Instead, the search for ideas about how to improve our schools has focused on quick fixes; researchers looked for the best curriculum, the best textbook, the best instructional method, the best kind of teacher, in the hope that once found, these solutions would make the schools work better. But the quick fixes have turned out to be as flimsy and evanescent as gossamer. An enormous volume of education research has turned up no curriculum, teaching technique, or special school program that consistently improves students' school performance.

"What has been lost in the whirl of controversy surrounding education is any real sense of what actually happens in a school. If asked, most people would probably agree with the proposition that education is built out of the ordinary, daily efforts of teachers and students in their classrooms. But education policy research, obsessed with the search for solutions to be imposed upon the schools, has shown little interest in ordinary school life or ordinary people in schools" [Pauly, 1991, pp. 1-2].

2. "That teachers and students do their work behind closed classroom doors makes many school officials and policy makers very uncomfortable" (p. 3).

3. Pauly presents "the radical argument that education is *the result of working agreements that are hammered out by people in each classroom, who determine the rules, the power relationships, and the kinds of teaching and learning that will take place there*" (pp. 13–14). This may seem to the reader to be a glimpse of the obvious but it is a glimpse, as Pauly demonstrates (proves would not be an exaggeration) that policymakers, administrators, and policy researchers have been incapable of seeing. The following points are crucial here.

4. The evidence is incontrovertible that there are large differences between the *average* test scores of students in inner-city schools and those in affluent, suburban schools. But it is no less incontrovertible that for rich and poor alike "most of the variation in student achievement occurred within schools, not between them, *thus ruling out school-wide policies as a principal cause of the differences in student achievement. Family economic status helps or hinders a student's achievement; school resources and policies . . . do not. . . . Some students learn more than others, but not for reasons that are traceable to differences in school policies*" (pp. 23–24, italics mine).

5. Existing research compellingly underscores the fact that when student test score gains are carefully examined "the important differences are between successful and unsuccessful *classrooms*, differences that cannot be traced to consistent school policies, characteristics or behaviors of teachers, curricula, teaching methods, or special programs" (p. 33).[1]

[1]In an earlier chapter I discussed the potential fruitfulness of the social sciences for how we think about classrooms and schools. Pauly's book confirms what I said in that the research he integrates for his particular purposes was done by social scientists. Unfortunately, it is a line of research which, despite its direct relevance to policy matters, has gotten very little play in the educational arena.

6. "The discovery of classroom differences in student achievement has not yet succeeded in changing the education policy debate, because people still equate education policies with controls and resources. As a result, the market for conventional policies continues to flourish, despite the lack of evidence that they work. Alternative kinds of policies do not yet exist. Politicians and education officials need practical education policy proposals, and since the new evidence on classroom differences did not immediately provide new policy ideas, the old ideas continue to hold sway" (p. 35).

Pauly is not saying that teachers are unimportant factors in explaining the wide variation among classrooms in regard to student achievement. He is saying that from day one of the start of the new school year a constitutional, political, social, interpersonal process begins in which *everyone* in the classroom acts and is acted on. It is an ongoing, never-ending process marked by conflict, struggle, problems, resolutions, and satisfactions; a process that is not characterized by one atmosphere but many over time, depending on events within and beyond the classroom; a process in which the teacher, no less than students, acts and is acted on, assimilates and accommodates, willingly or not, to the attitudes and behavior of others in the room. The process is truly dynamic in the sense that it never ceases, that it makes a mockery of the belief that what happens in a classroom can be explained only, or even largely, by this or that characteristic of the one adult in the classroom. It is a process that explains the findings of the research Pauly has integrated and something every teacher will attest to: "teachers who are successful with one classroom *may* not be successful with another, even if the students in the classroom are similar" (Pauly, 1991, p. 31).

Pauly is not downgrading the importance or influence of the teacher. He asks you to confront the reality that whatever you mean by learning is embedded in a complicated, subtle, ever-changing social context, a social "crucible" into which diverse humans are put; they change in predictable and unpredictable ways, for good or for bad, as a "new society" is created and developed. To explain classroom differences only in terms of teacher characteristics makes as much logical and theoretical sense as explaining our early history by saying that George Washington was our first president.

In *The Predictable Failure of Educational Reform* (1990b) I ask and discuss this question: why did it take decades for the rationale for family therapy to be formulated and accepted? Put in another way, why did it take so long to take seriously the obvious fact that the behavior and problems of a single member of a family is explainable only in terms of the reciprocal influences of those who make up the social system we call a family? So, when Pauly demonstrates that the variation among classrooms reflects differences in how each develops ways of dealing with the issues of *reciprocal power* — and he boldly and correctly states that those seldom-studied ways stamp everything and everyone in the classroom — he is advocating a rationale for practical action in principle identical to that of family therapy. Teachers, like mothers and fathers, are important but they are as much cause as effect in shaping the social system.

What are the implications of Pauly's conclusions for preparatory programs *and* primary prevention? It is clear from his discussion that altering and supporting what goes on in classrooms will require changes in the style of classroom and social governance. There are relationships between teacher and students, between teacher and parents, between one teacher and other teachers, between teachers and principal; when these power relationships change in ways that truly alter the decision-making processes governing the composition and atmosphere of classrooms, desirable educational outcomes stand a better chance of being realized. For example, how should we decide and who should participate in the decision about which children should be placed in which classrooms with which teacher? As any parent with more than one child will attest, he or she is not equally effective with or understanding of each of their children. And more than a few parents will own up to the fact that they do not like or love each of their children in the same way and to a similar degree. It is no different with teachers. The expectation that teachers must or can be equally effective with all children is worse than nonsense. It does make a difference what mix of students a teacher has; teachers cannot always be paragons of interpersonal adaptability; and they cannot (using David Hunt's apt characterization) always *flex* emotionally, cognitively, and appropriately to any child. Expecting teachers to interact the same with every child too frequently plays into the liabilities and not the assets of a teacher; it perpetuates a decision-making process in which teachers and parents have little or no role at the same time that the responsibility for the consequences of decisions are placed solely on the teacher. I share Pauly's mystification about the denseness of policymakers in regard to the significance of the diverse factors that, for good or for bad, become fused in the social crucible of the classroom. Far more often than not, it is fusion that engenders rather than prevents problems.

Preparatory programs are inadequate in several respects. The first is a consequence of casting issues of classroom management in terms of *discipline,* as if the power of the teacher is to be exercised for the purpose of rendering students powerless and conforming. The new teacher approaches the classroom expecting and armed to do battle, to win the war as quickly as possible, to subdue any sign of incipient insurrection. That classroom management always involves reciprocal powers; that power always flows from more than one source; and that the power of students is something to be capitalized on, not to be ignored or subdued, are issues about classroom life to which would-be teachers are, at best, superficially exposed and no less superficially helped on the level of practice. When I said earlier that I would require would-be teachers to read Pauly's book it would be not only as a means to raise, discuss, and illustrate the concept and facts of *reciprocal powers* but to bring to the fore these questions: What are the purposes of governance? On what conceptions of children's needs and responsibilities do those purposes rest? How do those purposes facilitate, inhibit, or even extinguish curiosity and commitment? How can the ways those purposes suffuse classroom relationships explain why schools are so uninteresting not only to most students but to most teachers?

The style of governance that characterizes a classroom has personal, interpersonal, and intellectual-educational consequences. It is not a creation only of one adult we call teacher. It is an outcome of myriad interactions, transactions, and events in which every individual is both cause and effect. It is not an outcome of which children are unaware, albeit they would have difficulty putting it into words. Nor are teachers unaware of the outcome, but their awareness almost always takes place *after* that outcome produces untoward consequences.

Let me offer an example that may strike some readers as coming from left field. Why do children "allow" themselves to be toilet trained? After all, the very young child urinates and defecates whenever and wherever the urge is felt and is unconcerned with what that means and does to others. What permits that child to agree, so to speak, to give up such an unreflective, pleasurable habit? The answer, most succinctly put, is in two parts: the parent is correct in the diagnosis that the child is *capable* of being toilet trained, and the child *wants* to please the parent, that is, the child does it out of love for the parent. When toilet training takes place relatively quickly, it signifies that the style of governance characterizing the parent-child relationships *before* toilet training began was one of trust and mutual respect. When toilet training becomes, as it often does, a prolonged battle, it signifies an earlier mode of governance featured by misperceptions, misreadings, and mismatches of intentions, needs, *and* capabilities. It is in these battles that parents "learn" that their child is very powerful, just as the child learns how to use that power to defeat the parent. The parent who views the child as powerless or, just as bad, decides to "tame" the child's power is, like too many new teachers, asking for war.

Toilet training does not take place in a social vacuum, just as Johnny's learning and actions in the classroom influence and are influenced by other children. The very young child has been with and observed other children (either in or out of the family), a fact that some parents use productively and others unproductively or counterproductively. And by productively I mean that the outcome of the process is the sense of accomplishment, growth, and satisfaction in child and parent. That means there are two outcomes: the child is toilet trained and a relationship has been strengthened, or, counterproductively, the child has been "finally" toilet trained after a long and bitter struggle, with the result that the struggle now moves to other arenas, the criteria of a Pyrrhic victory have been met. This is in principle identical to the learning of subject matter: children are required to learn subject matter in ways that have no personal or intellectual meaning, attraction, or utility; they learn it in differing degrees; they not only forget it, they come to devalue school learning in general. How style of governance develops in a classroom mightily determines students' attitudes toward and acquisition of subject matter. If the aim of schooling is to engender an attitude of *willing* pursuit of learning, we cannot be satisfied only with test scores independent of other outcomes. Unless, of course, you are satisfied with winning battles and losing wars.

Why do so many teachers feel so misunderstood, unrespected, powerless, and harassed? Why are so many of them (and others) advocating new forms or styles of school governance? Why do these proponents ask that teachers be given more responsibility to discharge their professional obligations? *Wrapped up in these questions about how teachers experience governance are the issues and problems of classroom governance.* In earlier pages I said that preparatory programs should enable would-be teachers to review their experience as students in order to distinguish between classroom contexts that were stimulating and productive and those that were otherwise, contexts in which they felt respected and those in which they were treated as ciphers incapable of assuming responsibilities. The would-be teacher is not without valuable experiential assets. The purpose of that review, of course, is to begin to sensitize the would-be teacher to issues of classroom governance and how that governance relates to learning. Here I would add that the review should not only direct the would-be teachers to begin to confront how they will experience school governance (as it currently is) but also how similar those experiences will be to those they had as students.

A major virtue of Pauly's book is the way he compellingly integrates research findings and penetrating observations to lead his readers to the crucial importance of the complicated governance process, one whereby teacher and students accommodate each other in ways that suffuse all activities and relationships. But, as Pauly reminds the reader, there is accommodation and there is accommodation. Teachers can respond to the governance of their schools in diverse ways: from resentment, uncooperativeness, lack of commitment, obstructional tactics, putting in for a change to another school, and forming adversarial groups to demonstrating respect, satisfaction, and a "beyond the call of duty" attitude. Students can also respond to their experience of classroom governance in diverse ways. *In the world of schools as they are, teachers and students have a good deal in common in regard to their experience of governance. Indeed, and far more often than not, what they have in common works against and not for productive personal and intellectual outcomes.*

Classroom and school governance are in theory and practice related arenas. A preparatory program that does not deal directly, systematically, and continuously with either arena *and* their interrelationships is contributing to future problems, not to their prevention. We hear often today that our schools ill prepare students for the world of work. We hear far less about how preparatory programs ill prepare students for thinking and dealing with the issues and problems of classroom and school governance, that is, their similarities and their attitudinal outcomes.

The current calls for changing the nature and style of school governance have one assumption in common: those who are or will be affected by a policy should stand in some relationship to the formulation of that policy. That political-moral assumption rests, in turn, on the belief that commitment, accountability, and desired outcomes are more likely to be achieved if those affected by a policy have meaningfully participated in the formulation of the policy or practice. That participation is not seen as a gift, noblesse oblige style, or a surrender of power as a political tactic, or a token gesture to a democratic ethos, but as the recognition that the way things are now reinforces adversarial stances that generate rather than prevent problems.

In the past few years I have taken advantage of every opportunity to talk with relatively new teachers about what and how they learned in their preparatory programs about issues of school governance. Had these issues been raised and discussed in all of their theoretical and practical aspects? Were the *predictable* problems of altering styles of school governance taken up? Were these teachers helped to become clear about and to be prepared for a new role in school governance? Were they clear about where they stood, what they "professed," about changing and participating in school governance? The answers I got were, unfortunately, what I expected. To say that teachers were unsophisticated in the *subject matter of school governance* is to state a truth and not a criticism. It was only after they became full-fledged teachers that issues of school governance became poignantly salient, not a salience that could lead to action but to a stance of retreat into personal and intellectual isolation. They quickly had come to see themselves as the have-nots at the foot of the mountain looking hostilely up at the castle on top where the haves lived.

Whenever I have talked to teachers, regardless of topic, at some point in the discussion the subject of the status of teachers would come up: how they were perceived by their administrative superiors, parents, the general public, and frequently their students. They saw themselves as misperceived, misunderstood, misled, and powerless. There were exceptions, of course; there always are. But even these exceptions seemed to agree that given the constant stream of criticism directed to schools in general and teachers in particular, it was understandable if so many teachers saw themselves as convenient scapegoats.

On several of these occasions I put the following prologue and question to the group:

> You regard yourselves as the objects of a policy, not as formulators of a policy. You are low person on the totem pole. Directives flow from others to you. It is a one-way street. You do not see light at the end of the tunnel. There is no real collegiality, no forum where your needs and ideas can be *safely* presented and discussed, no sense that life in the school will become more interesting, more stimulating, more chal-

lenging. What you fear is that it will become more challenging but in ways you prefer not to think about. I understand and sympathize with what you say and feel. But now I want to put a question to you, the intent of which I hope you will not misunderstand and/or take as criticism. Rather than put it in the form of a question, I will put it as an assertion: *The basis of your criticism of your powerless role in regard to school governance is similar to the basis of the criticism many students make of their lives in the classroom.*

Generally, students are given no role — either in discussion or formulation — in regard to classroom governance. They do what they are told to do, learn what they are told to learn, regardless of what they think or are interested in. They are expected to conform to what others require of them. They are *individual* learners, responsible only to themselves. There is no collegiality among students in regard to learning. There is no "forum" that allows them to learn with and from others. Indeed, learning with and from others, learning to help others learn, too frequently is verboten because it makes evaluation of individual accomplishment difficult. If my assertion is only 50 percent right, it helps explain why so many students find classrooms and subject matter uninteresting and see the light at the end of the tunnel as coming from some place other than school.

There have been two major reactions to my assertion. The first is one of surprise at the thought that teachers and students experience governance in similar ways. Some teachers quickly see and agree with the assertion; some think it wrong or unwarranted. Perhaps I am too partisan to my own assertions, but no teacher who disagreed with me could make anything resembling a case for his or her disagreement. The teacher's case was quite simple: the way things are is the way they should be. So speak those in the castle on the top of the mountain!

The second reaction is in the form of a question: am I advocating a cooperative-learning style of governance, the new panacea? My initial answer is definitely not. Before you latch on to the technology of cooperative learning, you have to work through your political-moral rationale for how people in a classroom should live with each other in regard to needs, responsibilities, obligations, decision making, and capabilities. Do you believe that children are "naturally" irresponsible, immoral, subversive, uncomprehending of the need for law and order, unformed organisms that need to be shaped, directed, and indoctrinated *only* by an adult, organisms possessing far more deficits than assets? My assertion is powered by the Deweyan maxim that the classroom is not a preparation for life; it is life itself. How should we live it? That question is precisely the one that is engendered in teachers by the ways they see themselves as being treated by their superiors.

My assertion *does* lead to the methodologies of cooperative learning in the classroom, just as it leads to alterations in governance in our schools. But let us not make the mistake of confusing a methodology with its political-moral-social rationale. Once you become clear about how life should be lived in classrooms and schools, the methodology you employ should be informed by that clarity. Methodology is a servant to our values and goals. There is no one correct way to employ that servant. Life, in classrooms, schools, or elsewhere, is not organized so as to permit us to assume that if you do A then B and C will inevitably follow. Values and goals are not maps; they are beliefs, imperatives, and stimulants on the basis of which we plan our actions. Between values, on the one hand, and actions, on the other, is a series of booby traps testimony either to our imperfections and inconsistencies, or an inhospitable social-institutional surround, or both. Methodologies are, in the abstract, morally neutral and useless. They become otherwise when we choose them to reflect our values and goals. And when we are unclear about our values and goals, and when our identification with and commitment to them are at best superficial and at worst mindless—they have not become part of our "guts" and what we call mind—we choose a methodology to which, when it fails as it must, we assign blame. Methodologies, no less than people, suffer the dynamics of blaming the victim.

Preparatory programs have been criticized for their emphasis on the methodologies of pedagogy. In the post–World War II era those criticisms have resulted in fewer such courses being required. To appease the critics, there has been an increase in subject matter requirements. That is what I would call shadow boxing, or window dressing, or the blind leading the blind. The point is wrapped up in the joke about the man who in dead winter became ill and went to his doctor who after a "thorough" examination said: "Go home, take off all of your clothes, open up all your windows, stand in front of them and breathe deeply for fifteen minutes eight times a day." The aghast patient replied, "But if I do that I'll get pneumonia." To which the healer said, "*That* I know how to treat." Our preparatory programs deemphasized pedagogy, emphasized subject matter, and neither prevented educational pneumonia. I take no satisfaction whatsoever from having predicted the pneumonia. But I do have a lot of anger at all of those people who *today* cannot face up to their egregiously mistaken diagnosis and prescriptions. And by people I mean both the critics and those who appeased them.

What the participants in this cyclical controversy seem unable to comprehend is that pedagogy and subject matter are experienced in a social context the features of which are reflections of governance. Pedagogy, subject matter, and curriculum are not independent variables like height, weight, or age. Their significances take on meaning only in the social actions and transactions of people governed by implicit and explicit rules about mutuality, obligations, power, and capabilities. You can substitute one curriculum for another because one is supposed to be more interesting or stimulating than the other, but if that alteration changes nothing else in the social crucible of the classroom, we end up confirming that the more things change the more they remain the same. For the teacher, a new curriculum poses two tasks: grasping the rationale for the new curriculum — not only its contents and sequences but its underlying logic and structure — and then, fatefully, setting the stage for students to grasp what the teacher grasped. If that "stage" is one that has all the political-moral-social psychological characteristics that make living and thinking in the classroom uninteresting, why expect that the new curriculum will make a difference? Have we learned nothing from the history of curriculum reform?

Readers of my previous books will know that I regard the constitutional convention of 1787 to be one of the most important and instructive events in human history. I shall not repeat here the justifications for such a judgment. Suffice it to say that the convention agonizingly wrestled with these questions: How do you protect the rights of individuals from the arbitrary exercise of power? How do you square those rights with the requirements of collective living? Can we devise a form of governance that gives citizens a voice, a role, a force in decision making? How can we ensure that those who govern will be responsive to and respectful of the ideas and needs of the governed? How should we distribute power so as to check and balance man's imperfections in handling power?

What went on in that amazing convention over several months in Philadelphia is no different from what Pauly describes in the crucible of the classroom, with one crucial difference: the founding fathers were excruciatingly aware of the important issues wrapped up in the question of how people should live with each other. They did not oversimplify the issues. They knew that questions of who should govern, in which ways, and for which purposes were complicated issues that had to be raised, thought through, and resolved, with full awareness that experience would require "amendments." That convention was an exercise, a most practical one, in philosophy, psychology, history, and politics.

Preparatory programs are most inadequate in how and how much they expose the would-be educator to the subject matter of governance. For the students in these programs governance is a method with the most shallow political-moral-psychological underpinnings. This is true not only for the teacher in the classroom but the teacher in regard to administrators and parents.

What do we mean when we say we should *respect* each other? That a teacher should respect his or her students? That parents should respect their children, and vice versa? What we mean is that we should realize that others, like ourselves, have

needs, rights, ideas, and feelings we should not ignore or derogate. "To refrain from interfering with" is one of the meanings
of *respect* in my dictionary, the implication being that we should
not do unto others what we would not want done to ourselves.
But, as our founding fathers knew, respect for the integrity of
the individual had to be seen in relation to the purposes of and
respect for the collectivity. Governance is the way we seek to
align those two objects of respect. In brief, governance is about
respect for what you think the rights, obligations, and capabilities of people are as individuals and as members of a collectivity.

It has not been my purpose to present a blueprint for governance in a classroom or school. Before you start making a
blueprint you have to be clear about what you want it to reflect.
A blueprint has a prior history. Our national constitution is a
written document reflective of two things: recognition that an
earlier written document (the Articles of Confederation) was dangerously inadequate, and agreement on the major considerations that should be reflected in a new document, discussed at
the constitutional convention. Our written constitution was possible only after consensus was reached about the rights and
responsibilities of individuals, states, and the federal government.

In matters of *school* governance a discussion of sorts has
started, albeit with a conceptual and philosophical shallowness
that does not bode well for the future. In matters of *classroom*
governance there has been little or no discussion. What I have
attempted to do in this chapter is to indicate that the issues of
classroom and school governance are in theory and practice identical, and to view them as different has two unfortunate consequences. The first is that it directs our attention away from how
the conventional style of classroom governance contributes to
a passive, conforming, disinterested stance in students. The second, a derivative of the first, is that this conventional style adversely affects how subject matter will be experienced and assimilated by the learners. Governance and subject matter are,
in a phenomenological sense, never experienced as separate variables. The effort to change attitudes toward subject matter and
make its acquisition more personally meaningful and productive is a doomed effort if it is not accompanied by a change in

power relationships in the classroom. The idea—I hesitate to dignify it by calling it a conception—that for *schools* to improve there will have to be changes in their governance, appears to be garnering support, albeit largely on the level of rhetoric. The idea that governance of *classrooms* will have to change if educational outcomes are to improve has yet to attain anything resembling currency.

There is another source for my reluctance to offer a blueprint: the empirical fact that when clarity about values and purposes have been achieved, there is not a single blueprint that alone will reflect that clarity and agreement. Our country has a written constitution. There are countries that have no written constitution, whose legal system differs in many respects from ours, whose culture is not ours, but who are no less wedded to the basic values and purposes that gave rise to our written constitution. And, let us not forget, there are countries that modeled their written constitution after ours, but that is where their resemblance to our society ends.

More important at this time than working on blueprints for school and classroom governance is gaining clarity about the values and purposes of governance, the challenge they present to the way things are, and what is personally required to act consistently in accord with an altered way of thinking. Put it this way: in relation to the governance of classrooms and schools, are we able to own up to the educational equivalent of the Articles of Confederation and, having done that, can we agree on a set of principles, values, and purposes whose meanings and force derive from personal experience? *That kind of question should occupy everyone at every point in a preparatory program.*

It would be grossly unfair to say that the literature on preparatory programs is without value. At the very least, it recognizes that preparatory programs are part of the problem and not of the solution. But it would not be unfair to say that the literature hardly alludes to the importance and complexity of issues—their political, philosophical, psychological facets—of classroom and school governance. And where there are allusions, they are no more than that.

When and how should these issues be raised? How can

and should the previous experience of would-be educators be mined? What is the relation between governance issues in the classroom and school? How does governance influence attitudes toward, the assimilation of, and the productive use of subject matter? What similarities exist between the needs, rights, and obligations of teachers and their students? These and kindred questions remain on the level of allusion, not confrontation. You can advocate the selection óf "brighter" candidates for preparatory programs, you can require more psychology courses, you can require a better grasp of subject matter, you can insist that preparatory programs be on the graduate level, you can require a longer practice teaching experience, you can require more and closer supervision. You can require any or all of these, as has been done, but they will not (have not) to any discernible degree prepare teachers productively to cope with those governance issues in classrooms and schools that will influence and shape their lives.

If the conditions that make for productive growth and learning do not exist for teachers, the teachers will be unable to help create and sustain those conditions for their students. When preparatory programs begin to take that seriously, they will be serving the purposes of primary prevention. What happens to teachers is no less important than what happens to their students. When the juices stop flowing in teachers, and Farber (1991) has noted that this happens too frequently, the juices will not flow in students. Blaming teachers for this or that on this or that basis is too easy. They are sitting ducks for those who are prone to blame the victim. Teachers, like the rest of us, are a product of how they have been taught. So, instead of taking aim at teachers, should we not focus on how they have been prepared for the complex, challenging, frustrating, demanding, energy depleting, satisfying role so inadequately reflected in the title "teacher"?

Chapter Eleven

Governance and
the Definition of Resources

In the previous chapter I stated that the rationale for governance in large measure determines how subject matter will be experienced and assimilated. In this chapter I attempt to show that this rationale also determines the resources available to a teacher and a school.

Let me start with the universal complaint of educators: they do not have the resources to deal adequately with the problems they face. In general, it is difficult for people to accept the fact that resources are always limited and finite. That difficulty in large part derives from the "habit" of defining a resource as what you pay for and, therefore, control. The less money you have, the fewer your resources will be. That, of course, is true; nothing I shall say should be interpreted as suggesting that money is not a problem. But it is also true that preparatory programs do not confront their would-be teachers with two questions. How do we explain why so many people (educators and the general public) are dissatisfied with our schools, even though in the post–World War II era billions of dollars have been poured into public education? Even if you believe that those billions were insufficient, is it unreasonable to expect that there would have been *some* discernible positive, general consequences? Does not the absence of those consequences suggest that money is not the panacea we like to believe it is? The failure of preparatory programs to deal with this question reinforces in people the belief that money is the universal solvent. They think that the major problems in education are the result of a niggardly public's derogation of education, a belief that robs educators of the ability

183

to consider ways of thinking and acting of which they are potentially capable and which would productively compensate (again
in part) for a perceived lack of money—ways of thinking and
acting that expose the fallacy that without money is to be without resources. Someone once defined money as a necessary
means of exchange among strangers. Schools are governed in
ways that, for all practical purposes, make the people within
them strangers to each other. They not only do not have money
as a means of exchange; they are, by virtue of being strangers
to each other, unable to exchange resources.

There is a second and related question: what are the
resources potentially available to educators that do not require
money? How do we, should we, define people as resources? By
people, I mean not only those with a direct interest in schools
(for example, educators, students, parents) but also others beyond the encapsulated schools. Is it possible to redefine people
as resources so that we capitalize on their assets and in the process
prevent that poignant feeling in teachers that they are alone and
lonely in a densely populated setting? I continue to be disheartened and surprised at the number of young teachers who are
disheartened and surprised by their feelings of loneliness, social isolation, and alienation. If walls do not good neighbors
make, neither do encapsulated classrooms in encapsulated schools.
Not only were they not "warned" about this, but in no way were
they provided with ways of thinking and acting to cope with
such a situation.

My colleague, Murray Levine, once wrote a chapter
(Sarason and others, 1966) entitled "Teaching Is a Lonely Profession." It was a chapter in a very thick book, but his was the
chapter about which we received the most unsolicited letters from
teachers around the country. Their message was simple and
clear: "Thank God you understand what loneliness means and
does to teachers." And that is the point: the dynamics of loneliness—the feeling that "it will always be this way"—over time
have adverse personal and professional effects. Those effects have
not gone unnoticed. They are one of the factors powering some
reform efforts, and those efforts are to be applauded. But as their
proponents well know, it is difficult to overcome experience from

which teachers conclude that it is safer to stay lonely than to participate in an altered governance requiring altered relationships which are unfamiliar and potentially dangerous. If educators had better preparation to think and act in regard to these issues, it would prevent or dilute the obstacles the reform efforts encounter. Is it asking too much of preparatory programs to prepare their students for a "real world" which they must understand and seek to change if as persons and professionals they are to grow, not only to survive?

Let us start with two examples that concern the definition and *re*definition of resources. The first example is a plan I devised whereby Yale University faculty and graduate and undergraduate students would set up, without cost, a department of psychology in a high school. And by department I meant one that spanned the traditional areas in the field.

Several school systems were quite eager for us to use their high schools. Although we monotonously repeated that there was a fair chance that we would fall on our faces, that we did not view ourselves as experts in high school teaching, that graduate and even (highly selected) undergraduates would be involved in addition to faculty, that we did not want to be viewed as in any way impinging on any one else's territory — the response was uniformly enthusiastic and for two reasons. First, in each school system there were some personnel who asserted that I was a responsible individual who knew something about schools. Second, they said they had so many unmotivated students, and since psychology was intrinsically fascinating to everybody (they obviously never sampled undergraduate opinion!), they could only see our involvement as helpful. In essence, we had no "port of entry problem" to speak of. The fact that we posed no credentialing issues was also a plus. The project lasted one year and could not be continued because of a variety of serious illnesses in my family that made planning and commitment an exercise in futility. The school was eager for us to continue. Not only was the teaching perceived as successful, but in diverse ways our group became involved with different individuals, groups, and departments in ways that we had hoped for and that were regarded by school personnel as extremely helpful in achieving desired changes.

And now for the major point: We came to the schools. We offered certain services and a long range plan which the schools saw as a possible help to a serious problem. It never occurred to them to come to us. Given their accustomed way of viewing the community, it could not occur to them that perhaps they had a "right" to request and even to demand help. They viewed the problems with which they were faced as their responsibility, solvable either by existing resources or additional ones they could buy (knowing full well that they would never be able to buy resources adequate to their needs as they defined them). They cannot take the stance that one of their major tasks is to refuse to assume exclusive responsibility for or to be seen as having the expertise to deal adequately with all the problems existing in schools. They cannot say aloud what they say privately: We will never have financial resources to cope effectively with our problems; unless we have call on community resources — unless we make the community share responsibility — the disparity between what we can do and what needs to be done will continue, and perhaps become greater [Sarason, 1976, pp. 26–27].

What deserves emphasis in this example is that it could never occur to school people that there could be people in the community whose professional self-interests might lead them to provide services to schools on a quid pro quo basis: "if you do this for us, we will do that for you." No one has to tell educators that they have problems for which they need help. No one needs to tell educators that there are people in the community who can be of help to them with those problems. But it is almost

axiomatic in the stance of educators that these community people cannot be approached without the carrot of compensation.
"They are busy people. They probably do not have enough time
in a day to do all they want and need to do. How can we ask
them to give us time free for nothing?"—that is the usual view
of educators of the availability of community resources. It is,
obviously, a realistic view but only if your approach is "We have
a problem. You can be of help to us. Are you willing to give
us that help for which we cannot pay?" In other words, you appeal to their altruism, not to their self-interests, that is, to the
possibility that providing the help will in some way have a significant payoff for them.

I have no objections to appealing to people's altruism. Indeed, as I stated in the example, educators have a "right" to request and even demand that community people and agencies
give of their time and skills to schools insisting they have an
obligation to do so. But as long as educators see themselves,
and therefore are seen by others, as solely responsible for what
happens in schools—a stance that keeps private inadequacies
that should be made public—they tend neither to request or demand. Instead, they devote their energies internally to getting
increases in school budgets that would permit them either to
add personnel or to pay for externally situated services. When,
as is usually the case, those increases are not forthcoming, educators feel rejected and derogated and resign themselves to making do with what internal resources they possess. Their feeling
of rejection when the political system fails to give them what
they perceive they need is precisely the feeling they would expect to have if they approached community individuals and agencies hat-in-hand, that is, as beggars. Educators have never been
able to say out loud, "We have never had, will not have, and
perhaps should not have, sufficient resources internally to accomplish our tasks the way we want and the public expects. Unless and until we have call on community resources we will be
unable to compensate *to any extent* for the brute fact of limited
resources."

If I have no objections to appealing to people's altruism,
neither do I expect such appeals to be very fruitful. It is not

that I think people generally are without altruistic feelings but rather that the appeal to self-interest (which is not to be confused with selfishness) is far more likely to be fruitful. If that is true, as my experience clearly suggests, the task of the educator is to be as knowledgeable as possible about the self-interests of community individuals and agencies so as to be able to determine when the self-interests of educators and others can result in an exchange of resources.

No money, no resources. When educators begin to see that this is not as true as it needs to be or should be, that what they have may be seen by others (in terms of their self-interests) as assets, that bartering for and exchanging resources can engender and sustain satisfying and productive relationships, that the failure to accept the fact that resources are always limited constrains creativity in thinking and acting—in short, when educators can begin to alter their way of defining resources, the concept of community participation will become more than what it now is: empty, unproductive rhetoric.

On any one day hundreds (perhaps thousands) of academics are carrying out research in schools. Their expectation is that schools have an *obligation* to permit research because the findings will add to the cumulative knowledge about how to improve schooling. I italicize obligation to emphasize that the appeal is to the altruism that schools should act on, that is, their permission will not bring them resources they can utilize to deal with the concrete problems of their concrete schools but rather it will discharge the moral obligation to contribute to knowledge. As generations of researchers can testify, schools have rarely enthusiastically rolled out the welcome mat. Schools have perceived, and rightly so, that they were entering a one-way street relationship. The researcher was crystal clear about his or her self-interests, but the schools felt they were being exploited, that whatever satisfaction they might experience from allowing the researcher to do his or her thing was small recompense for what they were giving. (But it does say something positive about the appeal to altruism that many schools have given permission.)

Why is it that I have never known school people to say

to a researcher: "We know what your needs are. Let us tell you what our needs are and see what you can do for us. Perhaps we can work out an exchange which would be mutually productive?" In order to adopt that approach several things have to be clear. The first, of course, is that you know what additional resources you would like to obtain for the school. The second is that you have determined the skills and interests of the researcher, neither of which may be fully (or at all) reflected in the research proposal. The third is that that determination suggests a possible match between a school need and a researcher's skills and interests. In other words, you do not look upon the researcher qua researcher but as a person with diverse skills and interests you can exploit for your self-interest, someone who can do something you would like done but for which you have neither the personnel or the funds. As long as you see a researcher *only* as a researcher, you have blinded yourself to and enormously narrowed your perception of the diverse "resources" the researcher *may* have that can be of use to you. "What do you have that I need, and what do I have that you need"—that is a stance that facilitates *redefining* people as resources, permitting you to go beyond stereotypes and categorical thinking. That point brings me to my second example.

> A colleague, Richard Sussman, visited a professor he had had in child development in Teachers College, Columbia University. He met with her and her graduate assistants to find out what research they were planning and carrying out in regard to schools. They outlined a series of researches they wished to do with elementary school children, research that would require several schools. However, they said, they had been unsuccessful in getting permission from schools to carry out the studies. At one point Sussman asked: "If I could make available to you a dozen highly selected high school seniors, would you and your assistants be willing to explain your study to them and train them to collect your data? [Asking that question reflected the fact that a high school with which he was

associated had a "problem" keeping bright, college-
bound seniors from goofing off in their final semester.]
Also, would you be willing to give them a mini course
in organizing and analyzing data?" Needless to say,
Sussman had determined that the high school students
were adequate to the tasks. Also, again needless to
say, the professor and her assistants did not look kindly
at his offer. Use high school students to collect data?
Teach them to organize and analyze data? Their reservations were dispelled when he played his trump card:
"If you are willing to use these students, I am quite
sure I can make available to you as many elementary
schools as you need." The project went so well that
at its completion the students were invited to give a
colloquium at Teachers College and later made a
presentation to their board of education. Money was
never in the picture.

To the college professor, high school students were high
school students, period. That is not unusual because when we
say that someone is a student, whether in the first grade or in
high school, we tend to be more impressed with what they do
not know and cannot do than with what they do know and are
interested in. It is only slightly unfair to say that our stereotype
of student emphasizes deficits and not assets. But it is not unfair to say that our tendency to categorize people — to attribute
to them all the characteristics of the abstract category — gets in
our way of redefining them, of seeing them as multifaceted individuals.

The above examples and discussion had several purposes.
The first was to show that the usual way educators (and people
generally) define people as resources adds, so to speak, insult
to the injury of limited resources. The second purpose was to
indicate that the usual way educators view the availability of
community resources limits using those resources in a quid pro
quo way. The third was to suggest that there are resources within
schools that are not exploited because they are seen (if not as
deficits) as without educationally exploitable assets. The fourth,

and most general, purpose was to alert the reader to the mischievous fallacy that there is nothing wrong with schools that increased funding will not correct. It was *not* among my purposes to deny in any way that there are many schools that lack the *minimal* (however defined) physical conditions, educational materials, and personnel required by considerations of equity and morality. Having said that, I must note that a few of these truly deplorable-looking schools seemed to have been forced to creatively redefine and exploit resources within and without the schools. These instances should not be used to buttress the argument that poverty is a good thing, but they do support the argument that there is a way of redefining resources that to a certain extent ameliorates the consequences of limited resources.[1]

Any form of governance justifies itself on assumptions about differences in the capabilities and knowledge of the governors and the governed. That is a glimpse of the obvious, but what is somewhat less obvious is that those assumptions lead the governors, far more often than not, to define the governed in unwarranted and narrow ways. The assumption that if you have no money you have no resources is a universal truth; so is the assumption that the governed lack all the resources possessed by the governed—if not all, then those that are perceived

---

[1] A number of years ago, in the process of collaborating on two books (Sarason and others, 1989 [1977]; Sarason and Lorentz, 1989 [1979]) concerned with resource exchange networks, I became aware of the obvious: between schools in the same system and between adjoining or nearby school systems, there was no exchange of resources, even though it was easy to demonstrate that an "asset" possessed by one school (usually a particular teacher of a particular subject matter) was a perceived "deficit" in another school, and that the latter school had an asset the other school lacked. That schools and school systems could or should exchange resources in mutually beneficial ways (to any degree for any length of time in any respect) is apparently unthinkable. I am indebted to my friend, Bruce Thomas, for bringing to my attention the Network of Complementary Schools, which is a group of schools around the country, public and private, joined together to serve their students in a unique way by sharing their specialized programs. "These schools, realizing that the number and range of options which they can individually provide their students is limited, saw that by pooling their offerings they could present their students a wider range of quality programs." I mention this network far less as a practical model for action but rather as an unusually clear instance of the principle of resource exchange. The interested reader should read the brochure of the network (79 Main Street, Dover, Massachusetts 02030).

as crucial by the governors. You can put it this way: if an individual in an organization has title A and his "superior" has title B, it is assumed that there is little or no overlap in the capabilities and skills between the two; there may be overlapping in sheer knowledge but not in skills, professional maturity, conceptual vision, and the ability to make appropriate decisions. Governors govern, the governed are followers — instruments of the governed.

More concretely, what has been the response of school administrators to the proposal that teachers have a more direct involvement in educational policy formulation and decisions? That proposal has been justified by its proponents on two grounds. The first is that because teachers are affected by policies and decisions they should have a voice in them. That is a moral-political argument. The second is that teachers have knowledge and capabilities which, if recognized and exploited, will contribute to more effective policies and decisions. That is the "resource" argument — that teachers are not simply teachers whose knowledge, skills, and capabilities are applicable only in encapsulated classrooms, but by virtue of their experience in classrooms they have much to contribute to educational policy and decisions. In brief, as long as you define teachers in the customary way, you cannot recognize and exploit the resources, actual or potential, that teachers possess. If you redefine what you mean by teachers, you increase the resources available to you.

The definition or redefinition of teachers as resources is barely alluded to in preparatory programs, even though the definition of self, both in the personal and professional sense, will predictably be a source of conflict and frustration. Almost every aspect of these programs focuses on the teacher in the classroom, that is, how he or she should govern students, ignoring how the teacher will experience and cope with the governors. It is not surprising, therefore, that only when teachers begin their careers do they experience what it means essentially to have no voice in school governance. Not only are they not prepared for that kind of experience; they do not possess a rationale for justifying redefining themselves as resources.

This glaring omission has had the unfortunate consequences of engendering in teachers a reluctance, even a fear,
to assume responsibility for anything beyond the confines of their
encapsulated classroom. That is bad enough, but in many instances — my experience, albeit obviously limited, leads me to
say all instances — where teachers have gained more voice and
responsibility, they find that nothing in their training prepared
them for how to cope with an enlarged role. No preparatory
program can do more than to alert its students to what they
predictably will encounter and to provide them technical, moral,
and political principles with which to cope with these predictable problems. No preparatory program can and should be a
complete substitute for learning by the seat of your pants. But
it is inexcusable for a preparatory program to fail to expose its
students to the predictable problems they will have to cope with
in matters of school governance, matters that directly or indirectly influence what goes on in the classroom. This omission
in preparatory programs can be justified only by those who believe that the phenomenology of teachers in regard to school
and school system governance has no bearing on what happens
in a classroom. That belief makes as much sense as one that
states how you conduct yourself at work is in no way influenced
by what is happening in your family.

How have school administrators responded to the proposal to redefine teachers as resources in regard to school governance? It should occasion no surprise that their response has
been, to indulge understatement, very negative. From what I
have said above, one has to conclude that their objections are
not wholly without merit. But when you examine their objections, they reduce to one major assertion: teachers lack the formal training (and the knowledge that goes with it) to appreciate and effectively contribute to the administrative complexities
that accompany policy formulation and decision making. This
assertion assumes that the resources necessary as a basis for effective policy and decision making can be learned, comprehended,
and utilized only by those who have completed a preparatory
program for administrators. Absent such formal training, what
does a teacher have to contribute to policy and decisions? This

stance implies that the teacher has seen and experienced nothing that would justify a role in policy and decision making. In such matters the teacher is without assets and with deficits. The governed should leave important educational matters to the governors whose superior training has equipped them for responsibility.

I am reminded here of a professional controversy that raged after World War II, a controversy that has lost steam and point. Who should be allowed to do psychotherapy? Psychiatrists-physicians said that *of course* only they had the training to discharge the responsibilities that come with the practice of psychotherapy. Over the next couple of decades that position was challenged by clinical psychologists, social workers, school psychologists, and others. They had no trouble pointing out nonmedical people who were incontrovertibly successful psychotherapists. They were able to demonstrate that by its nature, medical training contained features inimical to the practice of effective psychotherapy, and that the special training psychiatrists obtained was largely psychological and not medical. The medical community was in effect contending that the training and experience of the challengers, however valuable in other respects, did not give them the resources required to practice psychotherapy. The response of the challengers was this: "We will no longer permit you to define us as resources in your terms. We will no longer define ourselves in terms of the limitations within which you want us to stay. We have the knowledge, skills, and capabilities to contribute to the unmet personal needs of many people." There was, in the two decades after the war, a kernel of truth to the psychiatrists' position that the formal training and experience of the challengers was not all it should be. But it was *not* the psychiatrists' position that there was any basis on which one should be allowed to practice psychotherapy short of four years of medical school, internship, and special residencies. Absent that background, psychotherapy was off limits for you; you lacked the appropriate resources. Their stance, like that of school administrators, was "If you want to do what I do, get the formal training I did." That is defining resources only in terms of formal training, the kind of defining that all too often contributes to the most narrow, unwarranted perception of the resources possessed by those who lack that formal training—a way of defining that undergirds professional preciousness and imperialism. Today, the "psychotherapy wars" are over, a relic in the museum of fallacious assumptions behind conceptions of resources, human or otherwise, actual or potential. A fascinating feature of the post–World War II era is the number of groups who refused to accept any longer the way they had been defined by custom and tradition, and who then redefined themselves as possessing far more assets than their previous "governors" had conceded to them (Sarason, 1977).

I am not opposed to formal, preparatory programs, whether for teachers or administrators. I do argue against the assumption that anyone who has not been certified by a formal program has nothing to contribute to those who have been certified. When that assumption, rarely verbalized and even more rarely discussed, becomes in the most subtle ways part of one's outlook, it contributes to a devaluing perception of the assets of those in other roles and to an unreflective rejection and resentment of proposals in opposition to the assumption. To the extent that each type of professional within an organization defines resources only or even largely in terms of formally attained credentials, two things are guaranteed: limited resources will be more limited than they need be, and there will be interprofessional struggle and conflict. In order to redefine one's conception and definition of resources one has to be willing to alter power relationships, that is, the nature and direction of power relationships. That, apparently, is a type of change few people are voluntarily able to contemplate and implement. It takes the symbolic equivalent of a loaded gun to get most people to accept such a change.

Where I fault preparatory programs is their failure to deal with the psychological, political, moral, and economic aspects of the relationship between resources and governance—how governance style and structure affect and are affected by how resources are defined. My criticism is not that they do not (or may not) see that relationship the way I do but that it is handled in an egregiously superficial way. As I said earlier, when I have asked proponents of the status quo to spell out their rationale, what they offer cannot be labeled as a rationale but as rhetoric that has little depth or breadth; it is defensively reactive and raises visions of catastrophe if the status quo is changed, concluding that the problem is a need by the governors for more unfettered power. At the very least, I would expect that preparatory programs would enable students to understand the differences among competing views of the relationships between governances and resources. And by *understand,* I mean the ability to see these differences in a historical context in which issues of power and governance have been given salience and urgency which, in light of public dissatisfaction, will not go away and, indeed, will give rise to nostrums that bespeak more of desperation than of reasoned conviction. There are times when defense of the status quo is justified. Are these times, in regard to matters educational, to defend the status quo? If you so believe, it is in your self-interest to come up with a defense that is intellectually, philosophically, and empirically respectable. I have yet to hear such a defense.

What I have been saying has been in regard to how administrators see teachers as resources in the formulation of educational policy and in decision making. *In principle, the issues I have raised are identical to those in the case of teachers as governors and students as the governed.* The usual exceptions aside, teachers have been taught to view students as having few resources relevant to the attainment of educational goals. Their preparation has not enabled them to unlearn the attitude that students are, for all practical purposes, without resources. And by practical I mean in relation to having a voice (which is not to be equated with a vote) in classroom governance and in taking individual and group responsibility for learning. It is an attitude that says: "Students *need* to be governed, to be *given* the rules of governance, *to set aside* their diverse interests and curiosities, to learn what *we* know they need to learn, to conform *now* in order *later* in life to give expression to their interests and curiosities, to *respect* and *accept* the superior wisdom of their governors." It is an attitude based on the fact (and it is a fact) that students are inexperienced, unsophisticated, and in need of guidance and direction. But it is not a fact that students are uninterested in governance, that they are indifferent to it, that they neither want or need a voice in governance, that they do not relish a role of responsibility, that how they experience governance does not color their experience of subject matter, that their interests and curiosities are antithetical (or at least not relevant) to subject matter. Most teachers fail to recognize these truths. A glaring omission in their preparatory programs allows them to view students as without resources to partake in matters of governance or to assume significant responsibility for individual and small group learning of subject matter. In point of fact, students have the crucial resources of interests, curiosities, and a potent desire to feel worthy and "grown up."

Let us not overlook one other resource: however young the school child, that child has had experience in being governed. Being governed is not a new experience for the child. So when we say that students are inexperienced and unsophisticated, it does not mean they are without resources that can be capitalized on to begin to enlarge both their experience and their sophistication. The idea that "some day" far in the future they will be experienced, sophisticated, and responsible and until then we should regard them otherwise, is worse than nonsense. It is self-defeating of the purposes both of the governors and the governed.

Classrooms are, generally speaking, uninteresting places. They do not engender in students a commitment to and satisfaction from the pursuit of learning. This lack of personal commitment is kin to the lack of commitment that gets stronger in teachers in regard to their schools as the years go by. As teachers resign themselves to being perceived as having competencies only in their encapsulated classrooms — that what they know and have experienced is unwanted by their governors — why should one expect that they can sustain commitment? Similarly, indeed identically, as students with each passing year resign themselves to the role of passive, resourceless, powerless objects of the purposes of their governors, why should one expect them to feel worthy and growing up?

How you are governed is determined, among other things,

by how you are being defined—what resources, actual or potential, you are perceived as possessing. Governance and resources are not separate variables. *They are indissolubly related and very much determine how subject matter will be presented and experienced.* Far from being an "independent" variable, subject matter is enmeshed in the relationship between governance and the definition of resources.

Some school reformers will agree with everything I have said and will also know that it is a 1992 summary of what John Dewey said early in this century, what Alfred North Whitehead said in the twenties and thirties, and what John Goodlad has said (with data) in recent decades.[2] I lay no claim to originality. I do lay claim to the predictions I began to make in the sixties that if we do not take seriously the words of these and similar thinkers, the fruits of schooling will become increasingly unpalatable.

School reformers know one other thing: changing the attitudes and practices of school personnel is as difficult as it is necessary. I have never met a school reformer who did not struggle against the perception that he or she was trying to level a mountain with a teaspoon. I speak from a fair amount of experience with schools as they are. It took me years to begin to see clearly how the reform movement was one of repair, not primary prevention. It should not have taken years because the prevention theme was both implicit and explicit in *The Preparation of Teachers: An Unstudied Problem in Education,* written by Kenneth Davidson, Burton Blatt, and me in 1962, and reprinted in 1989. The question we posed three decades ago is what informs the present book: how can we prepare school personnel so that they are more sensitive to the realities of schools and less likely to need reformers to help them cope with problems that today suffuse the ambience of schools and the lives of their inhabitants?

---

[2]Misinterpreting, indeed misreading and misquoting, John Dewey has long been a cottage industry. There are people today—some who have read snatches of Dewey and many more who have read nothing—who identify "permissiveness" with him. Dewey was not the most felicitous writer but to identify him with permissiveness betrays either motivated ignorance or dyslexia. I urge the interested reader to read R. B. Westbrook's *John Dewey and American Democracy,* published in 1991, especially the chapters on education.

Just as we view Head Start as a deliberate preventive effort to inoculate children against the viruses of low achievement and disinterest, so must we view the preparation of school personnel. And, I must remind the reader, that preventive stance was what undergirded Abraham Flexner's 1909 recommendations about the preparation of medical personnel.

In an earlier chapter I discussed parents as educational resources, but only in regard to providing information about their child to the teacher and forging a collaborative relationship with the teacher. By collaboration I do not mean cooperation, which far more often than not in practice conveys a one-way street message: "Let me tell you what you can do for me." There is nothing inherently wrong with that message except when the conveyor implicitly conveys the additional message: "This is my turf so please do not intrude." The best example of this territoriality is the nature of PTA-school relationships in which parents are expected to be supportive in ways defined by school personnel; needless to say, that definition does not include meaningful participation in classroom practices and school policy. That stance, of course, is justified on the basis that parents do not possess resources relevant to either arena.

It is a stance by no means peculiar to professional educators. It long was a stance characteristic of the doctor-patient relationship. The doctor decided what needed to be done, frequently not telling the patient the universe of alternatives which the doctor had considered and the difference in consequences associated with each alternative. Doctor knew best. The obligation of the patient was to cooperate dutifully with the doctor's decision. Since when do you give patients the responsibility to decide what is the best course of action for their condition? Give patients that responsibility and God only knows what the untoward consequences will be! Until recent decades that stance was accepted by patients, no questions asked. It was accepted to the point that only the rare patient requested more information, let alone a second opinion. And it was very infrequent that a patient would sue the physician for malpractice. The patient was perceived as having no resources relevant to courses of action, and patients so perceived themselves. The patient's task was to cooperate with the physician, *not* collaborate because collaboration means, at least to me, that each of the parties has rights and resources that should be reflected by their explicit presence in decision making, and for two reasons. The first is, obviously, moral: if what my doctor is recommending will have significant effects on me, I have a right to decide whether I will go along. I do not want to feel that I am powerless to participate in decisions significant for my body and life. I do not want to feel that I am being "governed" in ways that assume I am an ignoramus incapable of seeking and contributing information, questioning opinions and practices, and making decisions. If this first reason is moral, it is also political because I do not want to feel or be powerless. I find it hard to label the second reason but it goes this way: "Of course my physician has much more medical knowledge and experience than I do. In this regard, we are not equals. But we are equals in our capacity to be wrong, to choose unwisely among alternatives, to ignore or overlook important factors. In addition, I am well aware that possessing as he does superior experience and knowledge, my physician, *like all other professionals,* may not take kindly to my need to understand what is at stake, to make decisions, and will view me as challenging his professional competency. He prefers that I cooperate, not collaborate with him."

I assume the reader is aware that in recent decades the moral and political nature of the doctor-patient relationship has undergone change. This shift is reflected in the exponential increase in malpractice suits, but that in turn is a reflection of a more widespread change in the attitude of people generally about having a voice in regard to policies (for example, environmental) that will affect them. Hospitals now have posted a "declaration of patient rights" and an increasing number of physicians — by no means a staggering number — are far more informative to their patients than in earlier decades. Indeed, in some states there is legislation that mandates "full disclosure."

A similar change has been occurring in education. The first and most dramatic example of the change is the "civil rights" section of the 1975 Public Law 94-142 for the Education of Handicapped Children. Those sections spell out in detail the rights

of parents to be informed about and meaningfully to participate in decisions about their handicapped children. One of the
people who helped draft that law told me that its aim was to
make it difficult, legally impermissible, for educators to make
unilateral decisions as they were accustomed to do. More recently, several states have mandated a role for parents in school
governance undreamed of two or three decades ago.

Again I have to say that nothing in my recent experiences
with new teachers alters my conclusion that preparatory programs are unconscionably deficient in helping their students understand the historical social context from which these changes
have emerged, the political-moral-philosophical issues involved,
the rationales for differing views, the predictable problems educators have and will confront, and the different ways these predictable problems might be coped with. These new teachers were
simply unprepared to think about the issues except in terms of
a power struggle. None of them saw kinship with parents redefining themselves as resources as *a reaction to the perceived inadequacies of schools and to the insensitivities of educators.* These teachers
have no trouble accepting the rhetoric of cooperation. Collaboration is another dangerous, power altering, governance changing affair. If these teachers see no similarity between how they
react to how they are governed and how students react to their
governors, they also do not feel kinship with how parents feel
about how educators prefer to govern them.

I am not partisan to the view that lay people (including
students) have a kind and degree of folk wisdom that professionals lack. That you are a parent (or a patient) does not mean
that you have a corner on truth or wisdom. What it does mean
is that you have a vested interest in what schools are and do
and that you see schools differently from the professionals. You
are a stakeholder with two obligations: to represent your interests
and to seek to understand the nature and complexity of *educational* issues. Those obligations hold no less for the professional
educator. But, as has been too frequently the case in recent days,
when parents and educators have been *required* to collaborate
we have gotten power struggles, direct and indirect, that have
had the unintended consequences of not coming to grips with

educational issues. If schools are not what we would like them to be, it is not *only* because of who had power to decide what, but also because of failure on the part of those with power to question the validity of their views about the social contexts that make for productive learning for everyone in the school: students, teachers, and administrators.

Let us also acknowledge that almost all the changes designed to make life in the classroom and school more intellectually and socially stimulating, to forge collaborative relationships between educators and parents, could have been recognized, accepted, and implemented before there was legislation, pressure, and exploding adversarial conflicts. It was not that power was an obstacle but that it was undergirded by conceptions of learning that were both invalid and self-defeating. Altering power relationships has no value if those alterations do not achieve the end of nurturing the needs of everyone in the school to experience a sense of intellectual and personal growth. The American colonists did not go to war with their English governors *only* to gain power but rather to gain that power to attain and protect articulated values.

Chapter Twelve

Collegiality, Resources, and Governance

My basic assumption throughout the previous chapters has been that preparatory programs should not prepare educators to conform to schools as they currently are. It is not sufficient for these programs to acquaint their students with the predictable personal and professional problems they will encounter, although that would be an improvement over what the programs do now. I have argued that they should provide their students with ways of thinking about how schools should change if life in school is to be more productive both for educators and students. Please note that I did not say "way" of thinking but rather "ways" of thinking about the universe of alternatives for change. However enamored I may be about my way of thinking — and I am quite aware of the deceptive consequences of enamorments — I have to assume that there is more than one way to think about the obligation of educators to seek and take responsibility for other than cosmetic changes.

If there is more than one way, I trust there is agreement that no preparatory program can any longer justify its existence if it does not provide its students a rationale for school change *and* the obligation to seek to act on it. In other words, these programs have a moral, professional, and educational obligation to try to prevent those predictable dynamics that have adverse consequences both for educators and for students. There are those who out of ignorance, lack of experience, or a resistance to reading proclaim that we know next to nothing about what and how we should improve schools. In reality, we have learned a good deal, albeit we would have preferred not to have learned

203

it as we have. One thing we have learned is that far too frequently a career in education has stultifying, self-defeating features that spread their effects to students.

Given the nature of life in schools, I would argue that the question is not why schools are as bad as they appear to be but why they are as good as they are. I do not say this facetiously. It is a conclusion that a noneducator could reach by reading Farber's recent *Crisis in Education* (1991). His book provides evidence as good as we have for recasting preparatory programs from the standpoint of prevention. We do know what we want to prevent; we just don't take that knowledge seriously. And by *we* I mean not only policymakers in officialdom but educators as well. Our knowledge notwithstanding, we want to believe that we can improve matters without altering governance, power relationships, and basic assumptions. I trust that what follows will not be seen as a digression but as an appropriate analogy to what has been happening in public education.

Today we are witness to one of the truly momentous events of this century: the dissolution of the Soviet Union. Why has this come to most people as a complete, bewildering surprise? To most people the tyrannical rulers of that empire not only were firmly in power but their governance structure and style, at least minimally, met the psychological and material needs of those they governed. In fact, our foreign policy rested on the assumption that the Soviet system of governance was sufficiently effective (economically, politically, and psychologically) so as to represent a threat we had to contain. If our leaders viewed the Soviet Union as an abomination, an "evil empire," they grudgingly respected its control and use of its human and material resources. We saw what we thought we saw, we believed the statistics the governors paraded before the world, despite two things. The first was the gut feeling that it was inconceivable that the Soviet people (and those in the Soviet satellites) were relatively content with the way they were governed, that is, it did not make sense to the "psychology" of Westerners. The second was that there were a few analysts who said that Soviet statistics, far from being either reliable or trustworthy, masked an egregiously inefficient and even a decaying economic system that inevitably would collapse.

Then came Gorbachev who confirmed the validity of the gut feeling and the economic disaster the Soviet Union was facing. What had appeared to be, again relatively speaking, a stable, self-sustaining society had been going downhill for a long time. When after the Russian revolution Lincoln Steffens visited the Soviet Union, he came back saying, "I have seen the future and it is here." Gorbachev forced people to say, "We have seen the past, and its barren fruits are here."

The point of these comments is not that *we* were surprised and had to change our views but that *Gorbachev* made the mistake of believing that the situation in his country could be improved without a fundamental, truly radical alteration in power relationships between the Communist party and the people. The governed knew, certainly felt, otherwise. Let us not forget that Yeltsin and Gorbachev were colleagues and friends and that they parted ways when Yeltsin concluded that the Communist party was a problem to be rendered impotent or abolished and in no way could be part of a solution. It was a conclusion the Soviet people had themselves reached.

Changing power relationships and governance in our schools is a necessary but not sufficient condition for the attainment of our goals (a fact the Russian people are today quite aware of). Unless those changes are informed by a redefinition of existing resources, the consequences of them are problematic. In previous chapters I have discussed and challenged the conventional view of teachers, students, and parents as resources. Here I wish to discuss other facets of the definition and utilization of resources. Let us start with a concrete, "live" example:

A suburban school was chosen as a demonstration site for the placement of certain community programs: a day-care center for prekindergarten youngsters, a center for parent education, and after-school programs for school children of working parents. In *The Predictable Failure of Educational Reform* I indicated why those demonstrations, which will become more frequent in the coming years, will fall short of the mark, given the way they were conceived and how they virtually lacked an implementation rationale. From what I and others have recently observed, my predictions are, unfortunately, being confirmed.

The future validity of my predictions is not at issue here. I mention this site in order to ask several questions: if a school (in this case a high school) has a day-care center, how can it be used for the intellectual-educational growth of students? Can, should, such a center be justified only in terms of the service it renders to parents and their preschool children? Is it a "resource" of no relevance to the education of older students? Is it a place about which the older students have neither curiosity nor interest? Is there no part of the formal curriculum for which this center can be exploited? When we say that schooling should be a "growth experience" do we mean experience only in encapsulated classrooms (except for the occasional bus trip to a museum or the local newspaper)? Is such a center lacking in resources for courses in biology, social studies, and (in many high schools) psychology?

Let me answer these questions by relating what has gone on for years in a *middle* school on Long Island. Each of two to three hundred students spend several hours in community agencies, for example, nursing homes, senior citizen centers, programs for cerebral palsied and other handicapped individuals, day-care centers, and so on. Associated with these field experiences is a "seminar" devoted to helping the students make personal-educational-intellectual sense of their experience. When the program started, the community agencies were by no means enthusiastic about having middle school "children" in their midst. Their reservations quickly dissipated as they learned to redefine and utilize "middle school children." That was no less true for parents who had to give permission for their children to participate.

I know and have met with the key people who created and sustained the Long Island program, an infrequent but not rare kind of program. I have not presented it here as meeting all of its goals in exemplary ways. My purpose has not been only to applaud what they *did* but rather the *thinking* that informed their actions. My purpose was really twofold: to suggest again how and why we must redefine what and who is an exploitable resource, and to contrast that program to those in the surburban high school *where there is absolutely no relationship between the day-care center and the educational program of the school.*

That there are few efforts like the Long Island program is explainable, in part at least, by the complete absence in preparatory programs of how one defines, redefines, and utilizes resources. In the coming years there will be a steady increase in the number of schools in which human services will be housed. This shift will come about on grounds of parental needs and efficiency in the provision of services. It has not, and apparently will not, come about because the advocates of such programs have any idea of the educational purposes these programs can serve for both students and teachers.

If these programs increase in numbers, what should preparatory programs do in preparing educators to capitalize on such changes in schools? What gives force to the question is not only that the world, educational and otherwise, is changing but that the introduction of these programs into schools is bringing a clash between the culture of the schools and the culture of the human services. In almost all the instances I know or have heard about, the clash manifests itself in walled boundaries between representatives of the two cultures; this phenomenon is a source of regret and disappointment. Especially worrisome is the frequency of open conflict on grounds of space, turf, and purpose. Should not preparatory programs help the would-be educator play a preventive role, that is, prevent walled boundaries and open conflict?

In earlier chapters and previous books I have suggested that schools will have to be more creative and courageous about their conceptions and use of community resources for educational purposes. I cannot deny that, generally speaking, educators have not been creative, courageous, or entrepreneurial in these regards. What I do deny is the criticism that implies (it is sometimes explicit) that *as people* (as "minds") educators are incapable of being more than they are. There are too many instances in which "ordinary" educators have demonstrated the contrary. And we have learned enough to know that the preparation for and a career in education are not embedded in contexts that engender and support creativity, courage, and educational entrepreneurialship.

It is strange that those who damn the intellectual and personal credentials of educators see no logical inconsistency when they go on to damn the intellectual ambience of schools, as if there is no possibility that the ambience may be, at least in part, as much cause as it is effect, as if socialization into a career is of no significance. Those kinds of critics seem completely unaware of the logical traps they set for themselves when they resort to ad hominem arguments, the kinds used in the past (and even in the present) in regard to women, minorities, and those who differ politically, religiously, and culturally from critics. Undergirding their reasoning seems to be the axiom that when in doubt blame genes and biology. Would that it were so simple!

Let us now look at another facet of the definition and utilization of resources. Here is how I have expressed it on several occasions in meetings with the faculty of a school:

> I am going to put to you some questions I would like you to ponder for several minutes. Really, it is one question with several variants. The first question is, what information, skills, hobbies, interests do you have that are or may be relevant to the education of children — not necessarily relevant to the particular age group you happen to be teaching but to some students somewhere in the school system. Some of you are married so I ask you also to think about the question in regard to your spouses. Is there anything they know, or have done, or are doing that would be education-

ally and intellectually instructive to some groups of students? The final question is similar but concerns the parents of your students. They may be parents of children you are now teaching or others you happen to know.

Please do not be concerned with the practical problem of whether the particular "resources" you and others possess can be made available for educational purposes. Assume that there is no practical problem. What are the special resources potentially available to you, resources that can have payoff for students? Please take a piece of paper and simply list what those resources are.

Several things were noteworthy about the reactions and responses of the groups to whom I put the questions. The first was from those teachers who had strong, long-standing skills, hobbies, or interests that they in no way utilized in their classrooms or who never thought that what they possessed could be utilized elsewhere. The best example was the teacher who only in discussion revealed that he had a large stamp collection that he had never considered relevant to social studies, geography, history, or arithmetic. Another example was the teacher who had a voluminous collection of photographs and newspaper accounts of Italian immigrants arriving at Ellis Island. It was not on her list of personal resources because it never occurred to her that it could have educational value for others. Generally speaking, the skills, interests, and hobbies of teachers were in a psychological world unrelated to that of children in classrooms.

The second interesting reaction had to do with spouses. Here, too, but to a lesser degree than with the teacher's personal resources, the educational relevance of what spouses did tended to be ignored on the lists of teachers. For example, the wife of one math teacher was the chief nurse in the operating room of the local hospital; this information came out in discussion but the teacher had great difficulty justifying its potential in instruction. One husband was a home builder, but his teaching wife had not listed this information and strenuously resisted my suggestion that building homes was a fruitful means of illustrating the significance of geometry, physics, economics, and more. Then there was the husband whose wife had not listed his occupation: owner of a large, regional private garbage collecting business. When this came out in discussion, I did not have to say anything because several teachers in the group immediately saw the relevance of his business to the chemistry, biology, economics, and quandaries of waste disposal. I bless the teacher in that group who had the courage to ask: "I really have long been curious about how human urine and feces are disposed of in a spaceship, especially the ones that stay in outer space for weeks or months." So was I and everybody else in that room.

The third noteworthy reaction was reflected in the fact that parents as resources appeared infrequently on lists. If I had to guess, I would say that three-quarters of the teachers knew little or nothing about parental occupations, interests, or hobbies. If I limited myself to high school teachers, the percentage would be nearer 90 percent.

The point of the exercise was to indicate that there are resources potentially available and, if available, quite relevant to educational purposes, to teachers. That was the obvious point. A less obvious one was that even if those resources were available, their utilization would be difficult given the way schools and school days are organized. It is unfair to say that schools are organized like an assembly line in a car factory. But it is not unfair to say that they are organized around and wedded to such narrow conception of curriculum as to make departures from routine require a degree of courage and innovativeness for which educational medals of honor should be given.

I do not believe that educators are uncreative and unimaginative but rather that those characteristics are neither nurtured nor reinforced in preparatory programs or schools. Beginning in preparatory programs and continuing into their socialization as independent practitioners they learn a rigid conception of the school day, week, month, and year, one that expresses a routine as ludicrous as the travel schedule caricatured in the title of the movie *If It's Tuesday, This Must Be Belgium.* We should remember, however, that a caricature is a reflection of reality; it has force for us to the degree that it distorts reality in order to emphasize one or several significant facets of it. The isolation of teachers and their students in an encapsulated physical space instills in them, subtly but pervasively, the narrowest of conceptions of who and what are educational resources, potential or actual. When, as in the exercise in which I engaged them, educators find redefining resources a difficult process and imagining ways of using them an exercise in futile fantasy, it should occasion no surprise. Creativity, imaginativeness, and spontaneity in individuals are almost always functions of present or past contexts. Neither for teachers or students are schools a nurturing context for these characteristics. To blame educators is to blame the victim.

There was one more not so obvious point to the exercise. It is less a point than a predictable consequence that teachers (on their own) found surprising. *Teachers knew amazingly little about their colleagues' or colleagues' spouses' interests, skills, and hobbies. The lack of collegiality in intellectual-educational issues was rivaled by a similar lack of personal collegiality.* Both lacks have no simple explanation but to an undetermined (and I would say large) extent they reflect a style of school governance that tends to make school personnel strangers to each other. And if strangers is too strong a word, I will accept any word or phrase that conveys the superficiality of relationships among personnel in a school. Of course there are exceptions. But that is what they are: exceptions.

Two "messages" are currently being broadcast. The first is that the traditional governance style of schools has to be altered. The second and related message is that high on the list of governance changes should be a greater role for teachers. There is really a third message: things are so bad that any suggested change that is not truly radical should be given short shrift. This last message comes almost exclusively from corporate executives (for example, see pp. 176–178 in *The Predictable Failure of Educational Reform* [1990b]). The latest and refreshing instance is the effort of the recently formed National Learning Foundation to bring attention to the approach of W. Edwards Deming, reputed to be the one individual most influential in helping

Japanese industrialists and business leaders adopt a new view of governance and its educational, resource-defining implications. Anne D. Forester prepared for the National Learning Foundation illuminating examples of and contrasts between Deming's and traditional approaches.[1] Tables 12.1 and 12.2 speak for themselves.

Explicit and implicit in these tables are, first, a change in power relations within the classroom; second, a challenge to the traditional ways in which educators, students, and community people are defined as resources; and, third, a view of collegiality in stark contrast to what school personnel view and experience.

There is always a "but." In the case of these increasingly frequent formulations my "but" is in two parts. The first is to confront realistically all the obstacles these reform efforts will encounter in getting educators to alter their accustomed view of their roles and responsibility. Not only educators in schools but boards of education, political leaders, and parents must be involved. Any meaningful effort at reform has to deal with a variety of people who differ in knowledge, attitudes, roles, power, and responsibility. So, when I hear the advocates of governance change make their persuasive case, and when I observe what too frequently happens where that change is being implemented, I applaud their efforts *but* at the same time have to conclude that the disparity between energy expended and results achieved is cause for appreciation and not enthusiasm.

As any psychotherapist will attest, changing the personal-psychological life-style of a single individual is no easy task. Effecting such a change in many individuals embedded in a com-

[1]The National Learning Foundation has an office in Washington, D.C. The rationale for and materials about this new foundation are contained in materials available from it. Whether this fledgling organization obtains support to sustain it and whether it succeeds in having an influence are open questions at this time. Nevertheless, it is a refreshing new voice. Those who have read *The Predictable Failure of Educational Reform* (1990b) may recall my discussion of Carl Frost's analysis and application of the Scanlon Plan to industrial organizations. His book with Wakeley and Ruh (1974) *The Scanlon Plan for Organization Development: Identity, Participation, and Equity* has many points of correspondence with Deming's rationale, and it has the virtue of greater specificity.

Table 12.1. Parallels Between Deming's Fourteen Points
for Management and Current Trends in Education.

Management	Education
1. Create constancy of purpose toward improvement of product and service, with the aim to become competitive and to stay in business, and to provide jobs.	1. Creates constancy of purpose toward improvement of service to students and the community, with the aim of enhancing learning for ALL students and making education relevant to their lives both in school and beyond.
2. Adopt a new philosophy. We are in a new economic age. Western management must awaken to the challenge, must learn their responsibilities and take on leadership for a change.	2. Adopts a new philosophy. We are in an information age, and leaders in education are shifting focus on curricula and products of education to a focus on learners and their best ways of functioning. By affirming that students are effective learners and building upon their strengths, teachers are creating a climate for lifelong learning in which creativity and productivity far outstrip the traditional curricula-driven model.
3. Cease dependence on inspection to achieve quality. Eliminate the need for inspection on a mass basis by building quality into the product in the first place.	3. Ceases dependence on tests and examinations to achieve quality. Eliminates the need for frequent testing by building ongoing evaluation into the teaching/learning interactions between teachers and students, students and their peers, and students with their own work. Instead of interrupting the flow of learning, the process-bound evaluation enhances it and teaches students how to examine their own work and improve it.
4. End the practice of awarding business on the basis of price tag. Instead, minimize total cost. Move toward a single supplier for any one item, on a long-term relationship of loyalty and trust.	4. Ends the practice of dwelling on the cost of quality education and looks instead for effective ways of fostering learning by using the loyalty and team work of a dedicated staff and the support services available in the community.
5. Improve constantly and forever the system of production and service, to	5. Improves constantly and forever the ways of delivering services to the

Table 12.1. Parallels Between Deming's Fourteen Points
for Management and Current Trends in Education, Cont'd.

Management	Education
improve quality and productivity, and thus constantly decrease costs.	students by observing closely what is productive for them, how they function best, and what encourages them to excel.
6. Institute training on the job.	6. Institutes in-house in-service training in which teachers collaborate in the same productive way their students collaborate in class working on issues and challenges that have direct relevance to their lives.
7. Institute leadership. The aim of supervision should be to help people and machines and gadgets to do a better job. Supervision and management is in need of overhaul as well as supervision of production workers.	7. Institutes leadership that encourages teachers and staff to function freely, to work as a team on all levels and that creates the same positive climate for working that teachers create in the classrooms for their students.
8. Drive out fear, so that everyone may work effectively for the company.	8. Drives out fear so that learning can flow unhampered by fear of failure, fear of reprisals, fear of ridicule or the embarrassment of low marks. Safety to learn for student and safety to function as competent professionals for teachers are high priorities and part of the new philosophy of teaching/learning.
9. Break down barriers between departments. People in research, design, sales, and production must work as a team, to foresee problems of production and in use that may be encountered with the product or service.	9. Breaks down barriers between learning disciplines and fosters writing across the curriculum, reading across the curriculum and content-learning through projects and themes that integrate all areas of learning. It also eliminates the barriers of age, sex and ability levels and encourages students to work in teams within their own class and with students from other classes. And it helps teachers to cooperate and network with one another by team teaching, combining classes, drawing an entire school into a project or collaborating with other schools.

Table 12.1. Parallels Between Deming's Fourteen Points
for Management and Current Trends in Education, Cont'd.

Management	*Education*
10. Eliminate slogans, exhortations, and targets for the work force asking for zero defects and new levels of productivity. Such exhortations only create adversarial relationships, as the bulk of the causes of low quality and low productivity belong to the system and thus lie beyond the powers of the work force.	10. Eliminates lectures and exhortations about doing quality work that is free of mistakes. Such lectures only intimidate and antagonize students as few of them are shown appropriate models of what constitutes quality work and fewer still have been invited to discuss the rationale for doing good work and to agree upon standards of quality.
11a. Eliminate work standards (quotas) on the factory floor. Substitute leadership.	11a. Eliminates assignment quotas and substitutes leadership in the classroom whereby the teacher and fellow students model learning behaviors, the production of writing, steps in research and, above all, enthusiasm for learning and inquiry.
11b. Eliminate management by objective. Eliminate management by numbers, numerical goals. Substitute leadership.	11b. Eliminates learning objectives that suggest limited goals for learning and substitutes leadership in exploring new ways of extracting, analyzing and presenting material. Curiosity, the drive to know, to get accurate information and to present it in interesting ways become the energy that fuels learning.
12a Remove barriers that rob the hourly worker of his right to pride of workmanship. The responsibility of supervisors must be changed from sheer numbers to quality.	12a Remove barriers that rob students of their right to pride in their work. Instead of evaluating work in terms of quantity and numbers of jobs completed, teachers encourage students to polish their writing to its fullest luster, to delve into questions of science or mathematics to their fullest and to follow a project to its conclusion based on the students' judgment, not a time or curriculum constraint.
12b Remove barriers that rob people in management and in engineering of their right to pride of workmanship.	12b Removes barriers that rob teachers and principals of professional pride. Instead of setting specifi

Table 12.1. Parallels Between Deming's Fourteen Points
for Management and Current Trends in Education, Cont'd.

Management	Education
This means, inter alia, abolishment of the annual merit rating and of management by objective.	objectives for the year, teachers and principals interact as autonomous, collaborating professionals.
13. Institute a vigorous program of education and self-improvement.	13. Institutes a vigorous program of overall self-improvement that includes physical, social, aesthetic and creative development along with intellectual growth. In the interactive, collaborative climate of the classroom teachers and students are co-learners who grow and develop together on all levels.
14. Put everybody in the company to work to accomplish the transformation. The transformation is everybody's job.	14. Puts everyone in the school to work on creating a climate that transforms education. The climate that empowers students to become effective, independent learners includes everyone in the school. From the support staff to the principal, everyone is collaborating in creating a learning community.

Source: Forester, Anne D. "An Examination of Parallels Between Deming's Model for Transforming Industry and Current Trends in Education." Paper presented at the National Learning Foundation's TQE/TQM Seminar, Washington, D.C., Oct. 10, 1991.

plicated human system is galactically more difficult. This is no argument, of course, against such efforts. All that I am saying is obvious: repairing, redirecting, and reorganizing complicated social systems is not only hard work but inevitably results in a "success rate" which, like the outcomes in psychotherapy, is both discouraging and dispiriting. The base rate for successful repair of human problems, individual or collective, is not robust.

My second "but" is in the form of a question I have asked many times in these pages: Given the difficulties of the repair process as well as the fact that prevention is far more efficient than repair, how can we prepare educators who will be more understanding of, sophisticated about, and articulate concerning the rationale for changes in governance? If preparatory

Table 12.2. Using a Management Model
to Compare Teaching Styles.*

The Boss Teacher	The Lead Teacher
Decides what will be taught and how it will be learned	Sets the framework for learning but leaves room for options
Keeps strict control of all aspects of the classroom	Encourages students to make choices about their learning
Decides on the rules and on how to enforce them	Discusses reasons for rules and asks for students' input to formulate and enforce those rules
Keeps a strong focus on the curriculum to shape lessons and is more concerned with the *what* of learning than the *how*	Observes learners and their needs and interests to foster learning that fulfills students' needs as well as curriculum requirements
Tends to use the lecture format to convey information	Models the skills to be learned and uses experimental, hands-on work
Relies heavily on Cazden's (1988) IRE model—teacher Initiation, student Response, teacher Evaluation	Engages students in discussions about the relevance and quality of work undertaken in class and makes information sharing reciprocal
Tries to have all students work on the same job at the same time	Offers choices that fit the work to students' interests, abilities, maturity, and experience
Generally has students work by themselves	Often uses teamwork and cooperative learning
Generally is the chief information giver and initiator of jobs, themes, or projects	Encourages students to share information and to initiate projects
Relies on outside motivation— grades, praise—to urge students to work hard	Relies on the inner motivation of students to excel and trusts them to work to the best of their abilities
Sees education as serious business that needs to be shaped by a knowledgeable leader—the teacher	Sees learning as exciting, as fun, and as arising from students' own needs and curiosity stimulated by interesting work
Generally feels that students must be closely supervised to ensure that they do the work	Trusts students to work in their own ways and at their own pace
Relies largely on tests, work sheets, and examinations to evaluate students' progress	Uses informal observation and ongoing anecdotal records to evaluate students' progress and to enrich information derived from examinations

Table 12.2. Using a Management Model
to Compare Teaching Styles,* Cont'd.

The Boss Teacher	The Lead Teacher
Generally sees record keeping and evaluation as the teacher's job	Has students keep many of the records and uses their self-evaluations to augment teacher observation
Holds the power in the classroom	Empowers students to work freely on academic tasks while observing social rules that have been established cooperatively
Focuses on the end product of learning	Focuses on the process of learning
Manages the curriculum	Manages people

*Derived from William Glasser's "The Quality School: What Motivates the Ants?" *Phi Delta Kappan,* Feb. 1990: 424–435.
    Source: Forester, Anne D., and Margaret Reinhard. *On the Move — Teaching the Learners' Way in Grades 4–7.* Winnipeg, Canada: Peguis Publishers, 1991, pp. 40–41.

programs changed in accord with these goals, would the alteration prevent some of the problems the advocates for governance change now encounter? If your answer is, as it should be, in the affirmative — and no advocate for change has ever answered it in the negative — is it not strange that these advocates have so little to say about preparatory programs?

Should teachers be prepared in an undergraduate program? Should such preparation only be on the graduate level? By what processes and criteria should the performance of educators be evaluated? Who should play what role in the preparation of educators? How should we judge knowledge of subject matter? Should the preparation of educators be more clinical in terms of orientation and duration? These and similar questions have been raised in regard to preparatory programs. They are legitimate and thorny questions. But (there is always a but) in my opinion, and especially in regard to matters of governance and the definition of resources, they do not address the issue of how to prepare educators for the real world of changing schools in a changing society, a preparation that seeks to prevent the

development of untoward attitudes and practices no less consequential for students than for educators.

No one quarrels with the statement that schools exist to
further the personal and intellectual development of students.
It is an assertion that is both egregiously incomplete and misleading because it is not accompanied by a second assertion:
if what you want for students does not exist for educators, it
is impossible for educators to create and sustain the conditions
in which what you want for students can be achieved. And few
things contribute to that impossibility more than a program that
ill prepares educators for life in schools as they are and fails to
provide them both with a rationale for and an obligation to seek
change. I am not advocating that educators seek to change the
world. What I do advocate is that they seek changes which, to
an undeterminable extent, will prevent the worst features of disillusionment, resignation, and routinization of thought and practice. What you don't know can hurt you. Unfortunately, the
truth in that cliché is learned by educators after they leave their
preparatory programs. *Then* it is not a cliché; it is poignant experience.

It may have occurred to the reader that what I have said
about governance and resources should be as appropriate to the
governance of preparatory programs as it is to the schools the
students will work in. After all, preparatory programs consist
of teachers and students, albeit all adults; and the values and
criteria used to judge the relationships between the classroom
teacher and students, between teachers and administrators, between a teacher and other teachers should be no different from
those used to judge the relationships in preparatory programs.

There is more at issue than taking seriously a democratic
ethos. No less important is for us to begin to see that how we
are governed (or how we govern) mightily determines how every actor in the educational drama is defined as a resource. The
less a setting rests on democratic values, the more those in it
define others and themselves in the narrowest ways. Unfortunately, if the setting rests on these values, there is no automatic
assurance that the actors will be defined in less narrow ways.

Our highly overlearned ways of defining people as resources are obstacles that will not be overcome merely by altering power relationships to be more in line with the theory and practice of democratic living. This is what I meant in *The Predictable Failure of Educational Reform* (1990b) when I emphasized that changing governance (altering power relationships) is a necessary but not sufficient condition for improving our schools. If those changes are not informed by new conceptions, values, and goals, or if they do not affect the ways we define and utilize people as resources, few positive differences will result. If people continue to be regarded in terms of the stereotypes custom has taught us to associate with labels — student, teacher, administrator, parent — if we continue to use those labels to identify deficits and to ignore assets, why should changes in governance have the desirable consequences we seek?

I confess that a part of me resents the label "human resources," a phrase relatively new in human history. In large part my resentment stems from my observation that many who use that label seem to imply that there is conceptual and practical virtue in regarding humans in much the same way we do minerals, oil, and wood. There would be no cause for resentment if those who use the label do so because they are knowledgeable about the history of nonhuman resource utilization, that they were taking seriously one obvious feature of that history. Any one of the major resources (for example, oil) initially was used in very narrow ways until the creative human mind "realized" that the resource potentially could be used in far more diverse, startling, and productive ways. Today we have petrochemical industries not dreamed of by those who saw oil only as a means of keeping people warm or a source of power for engines. Oil became, so to speak, more than oil. But that is not what most people mean or imply when they use the label "human resources." Indeed, it is unclear what they mean or imply. That is a charitable assessment. In my experience the label is devoid of any implication that people must not be regarded in such narrow ways as to blind us to their potential assets for *their* growth and *our* needs. If I resent the label it is because it has become empty rhetoric, and clearly not because it cannot have crucial significance for how we regard our potential assets and those of others. Humans are more than what we ordinarily mean by human. It was that belief that over the millennia kept alive the waxing and waning flame of the democratic ethos. It was (and is) a belief that said: we are capable of more than you think we are; you see us as having deficits, we see ourselves as having assets.

Chapter Thirteen

There Are
Two Subject Matters

With very few exceptions, the imagery that comes to mind when people use the word *teacher* is someone telling others what is to be learned and how it is to be learned. The teacher instructs and the learner is instructed. We gloss over the distinction between the active and passive connotations of the verb *instruct*. The teacher, so to speak, "shows and tells"; the learner mimics. The contract between teacher and learner is this: "I'm going to teach you what you need to learn. That's my job. Your job is to learn it. There is a lot you have to learn and you have a certain amount of time in which to learn it. You have to pay attention and, like me, do your best."

That contract is fulfilled, generally speaking, when the learners play their contractual role, regardless of whether they "like" what has to be learned. The students may have no intrinsic interest in the subject matter but they learn what needs to be learned in order to please the teacher, or meet parental strictures and expectations, or acquire the fruits of competitiveness. There is nothing explicit or implicit in the contract about whether the student needs to be interested in, fascinated, or captivated by the subject matter. The teacher performs the act of faith that what needs to be learned is good for the soul and mind. It is similar to requiring a child to take medicine. Some children will take the medicine, like it or not. Others will resist, struggle, engage in battle, even spit it out.

Obviously, some children dutifully fulfill their contractual role. It is no less obvious that for some of them the subject matter is entered into the file-and-forget compartment of their

222

minds. And is there anyone who would say that for the large majority of students learning subject matter is like taking an unpalatable medicine? Some people place blame on the students, or their parents and background. Even more blame educators. Very few see the objects of blame as unwitting, well-intentioned victims reflective of two things: the most narrow of conceptions of the context for productive learning, and an insensitivity to the differences between teaching children and teaching subject matter. Few teachers understand this, and they did not gain that understanding in preparatory programs.

Let me start with an observation for which I have found no exception. More correctly, it is an observation and conclusion I came to when I was a student; it has stayed with me and explains why in later life I made it my business to observe classrooms, especially at the beginning of the school year. I was a very good student. With one exception (algebra-geometry), I learned well what I was "supposed" to learn. Given my parents and background, it could not occur to me to question that my job was to learn what I was told to learn. And, it needs to be said, my working-class neighborhood was significantly homogeneous in terms of ethnicity and values. "You are there to do your best, do as you are told, learn what you are supposed to learn." It was a message that had the status of a biblical injunction.

The observation was that in regard to *any* subject matter *no teacher ever took up with the class why anyone should learn that subject matter.* Needless to say, the why question is, from the standpoint of the student, not satisfactorily answered by saying that the subject matter is both necessary and important. The student assumes that is true, but the explanation does not make sense in terms of his or her present or past experience. So, for example, when parents tell young children that there is a God, they just do not say, "There is a God and you have to believe in Him." What they do say, individual differences aside, is that believing in God explains how the world came into existence, why people are what they are, why the world looks the way it does, and more. It makes no difference if parents are aware that from a very early age children are asking, in their own ways (publicly or privately), questions for which the religious explanation makes personal sense, that is, the explanation has personal, concrete significance; it is not an abstraction; it is assimilated to questions asked and observations made by the child. The child accepts the explanation not as an act of faith but because it fits in with lived experience. It is when lived experience results in new questions and observations that the crisis in faith arises.

When my daughter was four or five, she asked me if I believed in God. My reaction time was by no means quick. I did not want to lie and yet I knew she was asking a question of great personal significance to her. So I finally said: "No, I do not believe in God but I can understand why some people do." She looked at me and then asked: "If you don't believe in God then how did the world start?" The point of the anecdote is that Julie was struggling with a concrete question to which she needed a concrete explanation. My answer was no explanation. I was faced, as teachers frequently are, with the difficult task, and it is *very* difficult, of how to adapt *my* explanation to *her* need and level of comprehension. I did not do a very good job. Adapting the "big bang" explanation of the origins of the universe to her needs and level of comprehension was beyond me. Julie was unaware that she had taught me about the gulf that exists between knowing the abstraction that children are question-asking organisms, on the one hand, and knowing how to apply that abstraction to the concrete questions of concrete children in search of answers, on the other hand.

Why should *anyone* learn *any* subject matter? That is a question that occurs to every child. It is not a question asked in the abstract. In the phenomenology of the child the questions take this form: "Why am *I* asked to learn *this?* What do I do with *this?* Of what *use* is *this* to me?" Although that kind of question occurs to every child, I have never heard a student ask that question out loud, just as I have never observed a teacher address the issue. If my talks with students are any guide, they support the conclusion that as students go through the grades they give up posing that kind of question to themselves. Schools are not for those kinds of questions, the kinds that power and reinforce intellectual curiosity only when there is a supportive response and ambience.

I have never heard an educational reformer (or read a commission report on reform) who did not stress the crucial significance of a teacher's knowledge of subject matter: the more the knowledge and grasp, the better. Basic to such a stance is the position that every subject matter has a conceptual structure, a logic, a cohesion, and organizing foci. If teachers do not possess a firm grasp of these features, they are unable to aid students in understanding the subject matter in productive ways. Indeed, teachers are missing the point, which is to get students to *appreciate* the internal logic of the subject matter — not only to know it but to appreciate it.

I have no quarrel whatsoever with that position. But it is egregiously incomplete and even misleading because it has ignored the "why" questions of students and the schooled incapacity of teachers to recognize and address those questions as the starting point for thinking about subject matter.

I am in no way suggesting that students need to be motivated to learn subject matter. *That motivation is there,* although it steadily loses strength over the school years. It is a motivation that early on collides with the question: "What is the point of all this? How does it relate to anything I know or do or think about or I would like to do? Why should I turn on and not off?"

The significance of the why question is contained in the joke about the person whose personal problems caused him to see a psychotherapist. On the first visit he spent forty-five minutes detailing his problems. When he finished the litany, the psychotherapist said, "Those are not your problems. The real problem is that you hate your mother." Just as the psychotherapist may be "right" from his way of thinking, the teacher is also "right" in saying that a particular subject matter should be, must be, learned. But when being "right" ignores the here and now phenomenology of the patient or student, neither of them has a way of assimilating what is "right." What is "right" is foreign to them; it has no relation to their problems or questions; it is a source of puzzlement, not a goad to meaningful inquiry. Psychotherapists and teachers are told that "you start where the person is, where he or she is coming from." And when we say "coming from," we mean the here and now questions or problems that are in their heads. If those questions or problems are not articulated, if they are not engendered and dealt with by the teacher, if students are immediately plunged into the formal subject matter, a boundary has been erected between the world of the classroom and the world of personal, lived experience. Students, like the rest of humanity, need reasons that make personal sense. When those reasons are not given, subject matter is medicine which, like Adelaide's lament in the musical *Guys and Dolls,* "doesn't get where the problem is."

University professors who, like me, have primarily taught graduate students tend to be insensitive to this issue. It would be more correct to say that they have little need to be sensitive because graduate students are a highly self-selected population who have already asked *and* answered the why question. They know why they chose graduate school and which courses they will and want to take. Indeed, they may find that they are not getting as much subject matter as they believe they should have. What the university professor can take for granted, the school teacher cannot. If that is obvious, it does not explain why the textbooks university professors write for students in preparatory programs only rarely confront the why question seriously and practically.

In regard to the why question, the teacher is in the role of the translator. Translators are two kinds, although that is an oversimplification. The first kind tends to translate literally, that is to do as little violence as possible to the words, sentences, and imagery of the language of the writer being translated. To the extent that the translator rigidly adheres to such a goal, the result tends to make life difficult for the reader, leading him or her to conclude that the writer could have benefited from a creative writing course. The second kind finds the task agonizing because he or she knows that the problem is how to go from one language to another in ways that allow the reader to assimilate the writer's intent without corrupting that intent. Put in another way, how do you convey ideas and imagery expressed in one language to a reader unfamiliar with that language and do this so that it is comprehensible but not misleading? That kind of translation is no routine affair. It is quintessentially creative. That a translator knows the two languages extraordinarily well is not enough. (Anyone who doubts that should compare Edith Hamilton's translations of the Greek dramatists with those of most others.) Similarly, a teacher may be quite knowledgeable about a subject matter, but unless he or she can make it meaningful to the personal-experiential world of the student, subject matter remains intellectually encapsulated and infertile. The teacher is a translator who melds two domains: that of subject matter and that of personal experience.

Some may hold that all I am saying is that teachers should know children, that is, their psychology, so to speak. I disagree, although how can you argue against that cliché? What teachers need to know are concrete children, in concrete classrooms, in concrete (no pun) schools, in a particular neighborhood populated by individuals and families who may or may not vary in race, ethnicity, religion, and social class. When you seek to enter the world of children, you find that it is a world that encompasses far more than the subworld of the classroom. For productive assimilation of subject matter, it is necessary but not sufficient to know that larger world. Beyond knowing is translating.

As I have emphasized, one of the major goals of the reform movement is to encourage and help teachers change their thinking and practices. Far less attention has been given to the preparation of educators so that when they became independent practitioners they would not require the degree of change reformers seek to effect. It is no secret that changing the thinking and practices of educators is very difficult both for the educators and reformers — difficult and not very effective, frequent characteristics of the repair effort. To illustrate these points, and again to alert the reader to the preventive stance, let us discuss a recent paper by David Cohen titled "A Revolution in One Classroom: The Case of Mrs. Oublier" (Cohen, 1990). It is an important paper deserving the attention of anyone interested in educational change. Below I present some of its major points.

1. David Cohen observed Mrs. O teach math to the second graders. He liked Mrs. O. "Mrs. O's story is engaging, and so is she. She is considerate of her students, eager for them to learn, energetic, and attractive. These qualities would stand out

anywhere, but they seem particularly vivid in her school. It is a drab collection of one-story, concrete buildings that sprawl over several acres. Though clean and well managed, her school lacks any of the familiar signs of innovative education. It has no legacy of experimentation or progressive pedagogy, or even of heavy spending on education. Only a minority of children come from well-to-do families" (Cohen, 1990, p. 311). It is fair to deduce from the paper that Mrs. O liked Cohen. It is also clear that Cohen did not come to her classroom with strong, predetermined biases, that is, seeking confirmation for conclusions to which he had previously come. The paper is a model of fairness and balance.

2. What apparently spurred David Cohen to make his observations was the new framework for teaching math developed by the California State Department of Education. The framework encouraged teachers to engender in students an attitude of curiosity and willingness "to probe and explore." However, even before this framework was developed, Mrs. O eagerly embraced change rather than resisting it.

3. "Make no mistake: Mrs. O was teaching math for understanding. The work with number sentences certainly was calculated to help students see how addition worked, and to see that addition and subtraction were reversible. That mathematical idea is well worth understanding, and the students seemed to understand it at some level. They were, after all, producing the appropriate sorts of sentences. Yet it was difficult to understand how or how well they understood it, for the didactic form of the lesson inhibited explanation or exploration of students' ideas. Additionally, mathematical knowledge was treated in a traditional way: Correct answers were accepted, and wrong ones simply rejected. No answers were unpacked. There was teaching for mathematical understanding here, but it was blended with other elements of instruction that seemed likely to inhibit understanding. The mixture of new mathematical ideas and materials with old mathematical knowledge and pedagogy permeated Mrs. O's teaching. It also showed up extensively in her

work with concrete materials and other physical activities. These materials and activities are a crucial feature of her revolution, for they are intended to represent mathematical concepts in a form that is vivid and accessible to young children. For instance, she opens the math lesson every day with a calendar activity, in which she and the students gather on a rug at one side of the room to count up the days of the school year. She uses this activity for various purposes. During my first visit she was familiarizing students with place value, regrouping, and odd and even numbers. As it happened, my visit began on the fifty-ninth day of the school year, and so the class counted to fifty-nine" (Cohen, 1990, p. 313).

4. "Mrs. O's class abounds with such [innovative] activities and materials, and they are very different from the bare numbers on worksheets which would be found in a traditional math class. She was still excited, after several years' experience, about the difference that they made for her students' understanding of arithmetic. Mrs. O adopts a somewhat cool demeanor in class. However, her conviction about the approach was plain, and her enthusiasm for it bubbled up in our conversations. After 3 years, she had only disdain for her old way of teaching math" (p. 314).

5. Mrs. O was very much influenced by Baratta-Lorton's book *Math Their Way* (1976) about which Cohen says: "In fact, the book's appeal owes something to its combination of great promises and easy methods. It offers teachers a kind of pedagogical special, a two-for-the-price-of-one deal: Students will 'understand' math without any need to open up questions about the nature of mathematical knowledge. The curriculum promises mathematical understanding, but it does not challenge or even discuss the common view of mathematics as a fixed body of material—in which knowledge consists of right answers—that so many teachers have inherited from their own schooling. The manual does occasionally note that teachers might discuss problems and their solutions with students, but this encouragement is quite modestly and intermittently scattered through a curric-

ulum guide that chiefly focuses on the teaching potential of concrete materials and physical activities. The book presents concrete representations and math activities as a kind of explanation sufficient unto themselves. Discussion of mathematical ideas has a parenthetical role, at best.

"All of this illuminates Mrs. O's indebtedness to *Math Their Way,* and her persistent praise for it. She used the guide to set up and conduct the lessons that I saw, and referred to it repeatedly in our conversations as the inspiration for her revolution. My subsequent comparisons of her classes with the manual suggested that she did draw deeply on it for ideas about materials, activities, and lesson format. More important, her views of how children come to understand mathematics were, by her own account, powerfully influenced by this book.

"Baratta-Lorton's book thus enabled Mrs. O to wholeheartedly embrace teaching math for understanding, without considering or reconsidering her views of mathematical knowledge. She was very keen that children should understand math, and worked hard at helping them. However, she placed nearly the entire weight of this effort on concrete materials and activities. The ways that she used these materials — insisting, for instance, that all the children actually feel them, and perform the same prescribed physical operations with them — suggested that she endowed the materials with enormous, even magical instructional powers. The lack of any other ways of making sense of mathematics in her lesson was no oversight. She simply saw no need for anything else" (Cohen, 1990, p. 317).

6. Mrs. O's class was spatially and socially organized for cooperative learning. But Cohen had to conclude that "the class was conducted in a highly structured and classically teacher-centered fashion."

7. "However much mathematics she knew, Mrs. O knew it as a fixed body of truths, rather than as a particular way of framing and solving problems. Questioning, arguing, and explaining seemed quite foreign to her knowledge of this subject. Her assignment, she seemed to think, was to somehow make

the fixed truths accessible to her students. Explaining them herself in words and pictures would have been one alternative, but she employed a curriculum that promised an easier way, that is, embodied mathematical ideas and operations in concrete materials and physical activities. Mrs. O did not see mathematics as a source of puzzles, as a terrain for argument, or as a subject in which questioning and explanation were essential to learning and knowing—all ideas that are plainly featured in the [California] framework. *Math Their Way* did nothing to disturb her view on this matter. Lacking a sense of the importance of explanation, justification, and argument in mathematics, she simply slipped over many opportunities to elicit them, unaware that they existed.

"So the many things that Mrs. O did not know about mathematics protected her from many uncertainties about teaching and learning math. Her relative ignorance made it difficult for her to learn from her very serious efforts to teach for understanding. Like many students, what she didn't know kept her from seeing how much more she could understand about mathematics. Her ignorance also kept her from imagining many different ways in which she might teach mathematics. These limitations on her knowledge meant that Mrs. O could teach for understanding, with little sense of how much remained to be understood, how much she might incompletely or naively understand, and how much might still remain to be taught. She is a thoughtful and committed teacher, but working as she did near the surface of this subject, many elements of understanding and many pedagogical possibilities remained invisible. Mathematically, she was on thin ice. Because she did not know it, she skated smoothly on with great confidence" (Cohen, 1990, p. 322).

Had there been a change in this teacher's thinking and practices? David Cohen answers in the affirmative but with the critical qualifications indicated above. The style of her relationship to her students has not changed: she is the sole initiator and judge of what students do; she determines the materials and problems children will use; and getting the *right* answer is the overarching criterion by which performance and understanding will be evaluated. An obvious source of regret to Cohen is

Mrs. O's failure to help students grasp the nature of mathematical understanding. "Had Mrs. O known more math, and tried to construct a more open discourse, her class would not have run so smoothly. Some of the tensions that I noticed would have become audible and visible to the class. More confusion and misunderstanding would have surfaced. Things would have been rougher, potentially more fruitful, and vastly more difficult" (Cohen, 1990, p. 323).

I have to disagree with Cohen's emphasis on this teacher's "modest grasp of mathematics" as the major source of the problem. To me at least, this emphasis has the ring of the position that if teachers knew subject matter better they would be more effective in helping students understand the nature of the structure and logic of subject matter. I have observed teachers far more knowledgeable about math than Mrs. O and I was quite underwhelmed by the understanding their students achieved. Indeed, these teachers were remarkably similar to Mrs. O in several respects. First, they determined when and how a particular math function or problem would be illustrated. As in the case of Mrs. O, I never saw a teacher who attempted to get students to relate that function or problem to something somewhere in their experience. Whatever math was in these classrooms was, so to speak, born and remained in those classrooms. Math had meaning in the classroom, not any place else. Second, token gestures aside, the ultimate criterion was whether the "final" answer was correct. Third, the level of question asking by students was very low despite the confusion and puzzlement obvious on the faces of more than a few students. Fourth, students were expected to work by themselves; that students could learn with and from others was an idea foreign to these classrooms.

I am suggesting that if Mrs. O had a far greater grasp of mathematics, it simply does not follow that Cohen would have come away less regretful. Grasping the nature of mathematical knowledge is one thing, a necessary thing, but it is quite another thing to translate that knowledge into the experienced world of children so that it not only has personal meaning but

becomes a goad for further exploration. The goal is not to enter
the world of students, period. The goal is to enter and utilize
it to engender the willing pursuit of further knowledge. How
to enter that world is in no way given by the nature of mathematics. There is nothing in Cohen's observations that directly
or indirectly suggested that Mrs. O sought to enter the world
of her students. As a result, math for her students existed in
an encapsulated space we call a classroom. It did not, could not,
exist in lived experience in the "outside world." What was going on in that encapsulated place that would make students eager
to pursue mathematical learning, to be turned on, not off, by
the subject matter? The answer, unfortunately, is nothing.

What I have said here has long been known by child de-
velopmentalists, and nowhere is this more clear than in regard
to imparting or acquiring sexual knowledge. Let us assume that
you are the world's leading expert about human anatomy and
sexuality. And let us assume that a parent of a young child seeks
your advice about when and how you should impart sexual
knowledge. I shall assume that you will *not* tell the parent to
give the child the "facts" about differences between boys and girls,
how the sexual act is performed, how and why conception occurs, and the nature of the birth process. If only on an intuitive
level, you will know that it is counterproductive to overwhelm
the child with facts, processes, and logic. You do not have to
be a psychologist to know that what you impart has to be as-
similable by the child; for the child it has to have something
akin to the ring of truth, albeit for you it is far from the "whole"
truth. What you impart has to be the kind of food for thought
that when digested and mulled over will require another serving of food.

So what do you say to the parent? I have always started
with the why question: "Why are you raising this question now?
What have you observed, what has the child said or asked, that
suggests you need to impart information?" Some parents, of
course, have observed nothing and report no questions asked
by the child. I shall not dwell on the significance of this except
to say that some parents have eyes that do not see and ears that
do not hear. There are parents who do see and hear, which is

why they seek advice about how to utilize their observations and how to answer the questions the child is asking. They sense, and you know, that what they say should in some way, to some extent, be able to be incorporated into the content of the child's concrete experience. So, in the world of the child the question is not why do men have a penis and women do not — a question intended to arrive at an abstraction — but rather why does Daddy have a penis and Mommy does not? To answer a concrete question with an abstract answer may satisfy the requirements of "truth" but at the expense of the child's understanding. *The overarching criterion by which to judge your answer to a child's question is the degree to which it facilitates new questions, the pursuit of more knowledge.* That explains why in anything I have ever written about classrooms I have riveted on the egregious discrepancy between the number of questions students and teachers ask. Children are quintessentially question-asking organisms, and their questions derive from personal, concrete experience. To forget or ignore that is to dam up the energies that power the pursuit of mind-forming knowledge.

Cohen is penetratingly correct when he says that if Mrs. O had more than a modest grasp of math "things would have been rougher, potentially more fruitful, and vastly more difficult." What I am adding to his diagnosis is that if Mrs. O had a better grasp of the world of children and of the characteristics of productive contexts for learning, things would indeed be rough, potentially more fruitful, and vastly more difficult. Absent that grasp, a more mathematically sophisticated Mrs. O would not likely be a contributor to the intellectual development of her students. There are always two subject matters: the kind we label math, history, social studies, science, or literature, and the kind we call children. The former cannot tell you how to approach the latter; the latter is the road map to the assimilation of the former. A most succinct, incisive commentary on the two subject matters is that by Cuban in *Education Week*, March 11, 1992. Let us listen to Cuban.

Yet to listen to the last decade of national and local debate over improving schools, what we have heard most is what students are supposed to study. Lists of facts are published for elementary-school teachers to teach. Children must learn them to become "culturally literate." More math, science, history, and foreign language. More multicultural content in all subjects. The bulk of the national discussion over school improvement has been how to jam more content into the curriculum. Thicker textbooks, longer tests, state curriculum guides for teachers to follow have spilled over the schools in the last 10 years.

Teachers have not been ignored, however. There has been concern over attracting high-quality newcomers to the classroom. Salaries have improved for entry-level teachers. Reforms are under way in teacher education. But reformers' attention to teaching? No, very little.

So what? Just because there appears to be a contradiction between citizens' focus on the importance of teaching and reformers' focus on content doesn't mean the agenda for school improvement ought to change. After all, these reformers have advanced degrees and are viewed as experts. Perhaps, common sense is wrong. I don't believe so. It is the assumption that content is more important than teaching upon which the national reform agenda rests that is fiawed. Why?

First, because at the heart of schooling is the personal relationship between teacher and students over content. Of course, Jaime Escalante taught math but it was his beliefs in his students and his personality harnessed to a way of teaching that inspired his Garfield High School students in Los Angeles to work hard at calculus. Of course, Eliot Wigginton teaches English but it is his willingness to plan with students how to use the richness of their family and community traditions that inspired his Rabun Gap, Ga., high schoolers to create Foxfire. Ask parents of students why their children performed their hearts out for a

football coach, band instructor, or a science teacher
at the annual science fair. Parents will point to the
personal connection that teachers have with their students and how those bonds saturate the daily teaching.

Second, just because policymakers mandate that
schools teach certain content doesn't mean it gets
studied or even learned. New state frameworks in
math, for example, or new district courses of study
in biology are what policymakers intend for teachers
to teach and students to learn. It is the official curriculum. Researchers have pointed out for years, however, that the official curriculum is not what teachers
teach. Nor is what teachers teach what students necessarily learn. Furthermore, what students learn is not
always what the nation, state, or district tests. There
are, in effect four curricula: the official, the taught,
the learned, and the tested.

Third, the content that teachers teach varies.
Researchers have known for years that three teachers
teaching 11th-grade English in the same school, even
on the same floor, from the same textbook would have
three different classes. Variation in what is taught
comes from the differences in teachers' personal traits,
their beliefs about how English ought to be taught,
their attitudes towards students, their teaching competency, their knowledge of subject matter, and their
experiences. Variations in teaching are most clear in
comparing, to cite a case, biology taught to college-
bound students and the same subject taught to students who are labeled "at risk" or who speak English
as their second language.

So pedagogy, the art and science of teaching,
is crucial to what students get from a subject. How
we teach becomes what we teach. If a 6th-grade teacher
only calls on the brightest, most verbal students in
the class, snipes at students' answers that call into question what the teacher said, and then provides few reasons for grades on paper, those 6th graders learn about

fairness, independent inquiry, and the moral character of the teacher. Yet pedagogy and teachers' personal qualities have been largely ignored by reformers. Instead there has been an unrelenting focus upon subject matter [p. 40].

The following excerpt from Kamii and DeVries's *Physical Knowledge in Preschool Education: Implications of Piaget's Theory* (1993) may also be helpful to the reader.

What we mean by "physical-knowledge activities" can be best explained by contrasting these with activities typically found in "science education." For illustrative purposes we shall present two different ways of teaching an activity on crystals. The first, quoted from a text on preschool education, is an example of the "science education" approach:

Theme: Crystals
Behavioral objective: At the end of the experience, the child will be able to

1. Pick out crystals when shown a variety of things.
2. Define what a crystal is.
3. Discuss the steps in making crystals at school.

Learning activities:

The teacher will show the children different crystals and rocks. She will explain what a crystal is and what things are crystals (sand, sugar, salt, etc.). Then she will show some crystals she made previously. The children are given materials . . . so they can make crystals to take home. A magnifying glass is used so the children can examine the crystals.

Method 1: Mix ½ cup each of salt, bluing, water, and 1 [tablespoon] ammonia. Pour over crumpled paper towels. In 1 hour crystals begin to form. They reach a peak in about 4 hours and last for a couple of days . . .

Maureen Ellis, one of our teacher colleagues, read the above lesson, modified it into a physical-knowledge activity, and wrote the following account of her teaching with crystals:

While looking through an early-education text, I found the "recipe" for making crystals. I decided to try it, but not as a science project because I had no idea why crystals formed. It was as much magic to me as to the kids; so we used it like a cooking activity. I told them that we didn't know why it happened, but they got the idea that when some things mix together, sometimes something extraordinary happens. The activity was such a success that for days individual children were showing others how to make crystals, and some made their "own" to take home.

This experiment inspired other experiments and a whole atmosphere of experimentation. One boy, during cleanup, decided to pour the grease from the popcorn pan into a cup with water and food coloring. He put it on the window sill until the next day. He was sure "something" would happen and was surprised when nothing much did. Another child said she knew an experiment with salt, soap, and pepper (which she had seen on television). She demonstrated for those who were interested. A third child was inspired by the soap experiment to fill a cup with water and put a bar of soap in. She was astonished by the change in water level and then tested other things in the water — a pair of scissors, chalk, crayon, and her hand to see the change in water level.

The next day, one child brought a cup filled with beans, blue water, styrofoam packing materials, and a Q-Tip. "This is my experiment. Cook it," he said. So I asked what he thought would happen to each of the things in the cup. He made a few predictions, and I told him we could cook it the next day. (I wanted to experiment first to see if there might be anything dangerous involved.) At group time, he told everyone about his experiment, and the group made predictions which I wrote on the blackboard. Among these were: "The whole thing will get hot," "The water will change color," "The beans will get cooked, and you can eat them," and "The beans will grow." When I asked, "Will anything melt?" the children predicted that the styrofoam would not melt, but that the Q-Tip would. The next day, the child did his cooking experiment, and wrote down the results with my help. Many of his predictions were found to be true, but there were some surprises: It smelled terrible, the Q-Tip did not melt, and the whole thing bubbled.

In the "science education" approach above, the teacher's objective is for the children to learn about crystals. More specifically, the objectives are to get children to become able to recognize and define crystals, and to describe how they can be made. In this content-centered approach, children listen to explanations, look at what the teacher shows, and do what he or she planned.

In the "physical-knowledge" approach, by contrast, the teacher's objective is for the children to pursue the problems and questions they come up with.

The purpose of making crystals is thus not to teach about crystals per se, but to stimulate various ideas within a total atmosphere of experimentation. In the situation reported above, the making of crystals inspired four children in different ways — to make "something" with grease from the popcorn pan, to make specks of paper "swim" in water, to watch what happens to the water level when various objects are dropped into a container, and to cook a variety of objects. It also stimulated other children to think about many possible outcomes and encourage decentering through exchange of ideas about what might happen. The physical-knowledge approach, thus, emphasizes children's initiative, their actions on objects, and their observation of the feedback from objects.

All babies and young children are naturally interested in examining objects, acting on them, and observing the objects' reactions. Our aim in physical-knowledge activities is to use this spontaneous interest by encouraging children to structure their knowledge in ways that are natural extensions of the knowledge they already have. Thus, learning in the physical-knowledge approach is always rooted in the children's natural development. As we saw in the lesson on crystals, "science education" basically unloads adult-organized content on children.

The child's action on objects and his observation of the object's reaction are both important in all activities involving physical knowledge. However, we see two kinds of activities based on the relative importance of action and observation. In the first type, activities involving the movement of objects (or mechanics), the role of the child's action is primary and that of observation is secondary. Aiming a ball down an incline toward a container is an example of this kind of activity. The role of action is primary here because there is a direct and immediately observable correspondence between where the child positions the ball and where it rolls down. If he varies his action by moving the ball six inches to the right, the ball rolls down about six inches to the right of the previous fall line, parallel to it.

The second kind of activity involves the changes in objects. Making crystals is an example of this kind of activity. In activities involving the movement of objects, the objects only move — they do not change. The role of observation thus becomes primary and that of the child's action becomes secondary. The role of action is secondary because the reaction of the object is neither direct nor immediate; that is, the outcome is due not to the child's action as such, but to the properties of the objects. Action is secondary also because, for example, mixing grease, water, and food color involves basically the same action as mixing salt, bluing, water, and ammonia. Yet the reaction of the second set of substances is very different, which leads to the conclusion that only under certain circumstances do crystals begin to form. Of primary importance, therefore, is the role of observation — the structuring of what is observable [Kamii and DeVries, 1993, pp. 1–3].

Several things are noteworthy in this excerpt. The first is the rejection of the practice of according to the pupil the passive role of listener and observer. The second is the recognition that when curiosity is aroused about something, the desire to act on that thing in some way — to change or control it in some way, to be part of it in some way — is also created. The third is that the process of asking questions and acting on them has or can have a self-sustaining quality that may take unpredictable but desirable directions in regard to the child's understanding of the nature of his or her world; it is not, and certainly need not be, a self-limiting process.

Fourth, what to an adult may not look like subject matter (such as science) is quintessentially that for a child: the experiential building blocks that sustain curiosity and give direction to action literally at the same time that internal thinking becomes more differentiated. Fifth, what we traditionally call "subject matter"—a set of facts and skills interconnected by concepts, all of which have been singled out by adults—attains its intended meaning for the child only through a process that takes account of the child's curiosity, interests, conceptual level, and need to act on the world.

There is another way one can articulate the differences in conceptualization and approach that Kamii and DeVries illustrated. It is an alternative that adults will readily comprehend because it involves a distinction that not only is central to their lives but also lies at the heart of a major social problem. I refer to the distinction between labor and work. When we say that a person labors we refer to an activity the end product of which in no way bears the doer's personal stamp. It is an activity so structured, ordinarily so predetermined, that there is no room for the product to reflect something distinctive about its maker.

So, when we say someone is a laborer or occupies a certain place on an assembly line, what is conjured up in our minds is an impersonal relationship between person and product: the product is independent of its maker. One maker can substitute for another but one would never know by looking at the product. The activity, of course, has meaning for the person but whatever that meaning may be, it is supposed to remain internal and not to affect the products. It is, so to speak, a mindless activity. The individual is active, he or she "acts on," but with the aim of further predetermined actions from which personal meanings are divorced. We know when we labor and why we dislike or abhor it.

The concept of work, in contrast, refers to an activity that in some way bears the personal stamp of its performer; the product or consequence has a signature that can be recognized by the maker and others. How clear that signature is, how large the area in which labor and work overlap, is not the issue. To the extent that a person's acting on the world is part of a continuing process in which what is acted on changes, in turn producing changes in the person that alter subsequent actions, we say that the individual is working rather than laboring. A

Supreme Court Justice said that although he had trouble defining pornography, he knew pornography when he saw it. Similarly, we may not be satisfied with our definitions of work and labor, but we know when we are either laboring or working.

This distinction between work and labor is precisely that between the two approaches to science education that Kamii and DeVries contrasted. In one approach the structure of the activity is so predetermined as to leave little room for active assimilation and accommodation. It does not capitalize on the child's curiosity and desire to explore and change what is out there, to digest and master a relationship between what is internal and what is external — a relationship that by its nature contains unpredictable features. The other approach is not a learning by doing, as if doing in and of itself has productive consequences. It is an approach, as Dewey and Piaget continually noted, in which activity (overt or symbolic) contains, expresses, and alters the relationships between internal schemas and external contexts. This kind of activity goes on willy-nilly, as Piaget amply documented. No one has disputed Piaget on that score. The educational task is to take that activity seriously, to transform the education process so that it maximizes the experience of working and minimizes the experience of laboring. If children say schooling is uninteresting, they are saying in their own way that they know the difference between work and labor. Boredom is one of the hallmarks of laboring.

It is noteworthy that in his preface to Kamii and DeVries's 1978 volume Piaget criticized, as he always has done, the efforts of educators to transform into standardized tests the "operatory tasks" used by him and his colleagues as the basis for asking questions in "free conversation" with children. However, he noted that Kamii and DeVries "centered their effort on inventing activities to permit children to act on objects and observe the reactions or transformations of these objects (which is the essence of physical knowledge, where the role of the subject's actions is indispensable for understanding the nature of the phenomena involved). The importance of errors is not neglected, as an error corrected is often more instructive than an immediate success" (Kamii and DeVries, 1978, p. vii).

The developmental principles on which the demonstrations of Kamii and DeVries with preschoolers were based are applicable at all levels of education and with any subject matter. That these principles are distinguished by their absence in our schools needs no documentation. It is true that here and there one finds that these principles are recognized and an effort is being made to act appropriately on them, but such instances are rare indeed as one moves from elementary to high school. High schools pay unwitting tribute to these principles. On the one hand, they are agonizingly aware of how difficult it is to engender and sustain in students an interest in subject matter (such as math, history, or science). On the other, in the past two decades many high schools have initiated programs that provide opportunities outside school for students to experience, explore, and act on some ongoing community effort. I am referring here to the upsurge of what has been called "experiential education," an upsurge (a cyclical phenomenon in American education) that explicitly reflects one fact and one assumption.

The fact is that attempts to harness and direct the energies and interests of students in the classroom have failed. That is not to deny that students can be kept in the classroom and that many will learn something about what others think they should learn, but rather to assert that this is achieved at very high cost: student boredom and loss of interest in learning and teacher burnout. The assumption on which experiential education rests is that students have both a need for and a desire to work: to be part of an environment on which they can act and from which they can assimilate knowledge and acquire skills that expand the range of their potential actions. Although the conceptual rationales put forth to justify experiential education never mention Piaget and his developmental findings and formulations, the assumption underlying experiential education obviously is consistent with what Piaget has given us. I have to add that if we view what Piaget has given us as a theoretical framework for mental development, then it is grossly unjustified to say that experiential education is based on an encompassing framework.

There is an irony here. To the extent that experiential education achieves its goals, it sharpens the contrast between what students experience in and outside school, with the class-room coming out a very poor second. This contrast is further sharpened because the thrust of experiential education very frequently is unrelated to subject matter. It is an add-on to the curriculum or a substitute for traditional courses. Far more often than not, experiential education is aimed largely at students for whom traditional courses are not deemed appropriate. At its worst, experiential education has to be put in the category of busy work, or make-work (the word *labor* would be more appropriate in these terms), mirroring what goes on in classrooms. At its best, experiential education provides a sustained out-of-classroom experience that requires observation, acting on, more observation, more acting on, all of this supervised in a way and to a degree so as to give structure, substance, and direction to the student's experience, knowledge, and outlook; this effort has all the characteristics of productive work.

Most of what I have observed or read about "experiential education" is not encouraging. The term *experiential education* has become a slogan, a rallying cry. It stands for the recognition of the limitations of classroom learning and of the frustrations they pose for the needs and the curiosities of students while, in practice at least, it justifies experience as if experience in and of itself has educational and intellectual value. The impression is also conveyed that if students are permitted to do something they want to do, the consequences will be educationally and intellectually desirable.

In no way am I suggesting that if someone does something he or she wants to do, the activity will be devoid of value. Nor am I suggesting that if a student participates in a project in which he or she has expressed no interest, the effort inevitably will prove counterproductive (although that is clearly the case with much classroom learning). What I am suggesting is that the term *experiential education* too frequently centers on experience and not on education. Put another way, when what the student experiences is not for the purpose of mastering the knowledge and acquiring the skills we associate with traditional subject matters, then the term *education* loses meaning; it becomes a term that refers to everything and, therefore, to nothing.

What we call "subject matter" is not an encapsulated body of knowledge and skills that exists for its own sake outside of time, something to be learned because of its longtime, systematic efforts to describe and understand the world in terms of numbers, history, chemistry, physics, literature, social process, and so on. At any one time a subject matter is the history of how people tried to understand, to explore, and to act on the world from a particular but ever-changing perspective. A subject matter is a record of our transactions with the world. Subject matter never existed, and does not now exist, independent of that kind of transaction.

Directly relevant here is Dewey's *Interest and Effort in Education* (1975 [1913]), a monograph that is rarely cited. From the standpoint of my argument, Dewey's small volume provides one of the most powerful arguments against the school as a site in which interest, effort, and subject matter can coalesce to serve productive thinking and doing. May I note in passing that it is in the 1913 publication that Dewey says, "The school for so-called 'free expression' . . . fails to note that one thing that is urgent for expression in the spontaneous activity of the child is intellectual in character. Since this factor is primarily the educative one, as far as instruction is concerned, other aspects of activity should be made means to its effective operation" (p. 83).

Let me end this chapter by returning to David Cohen's important paper for two reasons. The first is to emphasize his point concerning the (predictable) gulf between what a policy clearly intends and how, with the best of intentions, that policy is distorted in practice by teachers. Cohen makes the cogent point that at the same time the California policy statement implicitly criticizes the thinking and practices of teachers, it asks those teachers to change. That is an example not only of blaming the victims but of requiring them to heal themselves, a paradox that is as insensitive as it is unrealistic.

The second reason is more germane to the theme of prevention. As I have said in earlier chapters, it is not my position that we should to any extent reduce our efforts at repair. It is my position that we do this honestly, by which I mean that we should face up to — and help the general public face up to — not only how extraordinarily difficult that task is and will be but also how, at best, the desired results will be very modest. Indeed, to the extent that we continue to place the bulk of our energies and funding in repair, we are doomed to perpetual disappointment. That is why in this book I have focused on the preparation of educators as one available arena in which we can and should take prevention seriously. Should we not seek ways of preparing educators so that they will not require constant repair? Could not a Mrs. O—energetic, bright, motivated, self-questioning, concerned with her professional growth—have been prepared for her role so that David Cohen's observations would have been more reassuring? Granted that no preparatory program should be expected to produce a "final," polished professional adequate to meet any and all classroom contingencies and problems, should we not seek—indeed, are we not obligated—to prepare educators far better than we are now doing? Is there any knowledgeable person who takes the position that the cumulative knowledge and wisdom obtained over the decades are too unsubstantial to justify trying to change and improve preparatory programs? Was Abraham Flexner a fool for trying to change the education of physicians that was then far more scandalously inadequate than is the preparation of educators today? Or is it that we have been such poor advocates for the preventive orientation because it requires a long-term perspective and significant changes in the roles and self-interests of those of us who consider ourselves educators of educators? Should we not try to view ourselves in the dispassionate way Cohen viewed Mrs. O?

Those who have read Cohen's paper will raise one question to what I have said. It stems from his point that a stated policy that essentially sees teachers as the problem also sees and requires them to be the solution. Similarly, I have argued that the inadequacies of educators are, to a significant extent, the consequences of the inadequacies of their preparatory programs. If that is true, why and how do I expect them to be capable of "solving" the problem? That is a legitimate question that I will endeavor to answer in a later chapter. Suffice it to say here that I am less enamored with my inevitably incomplete answer than I am desirous to encourage others to explore the universe of alternatives available to us in regard to significant changes in preparatory programs. I have yet to meet anyone who is satisfied with these programs. Some people seem to take delight, orally and in print, in describing these programs and their faculty in derisive terms, as if their inadequacies were carefully planned and implemented. Scapegoating may make them feel superior but it is at the expense of the pursuit of understanding. The majority of those with whom I have talked seem to have resigned themselves to apathy. If I had to summarize their position it would be "the situation is both serious and hopeless." What surprises me is how many who are in this group are in the business of repair. That does not require justification. What does require justification is the tunnel vision that undergirds a dependence on repair.

Chapter Fourteen

Teachers and Administrators: Never the Twain Shall Meet

It probably has occurred to the reader that I have used the words "preparation of teachers" and "preparation of educators" interchangeably. That can be faulted on the grounds that all teachers are educators but not all educators are teachers. There are administrators, curriculum supervisors, and a variety of pupil and staff improvement personnel who do not teach children in a classroom. I justify the interchangeability on several grounds. First, a few exceptions aside, school personnel who are not classroom teachers begin their careers as teachers. (In fact, before World War II those exceptions, like school psychologists and school social workers, were usually required to have had previous teaching experience in the classroom.) The rationale for that requirement is obvious: if you have not experienced life in a classroom — with all of its problems, dilemmas, opportunities, frustrations, and joys — you drastically restrict the service you can render and equally drastically increase the chances of being irrelevant or even harmful. Put in another way, if the phenomenology of classroom teaching is absent from your experience, how can your service or help have intended positive consequences? There is still another way of expressing the rationale: whatever your role or expertise, the payoff for your efforts is how well you contribute to the personal *and* intellectual growth of teachers and students, and that contribution requires that you have had sustained experience in the classroom.

Does that mean that if you have not had such experience you cannot be helpful? Obviously not. But it does mean that lacking such experience is not an unalloyed asset. In general and in the abstract I accept the assumption that having had a sustained teaching experience is a necessary precondition for nonteaching personnel whose role it is to be helpful to teachers and students.

Although necessary, however, it is not a sufficient condition. If it were both necessary and sufficient, how would you explain why so many teachers (and in my experience they are a clear majority) regard administrators and others as, at best, unhelpful and, at worst, a source of mammoth insensitivity? It has never been a secret that teachers see themselves at the bottom of an organizational pyramid above which are levels of administrators and other personnel suffering from pervasive amnesia about their classroom experience. As one English teacher said to me, "They sit up there in Kafka's castle on top of the mountain dreaming up policies and programs that to them make sense and to us make nonsense." And the larger the school or school system, the taller is the pyramid and the greater the quantity of nonsense perceived by teachers.

I am not about to scapegoat administrators, as if they consciously collude to produce this too-frequent state of affairs. And I certainly am not suggesting that this condition is unique or even peculiar to the educational arenas. It is characteristic of *every* type of large organization: nonprofit, industrial, governmental, or religious. Indeed, the industrial-business sectors spend literally hundreds of millions of dollars for the purpose of understanding and diluting the destructive consequences of adversarialism. The problem is never "solved" in a once-and-for-all fashion. It is, so to speak, a built-in difficulty in all bureaucracies. What one seeks are modes of organization and problem-surfacing forums that will prevent the worst consequences of the situation. It is a problem you have to "solve" again and again and again. That simple and obvious fact is hard to face. We want to believe that there is a way of approaching these problems so that we never have to deal with them again.

There are many reasons (historical and otherwise) for the particular ways these difficulties manifest themselves in schools and school systems. It is beyond the purpose of this book to discuss most of them, but I wish to focus on one major reason that is not given the attention it deserves, one with such an apparent degree of self-evident validity that it goes without critical scrutiny. *There is no overlap whatsoever between preparatory programs for teachers and administrators. The two programs differ not only in substance (courses) but in the teaching faculty.* In my experience, the program for teachers has less institutional respect *and* power than the program for administrators. To become an administrator is regarded as an "advance" in career, to be in a "higher" and more "crucial" role, to be more "important" in furthering the goals of education. This is the perception not only of those who enter such a program but also of the faculty as well. There is nothing in the program for teachers to enable its students to challenge those perceptions.

The complete lack of overlap between the programs has a subtle but powerful effect on those in both programs, leading them to accept unreflectively that they are different kinds of people, that they live (or will live) in two different worlds, of which one is more important and powerful than the other. Those in the program for teachers not only regard administrators as more powerful but also more important. That needs emphasis because by the end of the first or second year of independent teaching most teachers come to three conclusions: *they* are more important in the education of children; as people rise in the pyramid of power their relevance to the classroom decreases; and those with the greater power seem unable or unwilling to provide the teachers with help in the way teachers define help.

The reader unfamiliar with preparatory programs has to bear in mind several things:

1. Preparatory programs for teachers contain, for all practical purposes, nothing that exposes their students to the nature, opportunities, dilemmas, and constraints of educational administration. As I have put it in earlier chapters, the would-be teacher is unconscionably and conceptually unsophisticated about issues of power and is unprepared for how to act in regard to those inevitable issues. It is not uncommon for a student to practice teach for weeks or months in a school and to have had no meaningful contact with the principal. That says as much about how

principals see their role as it does about the tunnel vision through which preparatory programs see teachers and schools.

2. Preparatory programs for administrators give little time to examining why, when, and how a principal relates to teachers. These matters are discussed, but because they are discussed on the level of abstraction or articulated in the language of behavioral formulas they ill prepare the candidates for the realities of live schools. For example, administrators spend a good deal of time in and planning for meetings with teachers. I know of no preparatory program for administrators that seriously and comprehensively discussed (and illustrates) the dynamics of and criteria for a productive meeting. Wrapped up in faculty meetings — undergirding the way in which an agenda is formed, purposes are articulated, the explicit and implicit "rules" governing discussion and decision making, the allocation of and uses of power — are all the issues subsumed under "how should we live with each other?" Those issues are no less relevant for the relationship between faculty and administrator than they are for teachers and students in the classroom. In no way do I derogate or dismiss reading about or discussing these issues as long as they do justice to competing conceptions of the philosophical, political, and organizational-educational functions of faculty meetings. But if I do not dismiss or derogate reading and discussion, neither can I ignore the opinion of most teachers (and, I suspect, many administrators) that faculty meetings are among their more boring, demeaning, and unproductive experiences in life.

3. Administrators do not regard themselves as teachers, with one enormously important consequence: occupied as they are with many tasks, their "feel" for and memory of life in a classroom fade. At the least, that feel and memory change markedly. Preparatory programs neither confront nor seek to prevent the subtle but powerful consequences of this process. The assumption seems to be that having been a classroom teacher provides forever the basis for understanding, helping, influencing, and changing the ways teachers think and act. That

this assumption is very frequently *not* valid has had little or no impact on preparatory programs.

4. To help a would-be teacher learn the difference between teaching children and teaching subject matter requires more than stating or discussing the difference in action (real or simulated). It requires having one's own actions observed and discussed by someone with *super* vision. The situation with administrators is in principle no different. In diverse ways the obligations of their role require them to go beyond articulating goals, standards, and expectations, if only because teacher-administrator agreement on these issues in no way ensures that in the realm of action spirit of intent is consistent with the letter of that intent. That means that the administrator is in the business of observing, analyzing, and evaluating what a teacher is doing in the classroom. For example, when we say that a principal is an "instructional leader," we clearly mean that he or she does not instruct in his or her office but rather that the office is where his or her direct observations are the basis for discussion. Discharging that obligation in a sensitive, productive way is the polar opposite of a routine process. It is in regard to these and other interactions between administrators and teachers that preparatory programs both for teachers and administrators are inadequate, and, far from serving the goal of prevention, they set the stage for problem production.

The imagery associated with the labels *teacher* and *administrator* has at least one common feature: each "tells" or "informs" something to someone in need of direction. Unfortunately, it is imagery that far more often than not mirrors reality but only a part of it because the other part, glossed over by the imagery, is the disinterest, or resistance, or surface acquiescence, or passivity these interactions generally call forth. I am not raising a technical or procedural issue, a kind of "how to do it" problem. I am calling attention to a central problem in the classroom and in a school: the relationship between means and ends, the always bedeviling problem of how the means one employs can be productive of the ends one seeks. That, I must repeat, is no less crucial for the classroom teacher than it is for the administrator (principal or supervisor) with responsibility for what goes on in classrooms. Would anyone deny that the way teachers and administrators are prepared to think and act regarding the means-ends issue is not productive of stated goals? That, I hasten to add, does not mean that the inadequacies of these preparatory programs are the sole cause of the problems in our schools, but it does mean that they no longer can be seen as improvable by doing better what they now do. John Goodlad was right when he called for a complete and radical redesign of the preparation of teachers. His point is no less applicable to the preparation of administrators. Both types of programs inadequately prepare people for the predictable and complex problems they will encounter.

I would go so far as to say that it would be a mistake to think of preparatory programs for teachers and administrators as unrelated arenas. I know that administrators have responsibilities teachers do not have. Two very frequent and related complaints of administrators are that teachers do not appreciate the diverse responsibilities of administrators and that people in general do not comprehend how those responsibilities prevent them from being "instructional leaders." The answer to the first complaint is this: why should teachers have such an appreciation when there is absolutely nothing in their preparation relevant to such an appreciation? And there is little in the preparation of administrators to help them think about why and how such an appreciation can be engendered.

The second complaint confirms the perception of the general public that whatever school administrators do, it has relatively little impact on the classroom. That complaint is grist for the mill of those who indict "bloated educational bureaucracies" as a major cause of the problems of our schools. I do not agree with that indictment for two reasons. The first is that it implies (and sometimes it is explicit) that the size and complexity of the administrative structure, especially in our urban centers, are creations of administrators, a kind of villainous conspiracy. Granted that bureaucracies seek to expand rather than contract, as local, state, and federal legislation and programs have multiplied (almost exponentially) in the post–World War II era—not only in number but in their demand for record keeping, criteria for implementation, and fiscal accountability—an increase in the number of administrators was guaranteed, as was an increase in their responsibilities.

The second reason is historical in nature: before the cascade of local, state, and federal interventions, the size of our schools, especially in urban settings, made a mockery of the idea that administrators could be "instructional leaders." Nowhere was that more the case than in our high and junior high schools. What went relatively unnoticed as growth of schools and programs occurred is that teachers and administrators had trouble comprehending who had power to do what, how parts were related to the whole, how anyone could make a difference anywhere in the system, why changing should take precedence over surviving.

There is a third reason: this crazy quilt pattern of growth had the effect of deemphasizing in preparatory programs for administrators whatever little attention had been given to the *direct* relationship of administrator to teachers and children in the classroom. *If anything was clear as that growth accelerated it was how inadequate the preparatory programs for teachers and administrators were for what was happening and would happen.* Whatever inadequacies were perceived were "solved" by add-ons to the programs, not by a rethinking of assumptions and practices.

An analogy is relevant here. Today there is recognition that American business and industry made two mistakes in the post–World War II era: they assumed that the future would be a carbon copy of the present and, as a result, long-range planning, in contrast to the pursuit of short-term profits, went by the boards. There was nothing to repair and nothing to prevent. We have had, so to speak, our comeuppance. One of the most frequent and major explanations is contained in this question: where did the executives and middle managers of our large corporations obtain their training? And the answer was our business schools, which prepared their students for a world that, so to speak, no longer existed. If that explanation is by no means a complete one, it has the virtue of directing attention to the

relationship between preparatory programs and the realities of
the arena to which their graduates go. It could be argued that
these business schools should not be criticized for supplying what
the corporations wanted. But if you accept that argument, you
are in effect saying that professional programs in our universities have no special obligation to seek new knowledge and understanding as a basis for changing their programs, to swim
against the tide. If preparatory programs in our universities (for
example, in medicine, education, and business) do not have,
or are not expected to have, that special obligation, the future
is even more gloomy than it appears.

    If today the state of affairs in education is grim, it is be-
cause preparatory programs have in no basic way been changed.
Cuban (1984, 1986) and others have pointed out that teachers
teach in much the same way they have always taught. Preparatory programs, both for teachers and administrators, are very
similar to what they have always been. And, yet, at the same
time that leaders in all walks of life publicly proclaim the necessity for our schools to entertain and implement "radical" changes —
frequently putting their money where their mouths are — they
strangely and unaccountably have nothing to say about radical
changes in programs that prepare educators. It is really not so
strange because, mired as they are in a repair orientation, they
cannot adopt the long-term perspective the preventive orientation requires. I am in no way suggesting that we cease our efforts
at repair, but when that is done at the expense of the preventive, long-term perspective, we are putting all our eggs in a
basket that is too fragile. That is not pessimism; it is an actuarially based conclusion we may not like but which we can no
longer afford to ignore.

    I have argued that preparatory programs for teachers
should have as their goals the prevention in teachers of the sense
of impotence to change anything, feelings of resignation and
unworthiness, the absence of a sense of personal-intellectual-
professional growth, the absence of a supportive collegiality, the
fear of and resistance to changing thinking and practices, and
conceptions of students and classroom organization that are
counterproductive. If the conditions for productive growth do

not exist for teachers, they cannot create and sustain those conditions for students. In the minority of instances where teachers do create and sustain those conditions for students, it is not because of their preparation but despite it, a very heroic feat we are far from understanding. Those instances aside, what we seek to prevent is what study after study has concluded about the development and phenomenology of teachers, especially of those in our urban centers.

The plight of teachers is not a pretty picture. What has gone unnoticed — at least it has not received discussion — is that the picture for administrators is essentially similar. At every level of the hierarchy, at least in my experience, is the feeling of surprise and disappointment that having *formal* power does not mean you are influential in ways that you expected. For those in the middle of the hierarchy there is resentment that they have little relationship to the formulation of policies; rather than having any sense of collegiality and collective purpose, they feel alone; they are at sea about how to deal with what they perceive to be the resistance of teachers to recommended changes and the adversarial relationship they have with teachers. These middle administrators spend too much time in "power games" with others in the hierarchy. Feeling as they do that they should be able to justify the existence of their roles by what happens to life and performance in the classroom, they are plagued by feelings of guilt that nothing they do really impacts on anything or anyone. They resent paper work, which they regard as a form of unintended harassment or as "spinning wheels" or as a source of their loss of self-respect; they feel that neither teachers or the general public appreciate what administrators are up against. Finally, in their heart of hearts they know that increased funding is no answer to their problems, although they respond to the perceived pressures from "above" publicly to adopt a stance they know to be, at best, minimally valid and, at worst, a moral charade.

Administrators did not seek to leave the classroom with regret but as a form of relief and with the expectation that as they ascend the hierarchy of increased power and responsibility they will be able to give tangible expression — incomparably more than when they were teachers—to their need to make a difference in their professional world, and that need is as real and praiseworthy as the result is disappointing.

The plight of administrators is also not a pretty picture. Some have said that it is overdrawn but *no one* has denied that the problem is "real." As one superintendent said to me, "Look, all you have to know is that the average amount of time a superintendent stays in the job is somewhere between three and five years. When the top honcho seeks to move from place to place, it is for greener pastures and that does not necessarily mean for more greenbacks. At some point he finds out that the grass is no more green in one place than in another. And at some point around fifty years of age he looks for a place that will not ruin his guts, where he thinks he can keep things from deteriorating and where he is not expected to make big changes. And I'll tell you one other thing: there are a lot of school administrators who, however unhappy they are, have learned enough to know that getting a superintendency is an invitation to trouble, personal, familial, and otherwise."

Let me now present the conclusions I have arrived at in light of the previous discussion. These are conclusions I have come to in regard to preparatory programs, although the first goes beyond such programs.

1. The first conclusion is that the effort to improve schools generally will be only minimally effective *over time* if the effort to repair existing schools is not explicitly, meaningfully, and ultimately associated with radical changes in preparatory programs that begin to take prevention seriously. To proceed, as we are now doing, as if repair and prevention are two separate issues, problems, or arenas denies the obviously symbiotic relationship between the two. It literally denies the reality of their symbiosis. That was a mistake that Abraham Flexner did not make in his 1909 assessment of medical practice and medical education. To continue to talk about repairing schools as if preparatory programs for educators as they now exist are pluses rather than minuses is worse than folly; it is egregiously unrealistic. If we seek to change the one without changing the other, we doom ourselves to the dubious fruits of repair. If those fruits

are unpalatable today, they are not likely to be more edible in the future.

2. The problematic, unproductive relationships between teachers and administrators derive, in part, from the lack of overlap in their preparatory programs. If the twain do not meet in preparatory programs, when they come together in everyday practice, the bond will be fragile and unreliable. The preparation of teachers is devoid of any substantive and experiential exposure to administrators and issues of power. Although those seeking certification as administrators are teachers, they quickly become insensitive — or at least seem to forget — that in the phenomenology of teachers, administrators are not in the category of helpers, let alone congenial colleagues. There is rarely any meaningful psychological sense of community among teachers, and that sense of community is virtually absent between teachers and administrators. Developing and sustaining such a sense is not easy and is not helped any by nonoverlapping preparatory programs that emphasize differences rather than commonalities, that assume agreements on purposes, values, and worth that everyday living in schools contradicts, that create two cultures at odds with each other. It is *not* self-evident that these programs should be nonoverlapping.[1] On the contrary, the realities demand some overlap.

3. For the movement to empower teachers to be even partially successful — to be more than a struggle for power — two

[1]An instructive analogy here concerns the preparation of nurses and physicians. The two preparatory programs always contained some overlap and, of course, these programs required face-to-face interactions. Up until World War II issues of power, worth, and respect rarely surfaced. They stayed underground but omnipresent, nevertheless. After World War II those issues began to surface and the struggle over power began. As a result, what had been a relationship marked by dramatic differences in parity is today very different, and that change has been reflected in changes in preparatory programs so that nurses and physicians are more like colleagues than they ever were when the former was the handmaiden of the latter. It would be more correct to say that not until those changes were given expression in the preparatory programs (especially those for nurses) that they got reflected in everyday relationships. The important point is that none of this could have occurred in nonoverlapping programs.

things have to happen. First, preparatory programs for administrators have to change markedly in regard to exposing their candidates to the complex interrelationships among power, authority, and responsibility. By expose I mean to introduce the history
of these interrelationships in public education and why today
so many people in and outside education are challenging the
customary way those interrelationships are conceptualized and
manifested in practice. For graduates of these programs to be
leaders in improving schools requires a breadth and depth of
the issues they now do not receive. The second thing that has
to happen is that preparatory programs for teachers have to expose their students to these same issues, an obvious basis for
overlapping in the two programs. Empowerment has become
a fashionable word. It has the ring of virtue and of an unques-
tioned morality. Some proclaim it as a panacea. If the empowerment movement is to avoid the worse excesses of sloganeering
and conceptual superficiality, it will have to come to grips with
issues that are as complex conceptually as they are on the level
of action. And if that does not begin to happen in preparatory
programs, it will happen nowhere. These are not issues peculiar
to education as a discipline and profession. That is why I, ap-
ing John Dewey in his presidential address to the American Psychological Association in 1899, plead for more overlapping between education and the other social sciences.

4. Preparatory programs for teachers and administrators
are faced with the same problem the teacher has in the classroom: how do you make subject matter intellectually interesting and personally meaningful? Courses and seminars have their
virtues but when they are the primary source of "learning," the
separation between theory and practice, between abstractions
and lived experience, leads to divorce. Courses, like the encapsulated classrooms, are limiting affairs. For would-be teachers,
the limitations of courses are hardly compensated for by practice teaching in a classroom under a supervising teacher, a kind
of quarantine that puts everything and everyone else off limits.
It would be both unfair and an exaggeration to say that that
kind of practice teaching is without benefits. But it is not unfair

to say that the degree of overlap between the experience of practice teaching and the experience of being a real teacher in a real
school is both small and, too frequently, maladaptive. In the
preparation of administrators the equivalent of practice teaching hardly exists.

The indictment of administrative bureaucracy as a contributor to the inadequacies of our schools is misleading because
it conveys the message that the problem is both quantitative and
structural. More correctly, the problem is *only* quantitative and
structural. There is a kernel of truth to the criticism but it confuses cause and effect. From the standpoint of teachers the problem is not the numbers of administrators but their inability or
unwillingness to understand and to be responsive to the perceived need of teachers. From the standpoint of administrators
the problem is the inability or unwillingness of teachers to change
their practices, to be responsive to new ways of thinking. Teachers see themselves as objects of change and blame, and administrators see themselves as frustrated agents of change. *Those different, conflicting perceptions and stances are not explainable by the size and
structure of the administrative hierarchy; they are, in fact, the cause of
the size and structure of the hierarchy.*

For example, in the post–World War II era many school
systems have added staff development and inservice training personnel to the hierarchy. These are not housed in schools but
"downtown." That did not occur because a self-serving, imperi-
alistic bureaucracy sought to feather its nest. It was not a case
of manufacturing a problem. Who would deny the crucial importance of creating conditions that stimulate growth, creativity,
and pursuit of the application of new knowledge in teachers?

Adding that layer to the hierarchy was an implicit admission: *schools were not places in which teachers and principals felt
and acted on an explicit responsibility to further their knowledge and growth.*
Schools were for the development of children, not faculty or principals. The implications of that admission were never explored.
Why were staff development and inservice training not taking
place in schools? If they were, why were they deemed inadequate? Was it because principals did not have to discharge such

a responsibility or that they perceived that teachers wanted to be left alone, or, if they so perceived, they did not want to deal with what teachers would regard as intrusions? In any event, instead of confronting what schools were (are) like and trying to help them be more adequate as arenas of learning for everyone in them, they "solved" the problem by setting up a new program outside the schools. Unless my experience is grossly atypical, it is a solution that has been far from fruitful at the same time that it has taken the personnel of a school off the hook of assuming the obligation of and the responsibility for their professional growth. John Goodlad argued most eloquently and persuasively that the object of change should be *the* school. He is as right as he has been ignored.

The implications of what I have described go beyond changing schools as they now are. One obvious direction is to the preparatory programs for teachers and administrators, unless, of course, you believe that what I and others have described in no way is related to these programs, and that there is no way preparatory programs can prevent in any significant way either the frequency or the destructiveness consequent to the adversarialism of the "two cultures." Neither belief merits rebuttal, even though basic to these beliefs is another implicit admission: preparatory programs are exercises unrelated to anything that happens in schools. With friends like that the educational community will never lack enemies.

If, as I have argued in this book, preparatory programs have to take prevention seriously, then whatever they do, however they are structured, they must confront in the most direct way that what they have done in the past has been inadequate. They have not adequately prepared their students for the real problems of real people in real schools. Good intentions aside, these programs have fostered rather than prevented conformity to the way things are. At the risk of narcotizing the reader through repetition, I have to say again that preparatory programs should instill in their students an obligation (moral and professional) to seek to change schools — not to seek to change society and the world, but to seek change in the arena of one's work to whatever extent is possible, always knowing that it is an uphill

battle that if not fought dooms you to disappointment, disillusionment, cynicism, and a reluctance to think.

It is hard in 1992 to remain unaware of President Bush's
"America 2000" program and of the New American Schools Development Corporation's "Designs for a New Generation of
American Schools." In the formal announcements, brochures,
and press releases about both efforts I have come across only
two references to the preparation of educators. The first is from
the "New Generation" initiative:

Q: Why try to "reinvent" schools when we already
know what works?

A: We do know what works on a general level in
today's schools—high expectations, strong school leadership, involved parents, dedicated and knowledgeable teachers, motivated students. But we have not
learned—on a large scale—how to create these conditions where they do not naturally exist. Nor have
we determined how to stitch together the many lessons learned from years of education research to create high-performance learning environments.

One thing we have learned: If educators and
communities are to break the mold, they must be
helped to imagine what is possible. Much of what is
possible today wasn't ten years ago: computer simu-
lations of experiments, entire encyclopedias on laser
disc, physics teachers beamed into classrooms via
satellite, voice mailboxes parents can call to get their
child's homework assignments and electronic networks
that allow teachers across states to swap teaching
strategies.

Technology is but one example. We've also
learned much in the last decade about how children
learn, about how to improve teaching and learning
in core subject areas (and others), and about *the importance of professional development for teachers.* The mission of the Design Teams is to help communities draw

on what's been learned—to imagine and then create
state-of-the-art schools that set the pace for the Nation and the world.

That is an interesting, even refreshing statement, in one respect:
it admits that the track record for creating "high performance
learning environments" has been poor, that repair is enormously
complicated and problematic in outcome. But when the statement says that the "professional development of teachers" is important, it is putting this preparation in the framework of repair
and not prevention. The hope is that these "break-the-mold"
schools, the bulk of which will be existing schools seeking to
change, will give a new lease on life to teachers. There is no
recognition that while these schools take on the obligation to
further the professional development of teachers, they should
also take on the obligation to influence and change preparatory
programs, and for two reasons. The first is that influencing
preparatory programs can lessen the time and energy required
by repair efforts. The second is that the explicit goal of this new
program is to select schools by several criteria, among the most
important of which is that they will have impact beyond their
immediate surround, that what they find to be productive will
be disseminated and applied elsewhere. No additional research
is needed to conclude that the professional development of the
teachers in the selected schools will require helping them either
to unlearn much of what they learned in preparatory programs
or to learn what they should have learned in these programs
but to which they were not exposed. To the extent that changes
in these schools are unrelated to changes in preparatory programs, repair will be the order of the day tomorrow, next year,
and in the distant future.

Note that there is no mention of the professional development of administrators. That is a puzzling omission considering that almost all the board of directors of the New American
Schools Development Corporation are executives of large corporations. They do not have to be told that when a large corporation has gone downhill and is unprofitable, you do not initially seek to change those at the bottom of the pyramid but you

look at those who have had administrative responsibility for policy and operations. Or do they unreflectively assume, as too many people do, that schools are a unique species of organization? It is one thing to say that schools are different from private sector organizations. It is quite another to say they are unique. They have not been, are not, and will not be unique in the world of organizations.

One problem these new schools will encounter is as predictable as sunrise tomorrow. Normally there is turnover in teaching and administrative personnel, and in our urban centers that turnover is considerable; but in schools that are radically changing themselves, the rate of turnover will frequently (not always) be high as the turmoil of radical change is experienced. The schools cannot count on a pool of replacements who will have been prepared for departures from convention. In the past I have seen too many of these efforts flounder and even vanish as principals and other administrators leave the scene, to be replaced by others who, however bright and well-intentioned, simply do not comprehend the whys and wherefores of the radical change effort. Unless over time such efforts are related to altered preparatory programs, the continuity and dissemination of the repair effort will fall short of the mark.

The second reference to the preparation of educators is from the brochure stating the rationale for President Bush's *America 2000: An Educational Strategy:* "*Alternative teacher and principal certification.* Congress will be asked to make grants available to states and districts to develop alternative certification systems for teachers and principals. New college graduates and others seeking a career in teaching or school leadership are often frustrated by certification requirements unrelated to subject area knowledge or leadership ability. This initiative will help states and districts develop means by which individuals with an interest in teaching and school leadership can overcome these barriers" (U.S. Department of Education, n.d., p. 16).

It is not a misreading of that paragraph to say that it implicitly criticizes preparatory programs *and* state departments of education. Nor is it a misreading to say that it regards the inadequate grasp of subject matter by many (really most) teachers

as a major cause of the problems in our schools. I have discussed
at some length why that truly simpleminded diagnosis — it is simpleminded, not simple — is so mischievous. It's like saying that
if you know all there is to know about human anatomy, physiology, and biochemistry, you can perform surgery.

What should we make of the targeting of "leadership ability"? Leadership of whom and for what purposes? Obviously
the aim is to attract and select leaders who do not fit the conventional mode. But how do you attract and on what basis do
you select? Is apparent success as a leader in a noneducational
setting an obvious plus for such a position in schools or as a
partial substitute for current certification requirements? I applaud the desire to experiment, to break conventional molds.
But at the same time we experiment should we not admit in
a loud, clear voice that we are experimenting and that it is the
obligation of the experimenter to carry out the experiments in
ways that permit us to decide whether the efforts were worth-
while? It is one thing to give brownie points for desiring to experiment; it is quite another to be able to praise demonstrable
results. And by demonstrable I mean both positive and negative results. To carry out an experiment and find that your initial assumptions are not confirmed is a contribution to knowledge. But there is nothing in that paragraph to suggest that that
is what its writers have in mind. If it was in their minds, candor requires that they would say that it will take a fair amount
of time before we would know whether alternatives to teacher
and administrator certification had their intended consequences.
Experimentation is not an amoral affair. Experimenters are and
should be held accountable. They should be encouraged and
supported even though we know ahead of time that most experiments deservedly end up in the dustbin of history. Pragmatic William James said that our actions have "cash value" by
which he meant the degree to which those actions can be demonstrated to have had their intended purposes. Some wit said that
there are two kinds of experts: those who say they do not know,
and those who do not know that they do not know.

Another reaction to that paragraph is that its message is
identical to paragraphs written many times before over past dec-

ades. That does not mean we should dismiss it out of hand, but does it not mean that those who write it should give their reasons for believing that their proposals will now have more productive consequences? A second reaction is, in my opinion, the most damning of all: *to a very large extent what the paragraph seeks to accomplish was and is implementable by states and districts and did and does not require federal grants.* Why should money be the carrot to stimulate states and districts to do what they already have the power to do? I can come up with scenarios, as I have in earlier chapters, in which altering preparatory programs radically would require funds not now available. However, when I put that paragraph in the context of the way the America 2000 program is being presented, I have no reason to believe that the presenters are talking about certification other than in the most narrow, superficial way. And when I receive and read, as I do, the weekly newsletter from the America 2000 office in the federal department of education, I have to conclude that performing in the role of cheerleader has nothing to do with leadership. I have to predict that America in the year 2000 will have little reason to be grateful to the America 2000 program of the nineties.

Chapter Fifteen

University Pecking Orders and Schools of Education

As David Cohen pointed out in Chapter Thirteen, it is para-doxical to criticize teachers and then to come up with guide-lines asking teachers to change themselves. I am in the same paradoxical situation. I have found preparatory programs to be inadequate and in need of change. Why should I expect that those who administer what I regard as inadequate programs can perform two heroic feats: to own up to the inadequacies and then to be able to make radical changes in their thinking and practices? I have, initially at least, no such expectation. For such an explanation to have a semblance of realism, several things must happen. The first is that preparatory programs have to become a focus of attention and discussion. In saying that I rule as off-limits polemics, venting of spleen, and resorting to ad hominem criticisms. The issues are real and complicated and are rooted in our national and institutional histories. If we ig-nore those roots we are not likely to go beyond the confines of conspiracy theories, which suggest that the problem was willed and that all we have to do is to change personnel and all good things will follow.

The task is not to come up with blueprints. Before you develop blueprints — whether for a home or a program — there has to be agreement about the functions and purposes you want that blueprint to reflect. When you want to build a new home, you do not go to an architect and say, "Build me a home." You want that architect to know what your needs, purposes, values, and vision are. The obligation of the professional architect is to help you clarify these features and, in light of your resources, to explore the universe of alternatives you should consider. The process of arriving at a blueprint is in principle identical to the preliminary sketches of the artist: they are both ways of clarifying what the problem will be in going from an internal vision to a finished product. Making sketches is a way of clarifying problems. It is a form of action, a kind of "playing around," a form of self-testing to gain confidence that you are on the right road to a final action.

In regard to preparatory programs we are neither at the blueprint or sketching point. We have not even arrived at the discussion point. John Goodlad has started the discussion in regard to the preparation of teachers, although anyone familiar with that literature will know that others in the past have toiled in the same vineyard. When I say that he "has started the discussion," I mean that he has made the most comprehensive effort to date to state the dimensions and complexity of the problem.

I may be wrong in saying that he has started a discussion. I am not aware that what he has written has spurred other educational luminaries to participate in the discussion. But not until that kind of professional and public discussion and debate pick up steam will the sketching process begin. If it does pick up steam, all those with a direct or indirect vested interest in these programs will have begun to *think* and, I would expect, to confront the necessity for change. What is a nonproblem today will have received the recognition it deserves.

During the time I was writing this book I had numerous opportunities to present to school personnel the ideas contained in previous chapters. It may be that they were overly polite, but in every one of those discussion no one even faintly disagreed with the importance and relevance of the problem. On the contrary, they were grateful that I was saying out loud what they had long been thinking. And, I should add, the audiences consisted of both teachers and administrators. I do not mention these experiencees as proof of the validity of any of the concrete recommendations I may have made but rather as evidence of sorts that preparatory programs have to be near center stage in the discussion of improving schools. If and when educational theorists, researchers, and policy experts in our universities participate in the discussion, we have reason to be somewhat hopeful. Absent their interest and participation — and given their influence on and even responsibility for preparatory programs — John Goodlad will conduct the discussion in a telephone booth.

I have no credentials for how you start a national discussion. I am a writer who writes as much to clarify my own thinking as to stimulate thinking in readers. Despite my lack of credentials there is one thing I have learned in regard to more circumscribed arenas of problem: any discussion has to involve those who have a stake in the problem, and that means that you do not begin by dividing the world into the good guys and the bad guys and consort only with the good guys. It also means that you avoid at all costs the consequences of scales of value that define who is powerful and who is not, who is prestigious and who is not, who is "bright" and who is "stupid," who is creative and who is a dinosaur. The important point is that they be stakeholders. I have participated in too many discussions in which power dynamics and arrogance of prestige defeated open discussion.

How do new ideas and practices spread? There is, of course, no one way they go beyond the institutional boundaries in which they arose and were tested. Insofar as schools of education are concerned, however, one of the ways this comes about can be called the trickle-down process. Concretely, when prestigious schools of education proclaim a new idea and describe a new practice — especially when the change is a marked departure from past practice or conventional wisdom — it is highly likely that a number of less prestigious schools of education will reflect both on the change and their need not to be far from the avant garde. What the Harvards, Columbias, and Stanfords of this world proclaim as new knowledge or as direction or as "basic," similar and less prestigious schools hear and think about, if only because they are likely to have graduates from these schools on their faculties. Macy's not only tells Gimbels (of sainted memory!) but it seeks to tell as a way of demonstrating leadership.

The reader not knowledgeable about academia needs to know that there are three categories of schools of education. The first category, containing a relatively small number of schools, is regarded by everyone as prestigious and influential. The second category, somewhat larger, are the semiprestigious schools whose influence tends to be more local than national. And then there is everybody else: a large third category. Influence is almost always top down. To be a tenured professor in a prestigious school is to have entered the academic college of cardinals. Having been anointed through a tenure process that, phenomenologically, makes Mt. Everest seem like a tall hill, it is extraordinarily difficult to withstand the consequences of being perceived by the field at large as deserving of the honor.

As a personal example, shortly after I joined the Yale faculty as a beginning assistant professor — please believe me when I said I did not know what tenure was and meant — I went to the convention of the American Psychological Association. I had been previously to such conventions but my name tag had said Seymour Sarason, Southbury Training School, Southbury, Connecticut. I was guaranteed anonymity and loneliness. But when my name tag said Yale University, it was a different, seductive game. I instantly became somebody, causing me to question whether indeed I was, as I felt, at best a nobody and at worst an imposter who would be found out.

Make no mistake about it: these prestigious schools of education have on their faculties people who are as bright, ambitious, creative, and hardworking as they come. I would wager that the average quality of the faculty is higher than that of many other departments in their universities. The point of all this is that these people see themselves and are perceived by others as leaders in their field. They do not arrogate the leadership role to themselves, they are *accorded* it. And that is the point: anything these schools advocate — and, again, especially when it is a departure from what is customary — will get a hearing and will engender discussion and debate. Anyone who lived through the curriculum reforms of the sixties will find nothing new in what I am saying.

Again I have to remind the reader of the scandalous state of medical education at the turn of the century and the impact of Abraham Flexner's report containing proposals for change.

Flexner was very explicit in holding that if the handful of medical schools that deserved being called educational institutions adopted his recommendations, the less deserving medical schools would be unable to remain what they were. That was the strategy he employed, although there is more to the story than that.

I would argue that in regard to the radical altering of preparatory programs, few strategies would be as effective and as quick as one that can engender in the prestigious schools of education a willingness seriously, systematically, and sincerely to, in Goodlad's terms, completely redesign their programs. It has to be a willingness, of course, that is *not* a response to being asked but of having arrived at the point where they *want* to change.

Now for the obstacles to the strategy. The status of the prestigious and semiprestigious schools of education does not rest on any hard evidence demonstrating that their preparatory programs are affective by criteria other than placing their graduates in prestigious positions. Their reputation rests on the theoretical research publications of a relatively small number of the faculty, and very few of this number focus on issues of preparation. Put in another way, the deserved acclaim of these individuals does not come from the programs of which they may or may not be a part, but from their individual accomplishments. It has long been the case that faculty with primary responsibility for preparatory programs have far less status and influence in these schools than those whose time is devoted mostly to research, theory, and policy. That is not peculiar to schools of education. In these universities there is a pecking order and those faculty in any department whose responsibility is to deal with the nitty-gritty of professional preparation are considered valuable, but not as valuable in some ultimate sense as the researchers and theoreticians.

These universities see themselves as places where their faculty can contribute to knowledge, an unassailable stance. But (there is always a but) does that justify regarding as second-class citizens the faculty who "only" prepare students for the realities of their professional careers? The public answer is no; the informal answer is yes. With few exceptions, the most prestigious members of the faculty have next to nothing to do with the details and substance of professional preparation. I am not suggesting that these individuals stop what they are doing and devote themselves to the preparatory process. I am indicating that the value system in these universities has the effect of making radical and creative changes in professional preparatory programs difficult and unlikely.

The value system shows up in another way: preparatory programs for administrators have markedly greater status than programs for teachers. Teachers are "only" teachers whose impact is restricted to an encapsulated space we call a classroom. The impact of administrators is more widespread. So, if you are preparing administrators, you are in a role presumably far more consequential for education than one in which you prepare the single teacher for the single classroom. It is an argument that in the abstract sounds both valid and compelling. But if you accept that argument, do you not have to accept *some* responsibility for the failure of several generations of administrators to have the sought-for, desirable impact?

Almost seventy years ago Yale decided that it should make some impact on public education. It is not irrelevant to what I said earlier that Yale's decision was a competitive response to Harvard's prestigious school of education. Given Yale's history, traditions, and self-perception, it was unthinkable that it would have anything to do with the preparation of teachers. Yale trained leaders, not followers! So it created a graduate department for the training and education of researchers and administrators. The department was eliminated by presidential fiat in the fifties. Anyone who is interested in how to create a new program guaranteed to fail should read Cary Cherniss's unpublished doctoral dissertation (1972).

The reader may find it hard to believe that I am not being critical. I am being descriptive, primarily to make the point that any effort to change preparatory programs should not ignore the *predictable* problems.

A second obstacle is that among the most prestigious schools there is a fair number that have no preparatory program for teachers. If, as I believe, programs for teachers and

administrators should no longer be kept *completely* unrelated —
that to continue to do so is more than a little defeating — one
must hope that these schools will come to see it in the public's
and the school's self-interest to have and to interconnect both
programs. On the very day I wrote these words I received in
the mail my copy of *Education Week* (March 4, 1992). On the
commentary page is an excerpt from a new book by Patricia
Albjerg Graham, former dean of the Harvard Graduate School
of Education. Here is an excerpt from the article, which requires
no commentary on my part.

> Finally, leaders of schools of education and of univer-
> sities need to continue their efforts to strike the proper
> balance in their faculties between issues of school im-
> provement and broader educational issues. Both foci
> are vital for a first-class professional school. Today
> some schools of education concern themselves solely
> with preparation of school teachers and school ad-
> ministrators in their locale, while others concentrate
> entirely on other more expansive educational ques-
> tions to the exclusion of schooling. Some are too nar-
> row, and some are too broad. Finding and maintain-
> ing the proper balance between research and practice
> is the key.
>   The difficulties schools of education have faced
> in their universities — low prestige and often low funds —
> mirror many of the problems that elementary and sec-
> ondary schools face in American society. Like the
> schools they serve, schools of education are much bet-
> ter than they were in the early years of this century,
> but again like the schools, they have plenty of room
> for improvement. Faculties of schools of education are
> no longer largely populated by former school superin-
> tendents who regale their classes with the educational
> equivalent of war stories. Nor are there as many ex-
> teachers who bask in the greater professional respect-
> ability of university faculties and professional orga-
> nizations. Most schools of education have not made

smooth transitions from faculties of ex-school people to researchers who eschew the schools to professors who combine skill in research and in practice. Like their colleagues in the arts and sciences, most ed-school professors today would rather explain a problem than solve it. Partly this is because the university culture in which they live and work places a higher value on explanation than on solution, and partly it is because the educational problems presented in America today are so daunting and are only partially rooted in issues of improved schooling and research.

The vineyard in which professors of education labor is one in which knowledge is important, but knowledge alone will not solve the educational problems of America. It can help, though, and faculties of education can make a limited but crucial contribution to improving the lot of American children and schools. Schools of education do not have it in their power to eliminate poverty, or to make American society place a higher value on its children or its schools. Graduate study in education should increase teachers' and administrators' understanding both of how children learn and of how institutions function, as well as improve their skills at enhancing both the learning and the functioning. These are no small accomplishments, and at a time when higher education's utility to society is being questioned, universities ignore them at their peril [p. 36].

My suggestion to the prestigious *and* semiprestigious schools of education has the virtue of having a specific target, but in no way should it be interpreted as other than one of numerous ways preparatory programs can become more effective and relevant to the needs of our schools. My proposal is not *an* answer but one of a number of potentially productive answers. My proposal deserves discussion from which its pluses and minuses can be gleaned. It is not arrogance on my part to say that anyone who dismisses the proposal out of hand should have his or her head examined. Do not confuse the reality of the problem of preparatory programs with the substance of my proposal, which is, I know, narrow in light of the complexity we face.

To those readers who do not need their heads examined I have one more obstacle to discuss. It concerns funding. In earlier chapters, as well as in earlier publications, I have said that increased funding for educational change not based on new assumptions and diagnosis guarantees failure. In the case of preparatory programs — regardless of where they are and how they are labeled in terms of prestige — funding will be a problem to the extent that they radically seek to change. That, of course, will be true in spades for those schools of education that now do not have either teacher or administrator preparatory programs. It does not mean that without funding the reformers are unable to think through what they want to do and why and to take initial actions consistent with the new goals. An individual or group does not need the carrot of funding to begin to think and to initiate actions. *Funding should not be the stimulus for change but an encouragement to continue what has demonstrably started to happen.* It will not be inexpensive. And the purposes of the funding will be inherent if that funding is not assured on a long-term basis. Here again, Patricia Graham (1992) has put it well:

> No highly regarded professional programs in medicine or law are part-time, and for good reasons: The university cannot immerse the students in the culture of the profession unless they are present on a full-time basis. Students who are working full time at a job inevitably must give their major attention to that obligation, and the occasional university course in education cannot command their full attention. Few graduate schools of education enroll predominantly full-time students, largely because most cannot provide the financial aid that would be necessary to support such experienced practitioners. Hence, the model of the Harvard Business School with its intensive, focused two-year program to train general managers is not

available to schools of education, and the preparation of school people suffers.

Since graduate study in education is almost always part time, it is fitted into the crevices of a life already overloaded with professional obligations that cannot all be fulfilled adequately. Under such circumstances, professors limit their requirements, and the graduate-student educators rarely visit the library, attend lectures by distinguished scholars or educators, or join informal discussions with other students and faculty about educational issues. Professional bonds are not formed through university study but rather with colleagues in the schools, thus vitiating significantly the influence of the university upon educators. No self-respecting professional school should let such a pattern develop in which its influence is inevitably minimized.

Schools of education must adapt their programs so that they can attract and support for full-time study able persons seeking to be practitioners: teachers, superintendents, and other types of administrators. Such programs will be expensive if they are done well and hence they will need financial help not only from the university but also from government, philanthropy, and business. The current lack of financial support for the education of all but a tiny fraction of our school administrators and teachers is an example of society's unwillingness to invest in the preparation of those who educate our young. It is, thus, another expression of America's ambivalence about the importance of education for everybody [p. 36].

It is inherent in my proposal that radical changes in the preparatory program for administrators, involving as they should an interconnectedness with programs for teachers, require full-time candidates *and* faculty, which is not to say that there is not a crucial role for teaching faculty from the real world.

Let me now turn to some considerations and suggestions

that may be helpful to those who see fit to pursue my proposal, be they in schools of education or in funding agencies or elsewhere.

1. Initially at least, thinking in no way should be influenced by the current length of preparatory programs. The question is this: given our goals, what do we want our students to know and experience? It is not sinful to be idealistic; it is sinful not to have ideals. More correctly, it is sinful not to try to clarify ideals and their implications for your actions. It is obvious from what I am saying that both length and substance of these programs will have to be changed. Length of training depends on goals of training.

2. Changes in programs require a supportive constituency, and that means a clear majority of the faculty of a school of education has to give its ungrudging support. Unless that kind of support is forthcoming it is best not to proceed. What are the minimal criteria to be met if one is to proceed? One of these criteria is a supportive, nonpassive constituency.

3. The low status of schools of education in our universities has diverse sources and among them are ignorance and misplaced values. How does a university justify programs for the preparation of physicians, or architects, or business personnel and not one for the preparation of teachers? In the case of Yale and similar colleges and universities, how do they justify having, for all practical purposes, no programs in education? The answer has nothing to do with money but everything to do with an insufferable elitism that goes back far in our national and academic histories. I am not scàpegoating university leadership or their faculties, and I am not suggesting that schools of education have not played a role. As individuals, everyone is enthusiastically in favor of school improvement, but the gulf between personal enthusiasm and informal and formal policy (and the institutional values on which they rest) is vast indeed. Leaders are not managers, which is not to disparage managers. Leaders, we hope and expect, are visionaries capable of conserving the best of tradition but at the same time capable of questioning

tradition. In any event, if radical changes are to occur and be sustained, they will require not only *some* new resources but also some evidence that the change agents know the changes will be predictably difficult. If I were czar of funding, I would disapprove of any request that conveyed the message: we cannot do *anything* to move in new directions unless we have funding *now*. There is a maxim among psychotherapists that the decision to seek help means the person is already halfway to the goal of meaningful change. The person has taken a decisive step. Similarly, in regard to preparatory programs, there must be grounds for believing that funding is deserved because actions for change have already been taken.

4. In the case of programs for administrators this question deserves discussion: should administrators be asked or required to return at stated intervals, for one year, to the classroom? I have recommended that programs for teachers and administrators overlap to a certain extent. Should not that overlap be reflected in subsequent years? In reacting to that suggestion I ask the reader to remember my saying that the preparation of educators should better prepare them for altered power relationships and governance because without those alterations efforts at school improvement will fail, as they have in the past. If those alterations take place, then the question I have raised will not be as thorny or as unthinkable as it now will seem to some, especially administrators.

5. Again, if I were czar of funding I would be suspicious of any grant request that failed to indicate that its writer did not feel absolutely certain that all it had done or proposed to do was unassailably the best and wisest course of action, that one had to expect in ventures of this sort that mistakes will be made. Put another way, and again borrowing from John Dewey, if you wait to act until you have achieved certainty and the evidence from research is overwhelming that your proposed course of action will succeed, you will never leave your armchair. That is not a case for sloppy thinking and ignorance of what others have experienced and researched or for rewarding failure to

become sophisticated about *predictable* problems. It is a case for truth in advertising. It is unfortunately true that today we have a "grant culture" in which candor, far from being rewarded, is the kiss of death. No good deed goes unpunished. . . .

In these concluding paragraphs I wish to emphasize several points. The first should be obvious, but experience dictates that it be stated again: many of the problems schools confront— academic, educational, or social—are not of the schools' making, and schools should not be expected to be able to affect those problems. Whatever the consequences for school children of marital discord, of single parenthood or working parents, of unemployed parents, of neighborhood violence, of drug and alcohol addiction and more, those consequences should be acknowledged to place a burden on schools that they cannot and will never be able to handle even semi-adequately.

Some will argue that schools must respond to these consequences. If you do so, you can go in two directions. The first is to prepare educators to be better psychiatrists, social workers, health providers, and paralegals. This is possible in preparatory programs at least four to six years in length. The cost would be staggering.

The second direction, the current one, is to place the human and health services and personnel in schools. This solution is not only expensive but inevitably increases the size and complexity of the administrative superstructure of school systems. In addition, as I have pointed out in *The Predictable Failure of Educational Reform,* there is nothing in the preparatory programs of educators and of human services personnel to alert them to the predictable problems resulting from attempts to meld two very different professional cultures.

My point here is not to discourage, let alone disparage, either direction but rather to indicate that the consequences of the problems of our society for our schools set a limit on what one can realistically expect from any effort to improve education. That is why I titled one of my books *Schooling in America: Scapegoat and Salvation* (1983). At the same time we look to schools as a universal solvent for society's inadequacies, we scapegoat them for not doing the impossible. That action is as reasonable as indicting the medical community for not preventing illnesses due to pollution, smoking, drug addiction, obesity, and more.

But if there are limits, a ceiling effect, that is no warrant for packing our bags and leaving the scene. We have knowledge and experience about why past efforts at improving the intellectual and social life in classrooms have been inadequate. The good news is that we have gained clarity about the contextual ingredients without which productive learning in classrooms will not occur. That is no small accomplishment. The bad news is that, the usual exceptions aside, we have not learned how to get the benefits of that clarity to be understood *and* appropriately reflected in action by teachers and administrators.

I have argued in this book that the benefits of that clarity will always fall far short of the mark because "repairing" any serious social problem has a built-in, high rate of failure, if only because we cannot control the many variables in and around these problems. That is no reason to give up on repair, but it is a reason to avoid raising public expectations that we are on the road to salvation, expectations which when they will not be met will mark the beginning of an era of scapegoating. When President Kennedy in his inaugural address said that by the end of the decade we will have put a man on the moon, the public had reason to believe that he was not indulging fantasy. So let me present the six national education goals that President Bush and the governors of the fifty states agreed would and could be met by the President's America 2000 program:

1. All children in America will start school ready to learn.
2. The high school graduation rate will increase to at least 90 percent.
3. American students will leave grades four, eight, and twelve having demonstrated competency in challenging subject matter including English, mathematics, science, history, and geography; and every school in America will ensure that all students learn to use their minds well, so they may be prepared for responsible citizenship, further learning, and productive employment in our modern economy.

4. U.S. students will be first in the world in science and mathematics achievement.
5. Every adult American will be literate and will possess the knowledge and skills necessary to compete in a global economy and exercise the rights and responsibilities of citizenship.
6. Every school in America will be free of drugs and violence and will offer a disciplined environment conducive to learning.

Educators regard achieving those goals by the end of the century (eight years from now) to be nonsense, and their attitude should not be surprising. I have not talked with any noneducator who believed otherwise. As the person with many broken ribs said in response to being asked how he felt: "It only hurts when I laugh." The scapegoating era is not far off.

If I do not criticize efforts at repair, I do criticize ignoring the preventive orientation. In this book I have essentially made two points. The first is that preparatory programs for educators inadequately prepare their students to cope with the realities of schools. The second point is that to the extent that these programs are radically changed educators will be better prepared to cope with and prevent some of the untoward consequences of those present realities.

References

Aikin, W. A. *The Story of the Eight-Year Study with Conclusions and Recommendations.* New York: HarperCollins, 1942.

Baratta-Lorton, M. *Math Their Way.* Boston: Addison-Wesley, 1976.

Brandt, R. "On Teacher Education: An Interview with John Goodlad." *Educational Leadership,* 1991, *49*(3), 11–13.

Carnegie Commission. *In the National Interest. The Federal Government in the Reform of K–12 Math and Science Education.* New York: Carnegie Corporation, 1991.

Cherniss, C. "New Settings in the University: Their Creation, Problems, and Early Development." Unpublished doctoral dissertation, Yale University, 1972.

Cohen, D. R. "A Revolution in One Classroom: The Case of Mrs. Oublier." *Educational Evaluation and Policy Analysis,* 1990, *12*(3), 311–329.

Cowden, P., and Cohen, D. "Divergent Worlds of Practice. The Federal Reform of Local Schools in the Experimental Schools Program." Unpublished manuscript. Available from Peter Cowden, c/o Transitions, Solutions Inc., 177 Worcester Road, Route 9W, Wellesley Hills, Massachusetts 02181.

Cowen, E. L., and others. *New Ways in School Mental Health: Early Detection and Prevention of School Maladaptation.* New York: Human Sciences Press, 1975.

Cuban, L. *How Teachers Taught.* New York: Teachers College Press, 1984.

Cuban, L. *Teachers and Machines.* New York: Teachers College Press, 1986.

283

Cuban, L. "Please No More Facts: Just Better Teaching." *Education Week,* Mar. 11, 1992, p. 40.

Dewey, J. *Interest and Effort in Education.* Carbondale: Southern Illinois University Press, 1975. (Originally published 1913.)

Dewey, J. "Democracy in Education." *Progressive Education,* 1931, *8*(3), 216–218.

Dewey, J. "Psychology and Social Practice." In E. Hilgard (ed.), *American Psychology in Historical Perspective.* Washington, D.C.: American Psychological Association, 1978.

Farber, B. *Crisis in Education: Stress and Burnout in the American Teacher.* San Francisco: Jossey Bass, 1991.

Flexner, A. *Medical Education in the United States and Canada: A Report to The Carnegie Foundation for the Advancement of Teaching.* Washington, D.C.: The Carnegie Foundation for the Advancement of Teaching, 1960. (Originally published in 1910.)

Frost, C., Wakeley, J., and Ruh, R. A. *The Scanlon Plan for Organization Development: Identity, Participation, and Equity.* East Lansing: Michigan State University Press, 1974.

Goodlad, J. I. *A Place Called School.* New York: McGraw-Hill, 1984.

Goodlad, J. I. *Teachers for Our Nation's Schools.* San Francisco: Jossey-Bass, 1990.

Goodlad, J. I. "A Study of the Education of Educators: One Year Later." *Phi Delta Kappan,* Dec. 1991a, pp. 311–314.

Goodlad, J. I. "Why We Need a Complete Redesign of Teacher Education." *Educational Leadership,* 1991b, *49*(3), 4–6.

Goodlad, J. I., Soder, R., and Sirotnik, K. A. (eds.). *The Moral Dimensions of Teaching.* San Francisco: Jossey-Bass, 1990a.

Goodlad, J. I., Soder, R., and Sirotnik, K. A. (eds.). *Places Where Teachers Are Taught.* San Francisco: Jossey-Bass, 1990b.

Graham, P. A. "Graduate Study and the Culture of the Profession." *Education Week,* Mar. 4, 1992, p. 36.

Hunt, D. *Starting with Ourselves.* Cambridge, Mass.: Brookline Books, 1987.

Kamii, C., and DeVries, R. D. *Physical Knowledge in Preschool Education: Implications for Piaget's Theory.* New York: Teachers College Press, 1993.

Kean, T. "The 'Imperative' of Arts Education." *Education Week,* Mar. 1, 1989, p. 36.

Levin, H. M. "About Time for Educational Reform." *Educational Evaluation and Policy Analysis,* 1984, *6*(2), 151–163.

McLaughlin, M. Vol. 7: *Factors Affecting Implementation and Continuation.* Santa Monica, Calif.: RAND Corporation, 1977a.

McLaughlin, M. Vol. 8: *Implementing and Sustaining Innovations.* Santa Monica, Calif.: RAND Corporation, 1977b.

McLaughlin, M. "The Rand Change Agent Study Revisited: Macro Perspectives and Micro Realities." *Educational Researcher,* 1990, *19*(9), 11–16.

Metropolitan Life Insurance Company. *The American Teacher, 1991. The First Year: New Teachers' Expectations and Ideals.* New York: Metropolitan Life Insurance Company, 1991.

Murnane, R. J., and others. *Who Will Teach? Policies That Matter.* Cambridge, Mass.: Harvard University Press, 1991.

New American Schools Development Corporation. *Designs for a New Generation of American Schools.* Arlington, Va.: author, n.d.

Pauly, E. *The Classroom Crucible: What Really Works, What Doesn't, and Why?* New York: Basic Books, 1991.

Sarason, S. B. "The Unfortunate Fate of Alfred Binet and School Psychology." *Teachers College Record* (Columbia University), 1976, *77*, 579–592.

Sarason, S. B. *Work, Aging, and Social Change.* New York: Free Press, 1977.

Sarason, S. B. *The Culture of the School and the Problem of Change.* (2nd ed.) Boston: Allyn & Bacon, 1982.

Sarason, S. B. *Schooling in America: Scapegoat and Salvation.* New York: Free Press, 1983.

Sarason, S. B. *Caring and Compassion in Clinical Practice: Issues in the Selection, Training, and Behavior of Helping Professionals.* San Francisco: Jossey-Bass, 1985.

Sarason, S. B. *The Making of an American Psychologist.* San Francisco: Jossey-Bass, 1988.

Sarason, S. B. *The Creation of Settings and the Future Societies.* Cambridge, Mass.: Brookline Books, 1989 (paperback). (Originally published 1972.)

Sarason, S. B. *The Challenge of Art to Psychology.* New Haven: Yale University Press, 1990a.

Sarason, S. B. *The Predictable Failure of Educational Reform: Can We Change Course Before It's Too Late?* San Francisco: Jossey-Bass, 1990b.

Sarason, S. B., Davidson, K., and Blatt, B. *The Preparation of Teachers: An Unstudied Problem in Education.* Cambridge, Mass.: Brookline Books, 1989 (paperback). (Originally published 1962.)

Sarason, S. B., and Klaber, M. "The School as a Social Situation." *Annual Review of Psychology,* 1985, *36,* 115–140.

Sarason, S. B., and Lorentz, E. *The Challenge of the Resource Exchange Network.* Cambridge, Mass.: Brookline Books, 1989 (paperback). (Originally published 1979.)

Sarason, S. B., and others. *Psychology in Community Settings.* New York: Wiley, 1966.

Sarason, S. B., and others. *Human Services and Resource Networks.* Cambridge, Mass.: Brookline Books, 1989 (paperback). (Originally published 1977.)

Sharan, S. "Group Investigation: Theoretical Foundations." In J. Pedersen and A. Digby (eds.), *Cooperative Learning in Secondary Schools: Theory and Practice.* New York: Garland, forthcoming.

Stevenson, H. W., and Stigler, J. W. *The Learning Gap: Why Our Schools Are Failing and What We Can Learn from Japanese and Chinese Education.* New York: Summit Books, 1991.

Stigler, J. W., and Stevenson, H. W. "How Asian Teachers Polish Each Lesson to Perfection." *American Educator,* Spring 1991, pp. 12–47.

Trickett, E. J. *Living an Idea. Empowerment and the Evolution of an Alternative School.* Cambridge, Mass.: Brookline Books, 1991.

U.S. Department of Education. *America 2000.* Washington, D.C., n.d.

Westbrook, R. B. *John Dewey and American Democracy.* Ithaca, N.Y.: Cornell University Press, 1991.

Index

287